MERRILL Science

AUTHORS

Dr. Jay K. Hackett
University of Northern Colorado

Dr. Richard H. Moyer
University of Michigan-Dearborn

Dr. Donald K. Adams
University of Northern Colorado

Contributing Writer
Ann H. Sankey
Science Specialist
Educational Service District 121
Seattle, Washington

Reading Consultant
Barbara S. Pettegrew, Ph.D.
Director of the Reading/Study Center
Assistant Professor of Education
Otterbein College
Westerville, Ohio

Safety Consultant
Gary E. Downs, Ed.D.
Professor
Iowa State University
Ames, Iowa

Gifted and Mainstreaming Consultants
George Fichter
Educational Consultant
Programs for Gifted
Ohio Department of Education
Worthington, Ohio

Timothy E. Heron, Ph.D.
Professor
Department of Human Services, Education
The Ohio State University
Columbus, Ohio

ACKNOWLEDGEMENT

The authors are deeply indebted to the late Robert B. Sund for his inspiration and guidance in the early development of this series.

Content Consultants
Robert T. Brown, M.D.
Associate Professor of Clinical Pediatrics
Director, Section for Adolescent Health
The Ohio State University/Children's Hospital
Columbus, Ohio

Henry D. Drew, Ph.D.
Chemist
U.S. FDA, Division of Drug Analysis
St. Louis, Missouri

Judith L. Doyle, Ph.D.
Physics Teacher
Newark High School
Newark, Ohio

Todd F. Holzman, M.D.
Child Psychiatrist
Harvard Community Health Plan
Wellesley, Massachusetts

Knut J. Norstog, Ph.D.
Research Associate
Fairchild Tropical Garden
Miami, Florida

James B. Phipps, Ph.D.
Professor, Geology/Oceanography
Grays Harbor College
Aberdeen, Washington

R. Robert Robbins, Ph.D.
Associate Professor of Astronomy
Astronomy Department, University of Texas
Austin, Texas

Sidney E. White, Ph.D.
Professor
Department of Geology & Mineralogy
The Ohio State University
Columbus, Ohio

MERRILL
PUBLISHING COMPANY

Merrill Science Program Components

Student Editions, K-6
Teacher Editions, K-6
Teacher Resource Books, K-6
  (Reproducible Masters)
Big Books, K-2
SkillBuilders: A Process & Problem Solving
  Skillbook, Student Editions, K-6
SkillBuilders: A Process & Problem Solving
  Skillbook, Teacher Editions, K-6
Poster Packets: Science in Your World, K-6
Color Transparencies, K-6
Activity Materials Kits, K-6
Activity Materials Management System
Awards Stickers
Science Words Software, 1-6
In-service Videotapes
Mr. Wizard Videos, 3-7
Science Fair Package

Dr. Jay K. Hackett is Professor of Earth Science Education at the University of Northern Colorado. He holds a B.S. in General Science, an M.N.S. in Physical Science, and an Ed.D. in Science Education with support in Earth Science. A resource teacher for elementary schools, he conducts numerous workshops and professional seminars. With over 20 years of teaching experience, he has taught and consulted on science programs across all levels and remains active in local, state, and national science professional organizations.

Dr. Richard H. Moyer is Professor of Science Education at the University of Michigan, Dearborn. He holds a B.S. in Chemistry and Physics Education, an M.S. in Curriculum and Instruction, and an Ed.D. in Science Education. With more than 19 years of teaching experience at all levels, he is currently involved in teacher training. He was the recipient of two Distinguished Faculty Awards. He conducts numerous workshops and in-service training programs for science teachers. Dr. Moyer is also the author of Merrill's *General Science* textbook.

Dr. Donald K. Adams is Professor of Education and Director, Education Field Experiences at the University of Northern Colorado. He holds a B.S. in Liberal Arts Social Science, an M.S. in Biological Science, and an Ed.D. in Science Education with support in Earth Science. In over 20 years of teaching, he has been instrumental in implementing personalized science and outdoor education programs and has served as a consultant to teacher preparation and science programs throughout the United States, Australia, and New Zealand.

Reviewers: Teachers and Administrators   **Joan Achen,** General Herkimer Elementary School, Utica, NY; **Mary Alice Bernreuter,** Mae Walters Elementary School, Hialeah, FL; **Jack Finger,** Waukesha Public Schools, Waukesha, WI; **Sister Teresa Fitzgerald,** CSJ, Office of Catholic Education, Brooklyn, NY; **Janice Gritton,** Gavin H. Cochran Elementary School, Louisville, KY; **Ann Hanacik,** Blair Elementary School, Waukesha, WI; **Barbara Kmetz,** Trumbull High School, Trumbull, CT; **Waltina Mroczek,** Beachwood Elementary School, Beachwood, OH; **Edith Mueller,** Northview Elementary School, Waukesha, WI; **Peggy Smith,** Special Education Resource Teacher, Fort Worth, TX; **Frank Stone,** Floranada Elementary School, Fort Lauderdale, FL; **John Varine,** Kiski Area School District, Vandergrift, PA; **Sue Ann Whan,** Greece Central School District, Rochester, NY; **Dr. Rosa White,** Cutler Ridge Elementary School, Miami, FL

Cover Photo: Robot by Commercial Image/21st Century Robotics
Series Editors: Karen S. Allen, Janet L. Helenthal; **Project Editor:** David Mielke; **Project Designer:** Joan Shaull; **Series Artist:** Dennis L. Smith; **Project Artist:** Michael T. Henry; **Illustrators:** Nancy Heim, Intergraphics, Kirchoff/Wohlberg, Inc., Jim Shough; **Photo Editor:** David T. Dennison; **Series Production Editor:** Joy E. Dickerson

ISBN 0-675-03513-9

Published by
Merrill Publishing Co.
Columbus, Ohio

Copyright © 1989 by Merrill Publishing Co.
All rights reserved. No part of this book may be reproduced in any form, electronic or mechanical, including photocopy, recording, or any information storage or retrieval system, without permission in writing from the publisher.
Printed in the United States of America

Table of Contents

UNIT 1

Seeds and Plants 2

1 Plant Beginnings 4

- **1:1** Seeds 5
  - Activity 1–1 Parts of a Seed 6
- **1:2** When Seeds Germinate 10
  - Activity 1–2 Light and Plant Growth 14
- **1:3** Scattering Seeds 16
  - Activity 1–3 Space and Plant Growth 17
  - Language Arts Skills 21

2 Plants from Seeds 24

- **2:1** Seed Plants 25
  - Science and Technology 27
- **2:2** Parts of Seed Plants 28
  - Activity 2–1 Water Transport in Plants 31
- **2:3** Flowers, Cones, and the Plant Life Cycle 34
  - People and Science 37

UNIT 2

Matter and Its Changes 42

3 Matter 44

- **3:1** Properties of Objects 45
  - Activity 3–1 Properties of Matter . 46
  - Activity 3–2 Measuring Mass 48
- **3:2** Matter 50
  - Science and Technology 53
- **3:3** States of Matter 54
  - Activity 3–3 States of Matter 57
  - Language Arts Skills 59

4 Changes in Matter 62

- **4:1** Changing Matter 63
  - Activity 4–1 Expansion of Air 67
- **4:2** Matter Changes State 68
  - Activity 4–2 An Ice Cube Race .. 70
  - Activity 4–3 Evaporation of Water 72
- **4:3** Combining Matter 74
  - People and Science 77

iii

UNIT 3
Earth's Rocks — 82

5 How are Rocks Formed? — 84
- 5:1 Rocks and Earth Layers 85
  Science and Technology 89
- 5:2 How Are Rocks Formed? 90
  Activity 5-1 Sedimentary Rocks.. 93
  Activity 5-2 Metamorphic Rocks 95
  People and Science 97

6 Nature Changes Rocks — 100
- 6:1 Weathering 101
  Activity 6-1 Weathering 102
- 6:2 Soil Formation, Erosion, the Rock Cycle 106
  Activity 6-2 Comparing Soils ... 107
  Language Arts Skills 111

UNIT 4
Forces, Work, and Machines — 116

7 Forces and Work — 118
- 7:1 Force 119
  Activity 7-1 Forces 120
- 7:2 Gravity and Friction 122
  Science and Technology 123
  Activity 7-2 Reducing Friction .. 125
- 7:3 Work and Energy 126
  Language Arts Skills 129

8 Simple and Compound Machines — 132
- 8:1 Simple Machines, Levers 133
  Activity 8-1 Levers 134
- 8:2 Inclined Plane, Wedge, and Screw 138
  Activity 8-2 Inclined Planes 139
- 8:3 Wheel and Axle, Pulley 142
  Activity 8-3 Pulleys 144
- 8:4 Compound Machines 146
  People and Science 149

UNIT 5

Water Around Us — 154

9 Weather and Climate — 156

- **9:1** Evaporation and Condensation — 157
  - Activity 9-1 Water Vapor — 159
- **9:2** Clouds and Precipitation — 162
  - Science and Technology — 163
- **9:3** Climate — 166
  - Activity 9-2 Climate — 168
  - People and Science — 171

10 The Water Cycle — 174

- **10:1** Runoff, Groundwater, and Storage — 175
  - Activity 10-1 Water Storage — 178
- **10:2** The Water Cycle — 180
  - Activity 10-2 Water Cycle — 182
  - Language Arts Skills — 185

UNIT 6

Life Around Us — 190

11 Living Things Have Needs — 192

- **11:1** Living Things Need Food — 193
  - Science and Technology — 195
- **11:2** Animals Are Consumers — 196
  - Activity 11-1 Green Plants — 197
- **11:3** Scavengers and Decomposers — 200
- **11:4** Food in a Community — 202
  - Activity 11-2 Food Chains — 204
- **11:5** Food Webs — 206
  - People and Science — 209

12 Habitats — 212

- **12:1** Habitats Are Important — 213
  - Activity 12-1 A Land Habitat — 214
- **12:2** Polar, Tundra, Desert, and Grassland Habitats — 218
- **12:3** Forest and Water Habitats — 222
  - Activity 12-2 Animal Habitats — 224
- **12:4** People Adapt to Many Habitats — 228
  - Language Arts Skills — 230

v

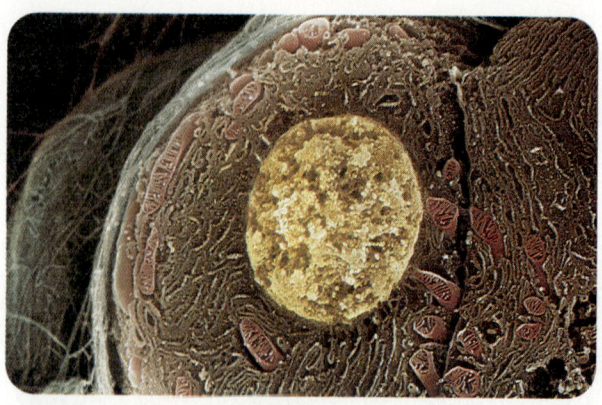

UNIT 7

Comparing Earth and the Moon — 236

13 Study of Earth and the Moon — 238

- 13:1 Earth and Moon Sizes 239
  - Activity 13-1 Spatial Relationships 240
- 13:2 Gravity 242
- 13:3 Earth and Moon Surfaces 244
  - Activity 13-2 Moon Craters ... 248
- 13:4 Equipment for Studying the Moon 250
  - People and Science 253

14 Earth and Moon Movements — 256

- 14:1 Movements in Space 257
  - Science and Technology 259
  - Activity 14-1 Earth and Moon Movements 260
- 14:2 Moon Phases 262
  - Activity 14-2 Moon Phases ... 266
  - Language Arts Skills 267

UNIT 8

Health and the Environment — 272

15 Cells to Systems — 274

- 15:1 Cells 275
  - Activity 15-1 Seeing Cells 276
- 15:2 Tissues, Organs, and Organ Systems 278
- 15:3 Circulatory, Skeletal, and Muscular Systems 280
  - Activity 15-2 Circulatory System 281
- 15:4 Digestive and Respiratory Systems 284
- 15:5 Urinary and Control Systems .. 286
  - Language Arts Skills 289

16 Staying Healthy — 292

- 16:1 Being Ill 293
- 16:2 Eating Well 296
  - Science and Technology 297
  - Activity 16-1 Healthful Foods in Your Diet 299
- 16:3 Drugs 300
- 16:4 Poisons 304
  - Activity 16-2 Design a Sign ... 306
  - People and Science 307

Glossary 312

Index 320

vi

Science in Your World

Science can help us learn about nature. It also can help us answer questions about our world. How are rocks formed? How does a giant oak tree grow from a small acorn? What finally happens to water that flows down a mountain stream? Questions such as these are studied in science.

Science, however, is more than a study of nature. Through research, science has helped improve your world. For example, cloth has been developed that can be used in winter clothes to make them both warm and lightweight. Safety devices have been invented to help make a safer family car. Toothpastes that help prevent tooth decay have been produced.

Science uses a special method for learning about your world. It is a method that involves observations. This girl is observing a rock. She is comparing it with other rocks she has seen. By comparing the similarities and differences of this rock with other rocks, she is able to identify it.

You can learn how to use this method to answer questions about your world. The information you learn can lead to many exciting new discoveries. One of the real joys of science is that the more you learn, the more questions you will want to try to answer.

UNIT 1
Seeds and Plants

For years, farmers and people such as John Chapman, "Johnny Appleseed," planted seeds by hand. Today, machines are used to scatter many seeds in a short amount of time. Sometimes areas of woodland are burned by fires. Trees are destroyed by the flames. Helicopters drop thousands of seeds into these areas. Why is it important to quickly reseed these areas?

John Chapman—1800

Helicopter scattering seeds

Chapter 1
Plant Beginnings

Many plants grow from seeds. Some seeds begin to grow into plants almost at once. Others do not begin to grow for a very long time. The seeds of the American lotus plant may not grow for years. What seeds have you planted? How long did it take before the plant started to grow?

Seeds of the lotus plant may not grow for years.

Seeds   1:1

LESSON GOALS
In this lesson you will learn
- there are many kinds of seeds.
- all seeds are alike in three ways.

Suppose your teacher put different seeds on a desk and asked you to sort them into groups. Figure 1-1 shows how one student grouped the seeds. In what other ways could the seeds be grouped?

Figure 1-1. Seeds can be grouped.

A **seed** is an undeveloped plant that may grow. There are many kinds of seeds. They have different colors, shapes, and sizes. Some seeds are as small as grains of sand while other seeds are as big and hard as buttons. Some seeds, such as those of the burdock plant, have small hooks. Others, like those of the maple tree, are winged.

Activity 1-1   Parts of a Seed

QUESTION   What is in a seed?

seed	Size (mm)	
	before soaking	after soaking
1		
2		

Drawing of tiny plant

Materials
2 bean seeds
hand lens
metric ruler
plastic glass
water
paper towel
pencil and paper

What to do
1. Observe the seeds with a hand lens. Notice how they look and feel.
2. Measure the seeds and record their sizes in a chart like the one shown.
3. Soak the seeds in water overnight.
4. Repeat steps 1 and 2.
5. Carefully peel away the outside of one seed. Look at this outside part with a hand lens.
6. Separate the two halves of each bean.

7. Using a hand lens, find the tiny plant in the seed. Make a drawing.

What did you learn?
1. How did the seeds change after they were soaked?
2. How would you describe the outside part of the seed?
3. Where in the seed was the tiny plant?
4. How does the size of the tiny plant compare with the size of the other inside part of the seed?

Using what you learned
1. How does water affect seeds?
2. Repeat this activity using different kinds of seeds. How are they like bean seeds? How are they different?

Parts of a Seed

Some plants have seeds with two halves. Beans, carrots, peas, and potatoes have seeds with two halves. The tiny plant is attached to both halves of these seeds. Look at Figure 1-2. Each of these seeds has two halves.

Figure 1-2. Some seeds have two halves.

Other plants have seeds that do not have two halves. These seeds are one piece. Corn, dates, tulips, and lilies have seeds that are one piece.

Seeds are different in many ways. They are, however, all alike in three ways. Each seed contains a tiny plant, stored food, and an outer skin.

In what three ways are all seeds alike?

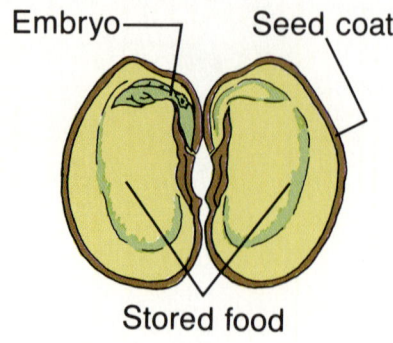

Figure 1-3. Each seed contains an embryo, stored food, and a seed coat.

Look at the parts of a seed shown in Figure 1-3. The tiny plant inside the seed is called an embryo (EM bree oh). A plant **embryo** is an undeveloped living plant.

An embryo in a large seed does not always grow into a larger plant than an embryo in a smaller seed. For example, seeds within the pods of peas are larger than cottonwood seeds. Pea plants, however, are much smaller than cottonwood trees.

Figure 1-4. The size of a plant cannot always be easily compared to the size of its seed.

Every seed also contains stored food. The **stored food** is used by the embryo when it begins to grow. Look at Figure 1-5 and compare the size of the embryo with the size of the stored food.

8

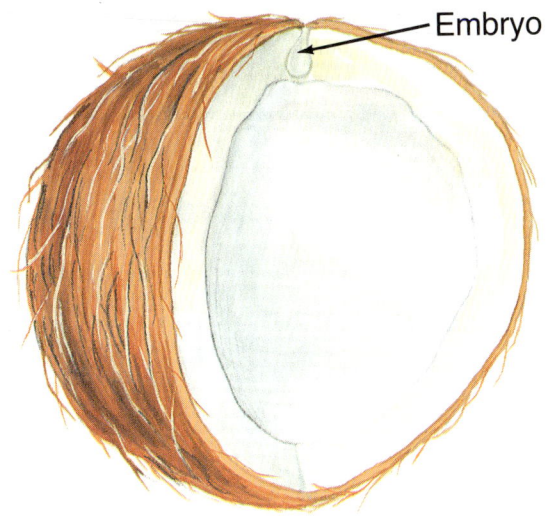

Figure 1-5. Coconuts contain a lot of stored food.

A seed also has an outer skin called a **seed coat.** The seed coat protects the other parts of the seed from injury, insects, and loss of water. In some plants, the plant embryo is not able to break through the seed coat unless the coat is cracked. The seed coat may be cracked by fire, freezing temperatures, or passage through the bodies of animals that have eaten the seeds.

What is the outer skin of a seed called?

Lesson Summary

- There are many kinds of seeds.
- All seeds contain an embryo, stored food, and a seed coat.

Lesson Review

Review the lesson to answer these questions.
1. What is a plant embryo?
2. What does the plant embryo use for food when it begins to grow?
3. Why is the seed coat important?

1:2 When Seeds Germinate

LESSON GOALS

In this lesson you will learn
- two things seeds need to germinate.
- four conditions seedlings need to keep growing.
- plants can make their own food.

Seeds germinate (JUR muh nayt) when they have everything they need to grow. **Germination** is the beginning of the growth of a plant embryo. Most seeds do not germinate right after they fall from a plant. Some seeds stay in the ground for a few months before germinating. Sometimes a seed may not germinate for years!

What is germination?

Figure 1-6. Seeds germinate when they have what they need to grow.

10

A seed needs water to germinate. Water can move through the seed coat. The water softens the hard seed coat. The seed coat splits as the embryo starts to grow.

Changes in temperature help germination. Many seeds begin to grow in spring because the temperatures of the ground and the air are becoming warmer. Perhaps you have planted seeds in the spring.

Figure 1-7. Many kinds of seeds are planted in spring.

Seedlings

After the seed germinates, the embryo grows into a young plant. The young plant is called a **seedling.** Seedlings need the right temperature and amount of water. They also need air and proper food in order to keep growing.

What do seedlings need in order to keep growing?

In the spring, the sun shines longer each day. The temperatures become warmer. The warmer temperatures speed the growth of the seedlings.

Figure 1-8. Warm temperatures speed the growth of seedlings.

Seedlings need air in order to grow. Just as you need air to breathe, a seedling also needs air. It needs air to make its own food.

Seedlings also need the right amount of water. Too little water will cause a plant to die. Too much water will drown a plant. The plant will not get air. When might a seedling have too much water?

The embryo uses the stored food in the seed while it begins to grow. This food lasts a short time. When the stored food has been used, the seedling must make its own food. Some of the food it makes is used by the seedling as it grows.

Plants need water and air in order to make their own food. Plants also need light to make food. Some plants need a lot of light. They grow where there is light most of the time. Other plants do not need much light. They grow in shady places. What might happen if plants that live in the shade were put in sunlight?

Figure 1-9. Not all seed plants need the same amount of light.

13

Activity 1-2   Light and Plant Growth

QUESTION   How does light affect plant growth?

Materials
3 paper cups
labels
9 bean seedlings
potting soil
water
2 tall boxes
pencil and paper

What to do

1. Label one cup **Light**, one cup and box **Some Light**, and one cup and box **No Light**.
2. Plant three seedlings in each cup. Add equal amounts of water to each cup until the soil is moist.
3. Place the box labeled **No Light** over the cup labeled **No Light**. Put the other two cups near a window.
4. Every day at noon, place the box labeled **Some Light** over the cup labeled **Some Light**. Remove the box each morning.
5. Check the soil in each cup every other day. Add equal amounts of water to each cup if needed.
6. After one week observe the plants in each cup. Record any changes you observe.

7. Wait a second week. Observe and record any changes.

What did you learn?
1. How did the seedlings in each cup look at the start of the activity?
2. How did the seedlings look after two weeks?
3. Which seedlings grew best?

Using what you learned
1. Why should all the cups receive equal amounts of water?
2. How is light important to the growth of plants?

Lesson Summary
- Seeds need water and the right temperatures to germinate.
- Seedlings need warm temperatures and the right amount of water, air, and proper food.
- Plants can make their own food.

Lesson Review
Review the lesson to answer these questions.
1. What is germination?
2. Why do many seeds begin to grow in the spring?
3. What is a seedling?
4. Why would seedlings not grow well in a flooded area?

1:3 Scattering Seeds

LESSON GOALS

In this lesson you will learn
- seeds are scattered in many ways.
- some seeds grow inside fruits.

Figure 1-10. Seeds are scattered in many ways.

In what five ways might seeds be scattered?

Most seed plants make many seeds. Some of the seeds fall under the plants, but not all of these seeds can grow. There is not enough room on the ground for all the new plants to grow. Seeds must be scattered so that more new plants can grow. Seeds are scattered in many ways. Many plants scatter their own seeds. Sometimes people scatter seeds on purpose. Seeds may also be scattered when animals feed. Other seeds are scattered by the water or the wind.

16

Activity 1-3 Space and Plant Growth

QUESTION How does space affect plant growth?

Materials
3 small milk cartons
labels
potting soil
22 bean seeds
water
paper cup
metric ruler
pencil and paper

What to do
1. Label the milk cartons **A**, **B**, and **C**.
2. Plant 2 seeds in carton **A**, 5 in carton **B**, and 15 in carton **C**. Space the seeds as evenly as possible.
3. Put the cartons in the light.
4. Keep the soil moist.
5. After one week measure and record the heights of the tallest and shortest plants in each carton.
6. Wait a second week. Repeat step 5.

What did you learn?
1. Which carton had the tallest recorded plant after 1 week? 2 weeks?
2. Which carton had the shortest recorded plant after 1 week? 2 weeks?

Using what you learned
1. How does the crowding of plants affect their growth?
2. Why should all plants get equal amounts of water and light?

17

Many plants scatter their own seeds. The flower part that holds the seeds bursts open. The seeds may land a long way from the parent plant. You may have seen a touch-me-not plant. It has a seed pod that bursts open if you touch it.

Farmers plant seeds to grow grains and other food. Gardeners plant seeds to grow flowers, grasses, and vegetables. When have you planted seeds? How else have you scattered seeds?

Figure 1-11. Some plants have pods that burst open to scatter seeds.

Animals scatter seeds. For example, squirrels gather acorns and other seeds for food. They eat some of the seeds. They store other seeds. Some of the seeds squirrels carry away may drop to the ground. The squirrels may not find all the seeds they stored. These seeds may germinate if water and temperature conditions are right.

Birds scatter seeds. They eat some seeds. The seeds pass through their bodies as waste and fall to the ground. The seeds may drop far from where they were eaten. Other seeds stick to the feet and feathers of birds. They drop to the ground as the birds fly.

Sometimes seeds stick to people or other animals, and are scattered that way. Other seeds float on water or are scattered by the wind. Look at Figure 1-12. Which seeds might be scattered by floating on water? Which seeds might be scattered by the wind? Which seeds might "catch a ride" on an animal?

In what ways might birds scatter seeds?

Figure 1-12. Seeds may be scattered in different ways.

19

Some seeds grow inside a plant part called a **fruit.** Some fruits are very dry when they are ripe. Seeds from these fruits may be scattered by the wind. Maple trees and milkweed plants, for example, have dry fruits with seeds that are scattered by wind.

Other fruits are soft and juicy. The seeds are inside a juicy layer or covering. This kind of fruit is eaten by many different kinds of animals. The seeds are dropped and scattered after the fruit has been eaten.

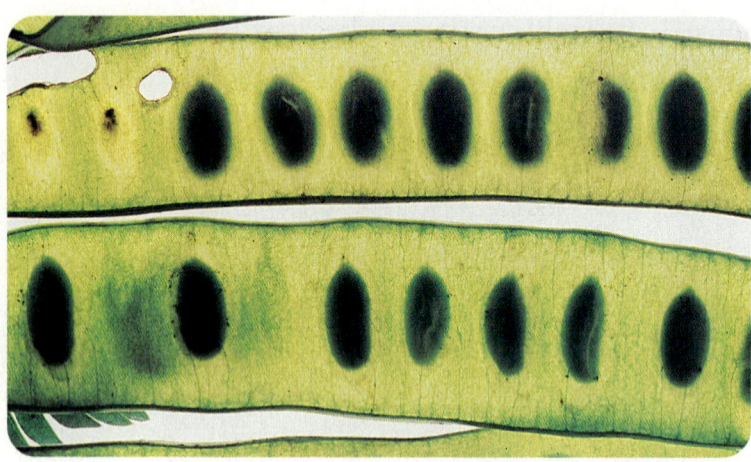

Figure 1-13. Some seeds grow inside thin, dry fruits.

Lesson Summary
- Seeds are scattered by plants, wind, water, and animals.
- Some seeds grow inside fruits that are dry or soft and juicy.

Lesson Review
Review the lesson to answer these questions.
1. Tell one way in which birds scatter seeds.
2. Name a group of people who scatter seeds on purpose.

Language Arts Skills

Using a Graph

People use different ways to give information. One way is by writing the information. Another way is by showing the information. There are many different ways to show information. People often use charts, tables, and graphs.

A graph is a drawing that compares certain facts. The graph at the bottom of this page is called a pictograph. In a pictograph, pictures are used as symbols. These symbols stand for something and are explained on the graph.

The title of this graph is "Number of Children Who Like to Eat Roots." The names of some roots are in the left column. The other column shows how many children like to eat each root. The symbol of the smiling face is explained at the bottom of the graph. *Use the graph to answer these questions.*

- How many children like radishes?
- How many children like turnips?
- Which root is most popular as a food?

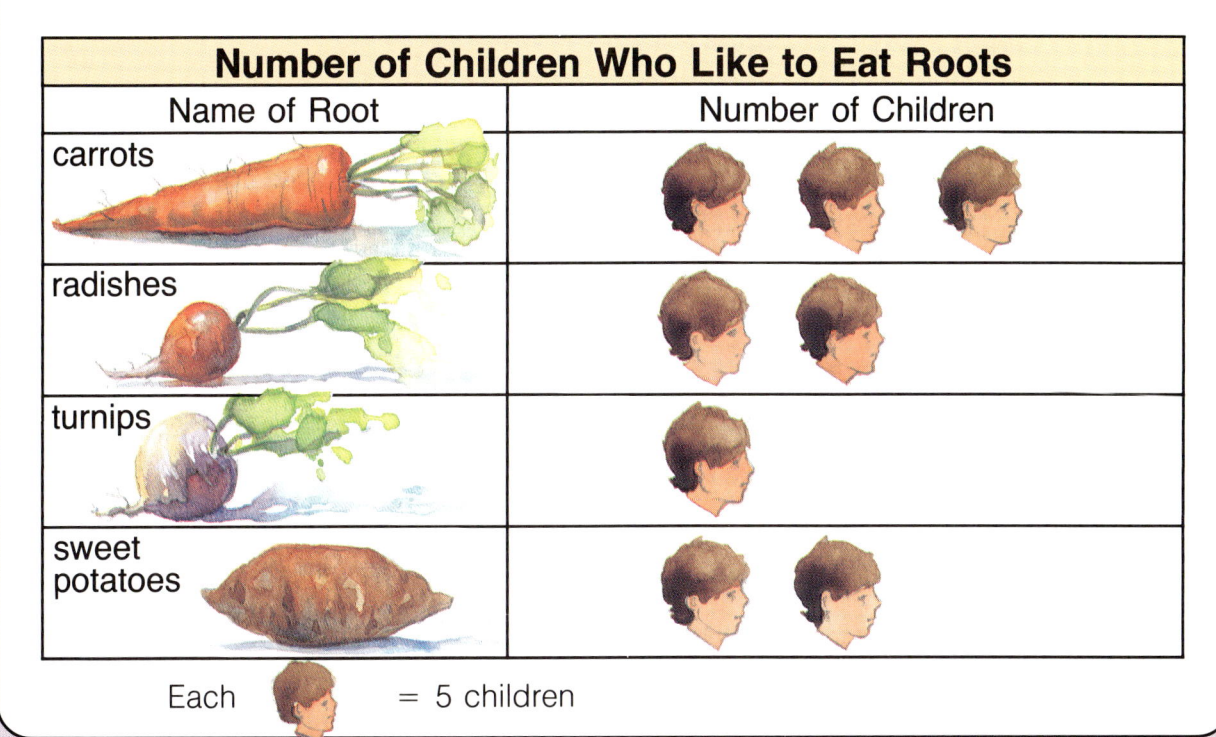

Number of Children Who Like to Eat Roots	
Name of Root	Number of Children
carrots	👦 👦 👦
radishes	👦 👦
turnips	👦
sweet potatoes	👦 👦

Each 👦 = 5 children

21

Chapter 1 Review

Summary

1. There are many kinds of seeds. 1:1
2. All seeds contain an embryo, stored food, and a seed coat. 1:1
3. Seeds germinate when they have the right amount of water and are at the right temperature. 1:2
4. Seedlings need warm temperatures and the right amounts of water, air, and proper food to keep growing. 1:2
5. Plants can make their own food. 1:2
6. Seeds are scattered in many ways. 1:3
7. Seeds grow inside plant parts called fruits. 1:3

Science Words

seed **stored food** **germination** **fruit**
embryo **seed coat** **seedling**

Understanding Science Words

Complete each of the following sentences with a word or words from the Science Words that will make the sentence correct.

1. The tough skin that covers a seed is called the _____.
2. The young plant is called a _____.
3. The undeveloped living plant is called an _____.
4. The beginning of the growth of the embryo in a seed is called _____.
5. The plant part in which seeds grow is called a _____.
6. The part of the seed used by the embryo is the _____.
7. An undeveloped plant that may grow is called a _____.

22

Questions

A. Recalling Facts

Choose the word or phrase that correctly completes each of the following sentences.

1. All seeds contain an embryo, a seed coat, and
   (a) stem. (b) root. (c) water. (d) stored food.
2. In order to germinate all seeds need
   (a) water.   (c) darkness.
   (b) sand.   (d) cold temperatures.
3. In order to keep growing, seedlings need warm temperatures, the right amount of water, proper food, and
   (a) darkness. (b) air. (c) rocks. (d) animals.
4. Seeds may be scattered by animals, water, or
   (a) light. (b) wind. (c) stems. (d) roots.

B. Understanding Concepts

Answer each of the following questions using complete sentences.

1. Name the different parts of a seed and explain the function of each part.
2. Tell what plants need in order to make their own food.
3. Why is it important that seeds be scattered?
4. Tell two ways in which seeds that develop in fruits might be scattered.

C. Applying Concepts

Think about what you have learned in this chapter. Answer each of the following questions using complete sentences.

1. A certain seed is covered with little hooks and is tiny. In what ways might it be scattered?
2. Suppose you found a seed believed to be 200 years old. What should you do to try to get it to germinate?

Chapter 2
Plants From Seeds

Many kinds of plants grow from seeds. This redwood tree is 84 meters tall. Its seeds, however, are very small. Each seed is only two millimeters long, about as long as this line: ⊢⊣ . What seed plants grow near you? How does their size compare to the size of their seeds?

Some plants are much bigger than their seeds.

Seed Plants   2:1

LESSON GOALS

In this lesson you will learn
- seed plants are different sizes and shapes.
- seed plants grow in different places.

Plants are all around you. What plants do you see on the way to school? What plants have you eaten this week? Many of the plants you see and use grow from seeds. A plant that grows from a seed is called a **seed plant.**

What are seed plants?

a

b

Not all seed plants look alike. Seed plants are different sizes. They may be large or small. A maple tree grows tall. The bluet plant, however, is sometimes overlooked because it is so small. The colors and shapes of seed plants are different also. The leaves of the coleus in Figure 2-1(a) have many colors. A lily plant has swordlike leaves. The elm tree in Figure 2-1(b) looks like a vase turned upside down.

Figure 2-1. Seed plants may have bright colors (a) or interesting shapes (b).

25

Figure 2-2. Seed plants may grow in wet places or dry places.

In what kinds of places might seed plants grow?

Seed plants grow in different kinds of places. Cattails grow in wet places. Other seed plants, such as cacti, are found in dry places. Some seed plants live in sunny, warm places. Others grow where there is shade and cool temperatures. Seed plants may be found in large fields or small pots. Where can you find seed plants growing near you? What are they like?

Lesson Summary
- Seed plants are different sizes and of various shapes.
- Seed plants grow in many different places.

Lesson Review
Review the lesson to answer these questions.
1. What is a seed plant?
2. Name two kinds of places where seed plants may be found.

Science and Technology

Providing Water For Crops

Rainy days may spoil picnics, sporting events, or camping trips. Farmers, however, need rainfall during the growing season. They worry when there are not enough rainy days. Their crops could die without enough water. Some farmers use irrigation to water their crops when there is not enough rain.

Farmers have used irrigation for hundreds of years. Irrigation is the watering of land by people. Most water for irrigation comes from lakes, rivers, streams, and wells.

There are many ways to irrigate crops. A farmer may flood a whole field. The water soaks into the soil. Sometimes pipes with tiny holes are placed between rows of crops. Water flows through the pipes and trickles out of the holes into the soil.

Another type of irrigation is sprinkler irrigation. The arms of the sprinkler stretch across a field. Some sprinklers are self-propelled and have an engine and wheels. The engine moves the sprinkler across a field without help from the farmer.

2:2   Parts of Seed Plants

LESSON GOALS

In this lesson you will learn
- why roots are important in seed plants.
- why stems are important in seed plants.
- the name of the plant part in which most food is made.

Remember there are many different kinds of seed plants. Most seed plants, however, have the same kinds of parts. These parts are found both above and below the ground.

Roots

What is a root?

A **root** is the plant part that holds a plant in the ground. You do not see the roots of most plants. The roots, however, form almost half the length of some plants.

Figure 2-3. Roots form a large part of some plants.

28

Most roots can be placed into one of two groups. Roots in one group are made of one main part that is long and thick. A carrot plant has a long, thick main root.

Roots in the other group are made of many small roots. These small roots spread out and look like branches or threads. Grass has threadlike roots.

What plant has a long, thick main root?

What plant has threadlike roots?

a

b

Figure 2-4. Roots of seed plants may be long and thick (a) or threadlike (b).

A **nutrient** (NEW tree unt) is a substance needed by living things for growth. Roots take in water and nutrients that move from the soil into hairlike parts on the roots. The water and nutrients then move up small tubes to the rest of the plant.

Notice the roots on each plant shown in Figure 2-4. Which plant might be harder to pull from the soil? Why?

29

Figure 2-5. Seed plants have different kinds of stems.

What is a stem?

Stems

Seed plants have stems. A **stem** is the part of a seed plant that holds up the leaves. Nutrients and water move through the stem to the leaves. Some stems are soft and green. Others are hard and woody. Name a plant with a hard woody stem.

Stems carry water and nutrients. Small tubes extend from the roots through the stems. Water and nutrients move up from the roots, through the stems, and into the rest of the plant.

Some plants have more than one stem. Find the stems of the plants in Figure 2-5. How are the stems different? How are they alike?

Activity 2-1   Water Transport in Plants

QUESTION   Where does the water go?

Materials
small jar
water
blue food coloring
spoon
celery stalk with leaves
colored pencils or crayons
dropper
pencil and paper

What to do
1. Fill the jar half full of water. Add six drops of food coloring and stir with the spoon.
2. Observe the freshly cut end of the celery. Place it in the colored water.
3. Observe the celery after two hours.
4. Take the celery out of the water. Your teacher will cut across the bottom and top of the celery.
5. Observe the cut ends of the celery.

What did you learn?
1. What did the ends of the celery look like in steps 2 and 5?
2. What happened to the celery after two hours?

Using what you learned
1. Why do we put cut flowers in water?
2. Why does a flower wilt when its stem is broken?

Leaves

What is a leaf?

What does a seed plant use to make food?

Most seed plants have green leaves. A **leaf** is the main plant part in which food is made. Air, water, nutrients, and sunlight are used to make food in the leaves.

Tubes in the roots and stems go into the green leaves. In leaves, the small tubes are called veins. Water and nutrients move through tubes in the roots and stems into the veins of the leaves.

Leaves can be put into groups. Some leaves are narrow and look like needles. Others are flat. Flat leaves may be broad or narrow. They have veins that form patterns. People use the pattern of the veins to tell flat leaves apart. Look at Figure 2-6. Which leaves look like needles? Which leaves are broad and flat?

Figure 2-6. Leaves of seed plants can be grouped.

32

There are two different types of broad leaves. Some broad leaves have only one part. A broad leaf with one part is called a **simple leaf.** Other broad leaves have several parts. Each part looks like a small leaf and is called a **leaflet** (LEE flut). A broad leaf with leaflets is called a **compound leaf.** How many simple leaves are shown in Figure 2–7? How many compound leaves are shown?

What is a compound leaf?

Figure 2-7. There are different types of flat leaves.

Lesson Summary

- Roots take in water and nutrients from the soil and hold the plant in the ground.
- Stems hold up the leaves of seed plants.
- Leaves are the parts of the plant in which most food is made.

Lesson Review

Review the lesson to answer these questions.
1. Compare the two types of roots found in seed plants.
2. What carries nutrients and water through the stem to other parts of a seed plant?
3. Compare the two types of broad leaves.

2:3 Flowers, Cones, and the Plant Life Cycle

LESSON GOALS

In this lesson you will learn
- seeds form inside special plant parts.
- all seed plants go through a plant life cycle.

Some seed plants have flowers. A **flower** is the part of a plant in which fruits and seeds form. Flowers may be brightly colored or plain. How are the flowers in Figure 2-8 alike? How are they different?

Figure 2-8. Flowers have different colors and shapes.

In flowering plants, seeds form inside fruits. Sometimes many seeds form inside one fruit. Sometimes only one or two seeds form. The number of seeds that form depends upon the kind of seed plant.

Figure 2-9. Some seed plants form their seeds in cones.

Some seed plants do not have flowers. These plants usually form seeds inside cones. A **cone** is a plant part in which seeds form in some plants. At first, cones are shut tight. Later, when the seeds have developed, the cones open. Then the seeds are scattered. They fall to the ground and may germinate. Pine trees and fir trees are two kinds of seed plants that have cones instead of flowers.

What is a cone?

Plant Life Cycle

After plants form seeds inside fruits or cones the fruits ripen or the cones open. The seeds are scattered and fall to the ground. They germinate if the conditions are right. The germination, growth of a plant, and formation of new seeds are parts of the **plant life cycle.**

What is the plant life cycle?

35

The life cycles of some kinds of plants are completed in one year. The life cycles of other kinds of plants take more than one year. No matter how many years are needed, all seed plants go through a plant life cycle.

Figure 2-10. All seed plants go through a plant life cycle.

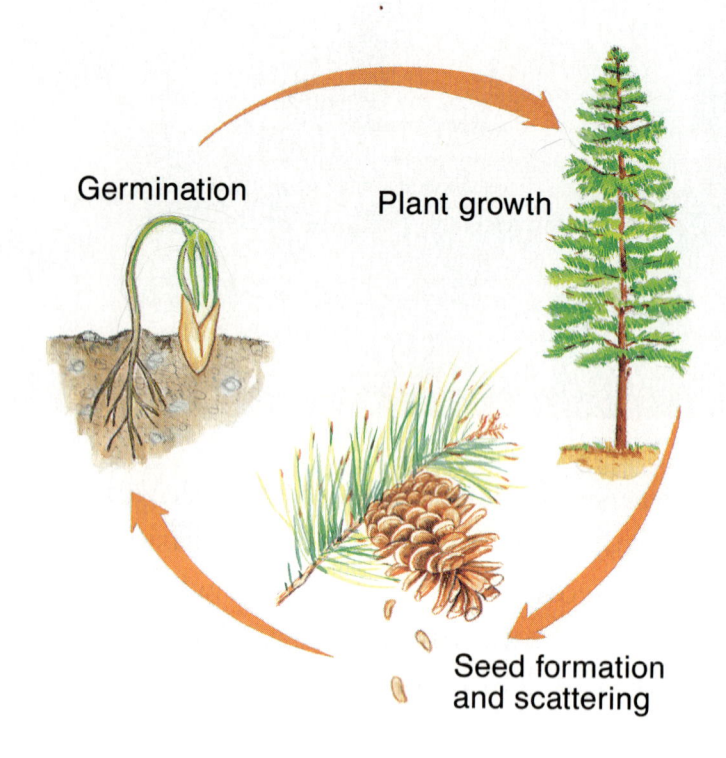

Germination

Plant growth

Seed formation and scattering

Lesson Summary

- Seeds form inside fruits or cones.
- The plant life cycle is the germination, growth, and seed formation of seed plants.

Lesson Review

Review the lesson to answer these questions.
1. Name the two different plant parts in which seeds can form.
2. Name the steps in the life cycle of a pine tree after a seed is released from a cone.

People and Science

Food Production is a Full-time Job

Farmers grow many of the foods we eat. George Andrews is a farmer. He grows corn, wheat, soybeans, and hay.

Farmers plan the planting and harvesting of crops. In April, George plants hay and corn. He plants soybeans in late May, when danger of frost is past. During late September, he plants wheat.

George rotates his crops. Crop rotation is the planting of crops in different fields each year. Soil nutrients are used up if the same crop is always planted in the same field.

Some plants, such as alfalfa, are important. They are used as hay because they contain many nutrients. They also add nutrients to the soil. This kind of plant returns more nutrients to the soil than it uses for growth.

Harvesting begins in summer when hay is harvested. Soybeans and corn are harvested in autumn. Wheat seeds sprout in spring. The wheat itself is harvested in July.

George and other farmers are busy all year. George is proud of his farm. He is glad to provide other people with food.

Chapter 2 Review

Summary

1. Seed plants are different sizes and shapes. 2:1
2. Seed plants grow in different places. 2:1
3. Roots anchor plants and absorb water from the soil. 2:2
4. Stems support plants and transport nutrients and water between the leaves and the roots. 2:2
5. Most food is produced in the leaves of plants. 2:2
6. Seeds form in fruits or cones. 2:3
7. Germination, growth, and seed formation are parts of the plant life cycle. 2:3

Science Words

seed plant	**stem**	**leaflet**	**cone**
root	**leaf**	**compound leaf**	**plant life cycle**
nutrient	**simple leaf**	**flower**	

Understanding Science Words

Complete each of the following sentences with a word or words from the Science Words that will make the sentence correct.

1. The main part in which food is made is the _____.
2. Seed plants that do not have flowers may form seeds inside a _____.
3. The germination, growth, and formation of new seeds are parts of the _____.
4. A leaf with one part is called a _____.
5. The part of many plants in which seeds and fruits form is the _____.
6. The part of the plant that holds it in the ground is the _____.
7. Each part of the compound leaf is called a _____.

38

8. A plant's leaves are supported by a _____.
9. A plant that grows from a seed is called a _____.
10. A broad leaf with leaflets is a _____.
11. A substance needed by living things for growth is a _____.

Questions

A. Recalling Facts

Choose the word or phrase that correctly completes each of the following sentences.

1. Plants that grow from seeds are called
    (a) mosses.   (b) seed plants.   (c) ferns.   (d) flowers.
2. Roots hold plants to the ground and
    (a) take in water.   (c) form fruits.
    (b) scatter seeds.   (d) make most of plant's food.
3. Water and nutrients are transported from one part of a plant to another through
    (a) roots.   (b) leaves.   (c) flowers.   (d) stems.
4. The main plant part in which food is made is the
    (a) root.   (b) stem.   (c) leaf.   (d) flower.

B. Understanding Concepts

Answer each of the following questions using complete sentences.

1. Name the parts of a seed plant in which seeds may form.
2. Tell how the two groups of broad leaf plants are different from each other.

C. Applying Concepts

Think about what you have learned in this chapter. Answer each of the following questions using complete sentences.

1. Describe the kinds of places where seed plants may grow.
2. Tell about the phases of the life cycles of a cone-bearing seed plant and a seed plant with flowers.

UNIT 1 REVIEW

CHECKING YOURSELF

Answer these questions on a sheet of paper.
1. In what ways are seeds different from each other?
2. In what three ways are all seeds alike?
3. Why is the seed coat an important part of the seed?
4. Why do most houseplants need to be placed near a window?
5. What do plants need in order to make their own food?
6. Name ways in which seeds are scattered.
7. Name two different types of fruit and tell how the seeds of each may be scattered.
8. In what way are an oak tree, a violet, and a pine tree alike?
9. Why are roots important for the growth of seed plants?
10. Why is the stem of a plant important to the other parts of the plant?
11. Why are leaves important for the growth of a plant?
12. What are the stages or parts of the plant life cycle?

RECALLING ACTIVITIES

Think about the activities you did in this unit. Answer the questions about these activities.
1. What is in a seed? 1–1
2. How does light affect plant growth? 1–2
3. How does space affect plant growth? 1–3
4. Where does water go in a plant stem? 2–1

IDEAS TO EXPLORE

1. Read about the life of Luther Burbank or George Washington Carver. Prepare a report.
2. Construct a terrarium using a clear plastic container. Use a resource book to identify the plants used.
3. Draw and describe a plan for a small garden. Tell the kinds and number of seeds planted and describe how you will care for the garden.

CHALLENGING PROJECT

Do plants move? Construct a plant maze to find out. Use a rectangular box and some cardboard. Cut four strips from the cardboard. Each strip should be as tall as the box and four centimeters narrower than the box. Divide the box into five equal sections by taping the strips on alternate sides. Make an opening at one end of the box and place a vine plant at the other end. Cover the box and put it where the opening receives light. Water the plant as needed and make drawings each week to record its growth.

BOOKS TO READ

From Spore to Spore by Jerome Wexler, Dodd Mead & Co.: New York, © 1985.
    Learn how seeds travel.

How Plants Grow by Steve Parker, Franklin Watts: Danbury, CT, © 1985.
    Read about the growth of plants.

Soils & Plants by Michael Eden, Merrimack Publishers Circle: Salem, NH, © 1984.
    Learn about different types of soil and plants.

UNIT 2
Matter and Its Changes

Years ago a Chinese man, Tsai Lun, invented paper. He used pieces of bark, fish nets, and rags. They were beaten to a soft pulp and mixed in water. The pulp was dried on bamboo screens. Today, paper mills use logs, cloth, or recycled paper to make paper. How was making paper in China like making paper today? How was it different?

Tsai Lun invents paper—105 A. D.

Today, machines change wood pulp into paper.

Chapter 3
Matter

Most things around you are matter. The balloons, clown, children, and juice are matter. Matter is often grouped as solids, liquids, and gases. What matter shown here is a solid? A liquid? A gas?

Matter is found everywhere.

Properties of Objects   3:1

LESSON GOALS

In this lesson you will learn
- that properties describe objects.
- two properties are common to all objects.
- two of the units used to measure mass.

Suppose your class is going to play soccer. You are sent to get the ball. In the storage room you find many kinds of balls. How will you choose the right one?

People describe or tell about objects in many ways. Size and shape are used to describe objects. Color and smoothness or roughness can also be used to describe objects. Size, shape, color, smoothness, and roughness are some properties of objects. A **property** (PRAHP urt ee) is a characteristic of an object. What are some properties of the objects in Figure 3-2? How can you use properties to tell the fish apart?

Figure 3-1. Objects can be identified by their properties.

Figure 3-2. Color, size, and shape can be used to group the fish.

45

Activity 3-1 Properties of Matter

QUESTION How can we use properties?

Materials
students' shoes
pencil and paper

What to do
1. Work with 5 other students. Put 1 of your shoes in a pile with 1 shoe from each of the other students.
2. Have 1 student group the shoes based on one property.
3. Take turns guessing what property was used to group the shoes.
4. The first student who guesses correctly then groups the shoes based on a new property.
5. Record the properties used.

What did you learn?
1. What properties were used?
2. What property was easiest to guess?

Using what you learned
1. Describe the properties of a piece of your clothing. See if a friend can tell what you are describing.
2. Compare the properties of shoes and dogs.

Look at Figure 3-3. The objects shown are all different. All of these objects, however, are alike in two ways. First, all of the objects take up space. No two objects can be in the same place at the same time. Think about books on a bookshelf. Each book takes up space. No two books can be in the same place at the same time.

Second, all objects have mass. **Mass** is how much there is of an object. An elephant, for example, has more mass than a park bench. The park bench has more mass than a bicycle.

You can measure the mass of objects. One unit used to measure mass is the **gram.** One gram is a small amount of mass. Two paper clips have a mass of about one gram. A nickel has a mass of about five grams.

Figure 3-3. All objects have mass and take up space.

What is mass?

What is the mass of two paper clips?

47

Activity 3-2   Measuring Mass

QUESTION   How much mass?

Object	Predicted Mass	Nickels Used	Paper Clips Used	Mass in Grams

Materials
nickels
paper clips
balance
4 small objects
pencil and paper

What to do
1. Predict the mass of each object in nickels and paper clips.
2. Copy the chart. Write your predictions in the chart. Start with the object you predict has the most mass.
3. Put one object on the left side of the balance. Place nickels and paper clips on the right side until both pans are balanced.
4. Record the number of nickels and paper clips used.
5. Repeat steps 3 and 4 for the other objects.

What did you learn?
1. How many of your predictions were correct?
2. What object has the most mass?

Using what you learned
1. How can you find the mass for each object in grams? Try it.
2. When would it be hard to find the mass of objects by using nickels and paper clips?

48

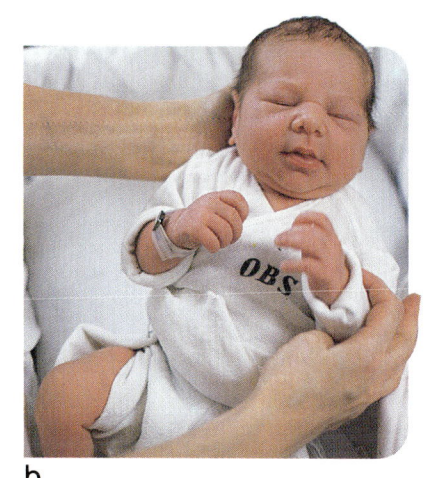

Figure 3-4. The dump truck (a) has a mass of about 10,000 kilograms. The baby (b) has a mass of 4 kilograms.

Sometimes you may want to measure a large mass. Large amounts of mass can be measured in kilograms (KIHL uh grams). A **kilogram** is 1,000 grams. The mass of the truck in Figure 3-4 is about 10,000 kilograms. The mass of the baby is 4 kilograms. What do you think your mass is?

What unit is used to measure large amounts of mass?

Lesson Summary
- A property is a characteristic of an object.
- All objects have mass and take up space.
- Two units used to measure mass are gram and kilogram.

Lesson Review
Review the lesson to answer these questions.
1. What are two properties of all objects?
2. What is the mass of one nickel?
3. What unit would you use to measure the mass of a person?

3:2 Matter

LESSON GOALS

In this lesson you will learn
- matter is found everywhere around you.
- all matter is made of atoms.
- some matter is made of one kind of atom.
- some matter is made of more than one kind of atom.

Figure 3-5. Matter takes up space and has mass.

Everything that takes up space and has mass is called **matter.** Rocks, clocks, bees, and trees are matter. Everything around you is made of matter. You are made of matter, too. Matter can be a solid, a liquid, or a gas. Figure 3-5 shows matter that is solid, liquid, and gas. The beach balls, for example, are solids and the water is a liquid. The air in the beach balls is also matter because air has mass and takes up space.

Figure 3-6. Just as the blanket is made of threads, matter is made of atoms.

From far away, the blanket in Figure 3-6 looks like it is all one piece. As you get closer, you see that the blanket is made of many small threads woven together. How might you get a good view of each separate thread?

Each thread in the blanket is made of even smaller parts. The small parts are called atoms. An **atom** is the smallest part of any kind of matter. Remember that all matter is the same in some ways. All matter has mass and takes up space. This is also true of atoms. Atoms have mass and take up space.

Matter made of only one kind of atom is called an **element.** Gold is an element. Gold is made of gold atoms. Oxygen is also an element. It is made of oxygen atoms. The properties of gold and oxygen are different. Gold is a heavy yellowish solid. Oxygen is a colorless gas that is part of the air. The properties of elements are different because they are made of different kinds of atoms.

What is an atom?

Name two elements.

51

From how many different kinds of atoms is table salt made?

Sometimes different kinds of atoms join together. Table salt, for example, is made of two kinds of atoms and sugar is made of three kinds of atoms. Table 3–1 gives other examples of matter made from more than one kind of atom. There are many different types of matter because atoms can be joined together in many ways.

Table 3–1 Matter With Different Kinds of Atoms	
	Number of Different Kinds of Atoms
Water	2
Rubbing Alcohol	3
Baking Soda	4

Lesson Summary

- Everything that takes up space and has mass is called matter.
- An atom is the smallest part of any kind of matter.
- An element is made of only one kind of atom.
- Most matter is made of different kinds of atoms that are joined together.

Lesson Review

Review the lesson to answer these questions.

1. What is an element?
2. Give an example of matter that is made of more than one kind of atom.
3. Is a shadow matter? Why or why not?

Science and Technology

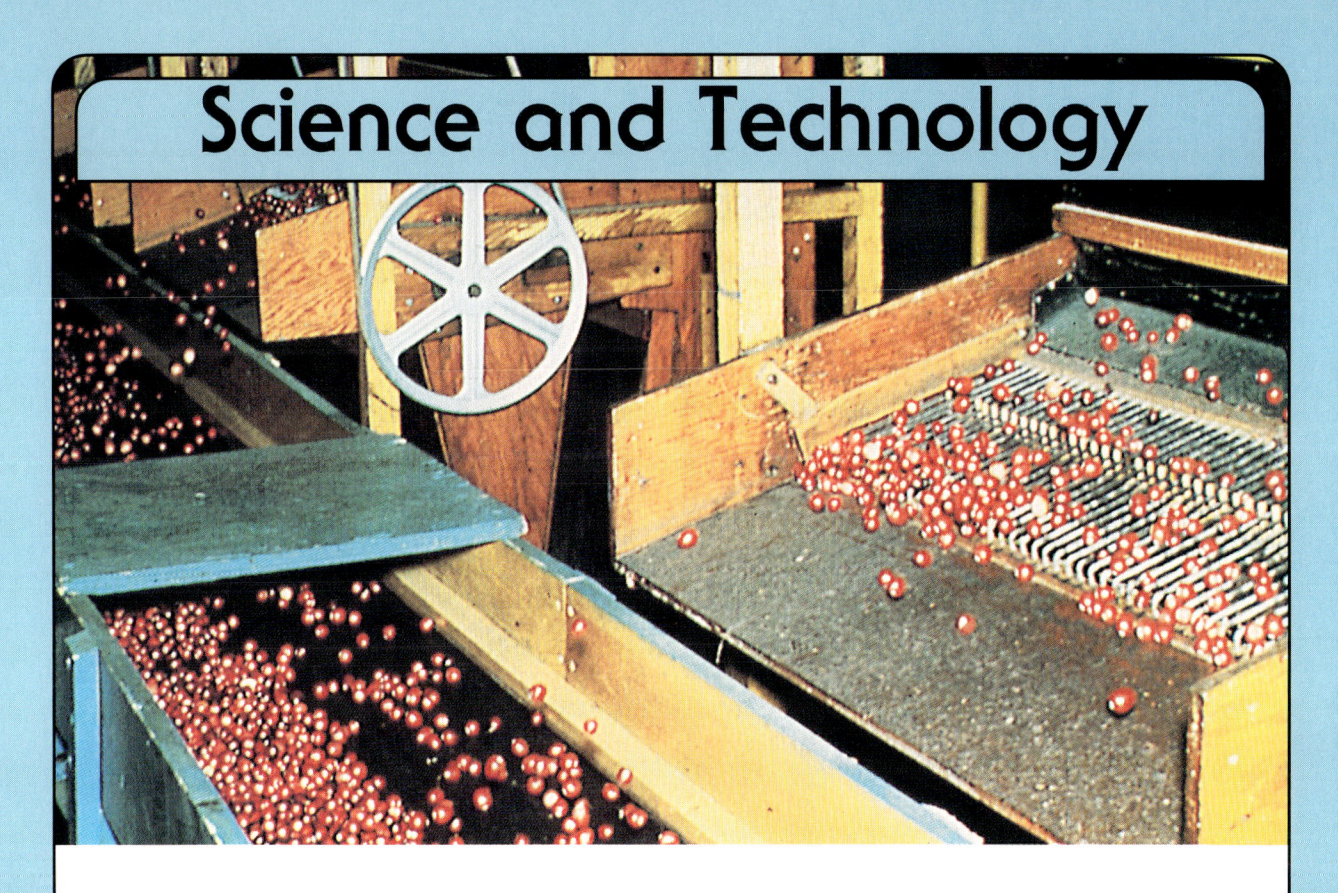

Bouncing Berries

People have enjoyed cranberries for many years. These berries are sold as whole fruit, juice, or sauce. Cranberries are usually sorted by a bounce test. Freshly harvested berries are dropped onto a slanted board from a height of about 20 cm. Firm berries will bounce over a short fence. Soft berries, used for juice or sauce, will not pass the bounce test.

Some berries get bruised in the bounce test. They get mashed when they hit the board. Scientists are trying to find a better way to measure cranberry firmness.

In a new method, berries are bounced off the paper surface of a radio speaker connected to a transmitter. When the berries hit the speaker a piece of metal moves through a magnetic coil. An electrical pattern is created. This pattern shows the cranberry growers whether the berries are hard or soft.

Using an electrical system to sort cranberries may someday be common. Until then, the cranberry juice you drink may be the product of berries that did not have enough bounce to get over a fence.

3:3 States of Matter

LESSON GOALS

In this lesson you will learn
- the properties of solid matter.
- the properties of liquid matter
- the properties of matter that is a gas.

Wood, milk, and air have different properties. They are put in different groups because of their different properties. Wood is a solid, milk is a liquid, and air is a gas. Matter can be grouped by whether it is a solid, a liquid, or a gas. Solids, liquids, and gases are called states of matter.

What are the groupings of matter as solids, liquids, and gases called?

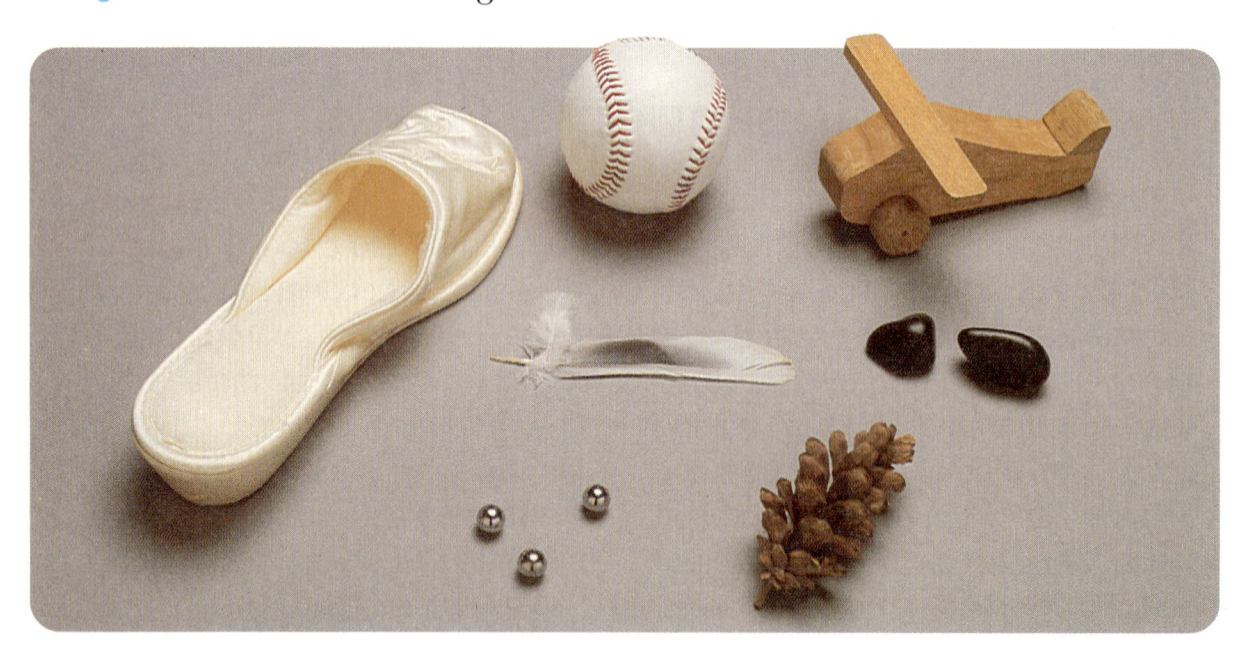

Figure 3-7. Solids have a certain size and shape.

Wood is a solid. A **solid** is matter that has a certain size and shape. Most of the objects you see are in the solid state. Your desk is a solid. It does not change its shape or size.

54

Atoms form particles of matter. These particles are moving but are too small to be seen. The particles in solids are shaking back and forth. Notice the particles of matter as a solid in Figure 3-8. In solids, the shaking particles are packed close to each other. In solids, they form a definite pattern. Solids do not easily change shape because of this pattern.

Milk is a liquid. A **liquid** is matter that has a certain size or volume but does not have a shape of its own. A liquid takes the shape of its container. Look at Figure 3-9. What shape is the milk in a pitcher? What shape is the same milk in the glass in Figure 3-9?

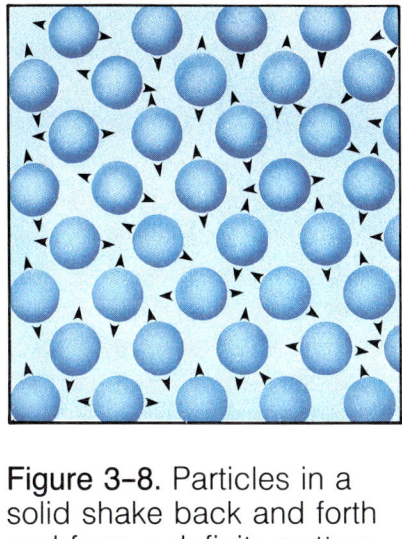

Figure 3-8. Particles in a solid shake back and forth and form a definite pattern.

Figure 3-9. The shape of liquids can change.

What can change in a liquid? What cannot change?

Figure 3-10. Particles in a liquid do not form a definite pattern.

Figure 3-11. Some matter is like a solid and a liquid.

Liquids flow. They can be poured. You can pour milk from a pitcher into a glass. Liquids also have a certain volume. When you pour milk from a small carton into a tall glass, the shape of the milk changes. The amount of milk, however, is still the same.

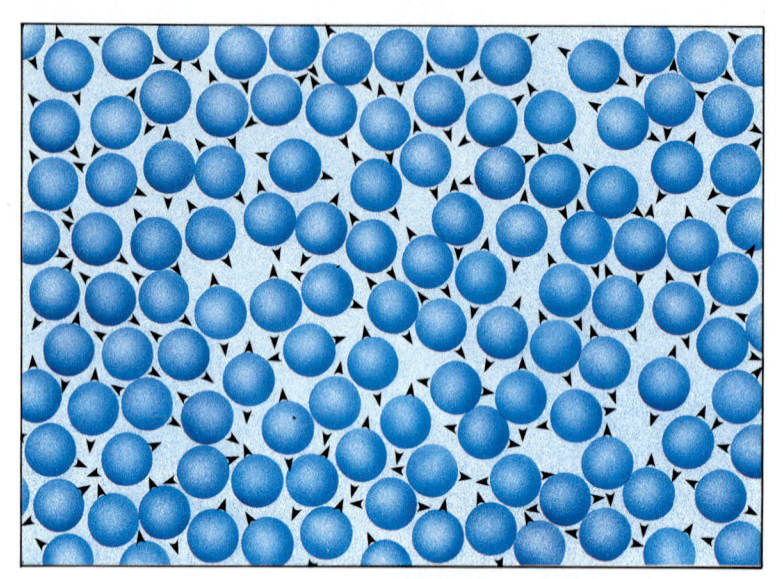

The particles in liquids move more freely than those in solids. Particles in liquids fall over each other. They do not form a definite pattern. Liquids pour and change shape because of the way their particles move.

Some matter has properties of both liquids and solids. This kind of matter does not seem to change its shape. Its particles, however, do not form a definite pattern. The shape of the matter changes after a period of time. How are the objects in Figure 3-11 like a solid? How are they like a liquid?

56

Activity 3-3 States of Matter

QUESTION   Is it a solid or a liquid?

Materials
newspaper
paper cup
mystery matter
paper towels
pencil and paper

What to do
1. Cover your desk with newspaper.
2. Get a cup of "mystery matter" from your teacher.
3. Carefully test the "mystery matter." Try the following things:
   (a) Try to pour it.
   (b) Poke it with your fingers.
   (c) Roll it into a ball and try to bounce it on the desk.

What did you learn?
1. How was the "mystery matter" like a solid?
2. How was it like a liquid?

Using what you learned
1. What other matter has properties of both a solid and a liquid? Make a list.
2. How is each type of matter on the list like a solid? How is each like a liquid?

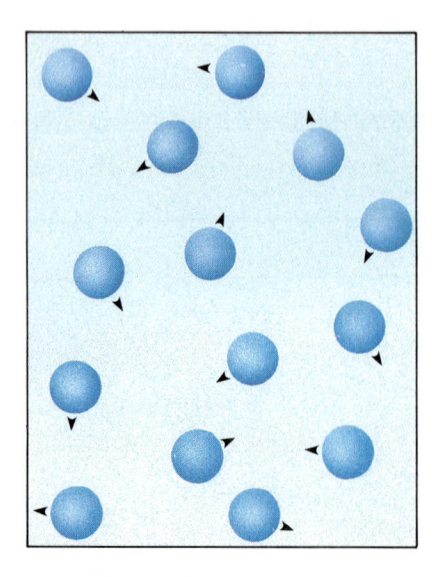

Figure 3-12. Particles of a gas spread out to fill any container.

A **gas** is matter that has no shape or size of its own. Air is a gas. Air takes the shape of any container it is in. It also spreads out to fill any size container. Air particles can spread out to fill a large container such as a barrel. They can also fill a smaller container such as a jar. What would happen to the space between particles if air were moved from a large to a small container?

Gas particles move very freely. They are also farther apart from each other than the particles of a liquid or a solid. The particles of a gas spread out to fill any container. The same amount of gas can fill a small jar or a large room.

What state of matter is air?

Lesson Summary

- Solid matter has a certain size and shape.
- Liquid matter has a certain size but does not have a shape of its own.
- Matter that is a gas does not have a size or shape of its own.

Lesson Review

Review the lesson to answer these questions.

1. What are three states of matter?
2. In which state are the particles of matter in a regular pattern?
3. In which state of matter are the particles farthest apart?
4. How are the properties of solids and liquids alike? How are they different?

Language Arts Skills

Similarities and Differences

Objects may be similar or different in their properties. Look at the pictures on this page. Think of ways in which these objects are similar and different.

The objects are alike because they float in the air. However, they are also different from each other. The kite has a different shape than the balloons. The toy balloon floats because it is filled with helium. The big balloon floats because it is filled with hot air. The kite flies because it is blown by the wind.

You may use pictures to find similarities and differences. Written information can also be used to find similarities and differences. *Read the following paragraph.*

Oxygen and gold are both elements. However, they are different in the way they appear. One is a colorless gas. The other is a heavy, yellow metal.

- How are oxygen and gold alike?
- How are they different?

Chapter 3 Review

Summary

1. A property is a characteristic of an object. 3:1
2. All objects take up space and have mass. 3:1
3. The mass of objects is measured in grams and kilograms. 3:1
4. Matter is anything that takes up space and has mass. 3:2
5. All matter is made of atoms. 3:2
6. An element is made of only one kind of atom. 3:2
7. Most matter is made of more than one kind of atom. 3:2
8. Solid matter has a certain size and shape. 3:3
9. Liquid matter has a certain size but not a certain shape. 3:3
10. Matter that is a gas has no size or shape of its own. 3:3

Science Words

property	kilogram	element	liquid
mass	matter	solid	gas
gram	atom		

Understanding Science Words

Complete each of the following sentences with a word or words from the Science Words that will make the sentence correct.

1. Matter that has no shape or size of its own is called a _____.

2. All objects that have mass and take up space are _____.

3. Matter that is made of only one kind of atom is called an _____.

4. Matter that has a certain size but no shape of its own is called a _____.

5. One thousand grams has the same mass as a _____.
6. A small unit used to measure mass is the _____.
7. We can describe a characteristic of an object as a _____.
8. Matter that has a certain size and shape is called a _____.
9. The smallest part of matter is called an _____.
10. A measure of how much there is of an object is called _____.

Questions

A. Recalling Facts

Choose the word or phrase that correctly completes each of the following sentences.
1. Particles move least freely in
    (a) grams.   (b) solids.   (c) liquids.   (d) gases.
2. A person's mass is best measured in
    (a) atoms.   (c) kilograms.
    (b) Celsius.   (d) properties.

B. Understanding Concepts

Answer each of the following questions using complete sentences.
1. What are two properties that all matter has?
2. Why are there so many kinds of matter?

C. Applying Concepts

Think about what you have learned in this chapter. Answer each of the following questions using complete sentences.
1. Most gases cannot be seen. How do we know they are there?
2. Compare the properties of solids, liquids, and gases.

Chapter 4
Changes in Matter

Matter changes. Some changes in matter are made by people. Other changes are made by nature. How did people change the rock to make this statue? How is nature changing this statue?

Matter changes.

Changing Matter 4:1

LESSON GOALS

In this lesson you will learn
- the properties of matter can change.
- matter can expand and contract.
- why heat causes matter to expand.

The properties of matter can change. In Figure 4-1, the boys are changing matter. How have they changed the properties of the airplanes?

People can change the properties of matter. Wood is changed when it is sanded. The surface of the wood is changed from rough to smooth.

Figure 4-1. Properties of solids can be changed.

63

The size and shape of matter can also be changed. Some solids can be broken, bent, torn, or stretched. When a solid is broken, bent, torn, or stretched, its shape is changed.

The properties of matter that is a liquid or a gas can also be changed. Look at Figure 4-2. How have the properties of the matter been changed?

Figure 4-2. The properties of a liquid can be changed.

Color, size, shape, smoothness, and roughness are some physical properties of matter. Physical properties of matter can be used to tell how matter looks or feels. A change in a physical property is called a physical change.

What is a change in the physical properties of matter called?

Heat can cause matter to change. Think of how a thermometer works. When the air warms, the liquid in the tube rises. It rises because the liquid expands when it is heated. Matter that expands gets bigger. It takes up more space. Most matter expands when it is heated. Most matter also contracts when it cools. Matter that contracts gets smaller. It takes up less space. When will the liquid in the thermometer contract?

Matter expands because heat makes the particles of matter move faster. As they move faster, the particles move farther apart. This movement makes the matter expand.

Look at Figure 4–3(a). In this photo, the students are sitting at their desks. They are not moving very much. In Figure 4–3(b), the students are running outside. They are moving fast on the playground. They use a lot of space as they move around. What would happen if the playground were the same size as the classroom?

Figure 4–3. More space is used on the playground (b) than in the classroom (a) because the speed of the students has increased.

a

b

65

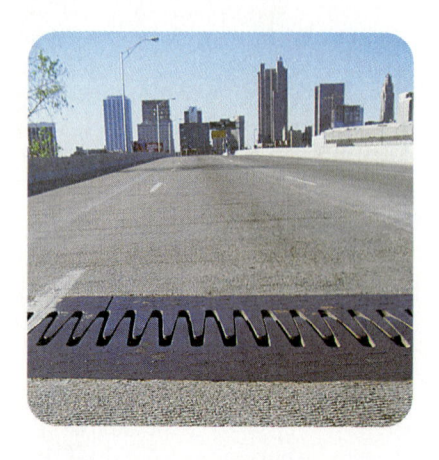

Figure 4-4. Expansion joints allow the concrete to expand without breaking.

Why is tar placed between sections of concrete in roads?

Sometimes problems take place when matter expands. Pavement in roads may expand and crack in hot weather. People want to stop the roads from cracking. Some roads are built with tar strips between the sections of concrete. The soft tar allows the concrete to expand. There is less chance that the concrete will crack. Some buildings are also built with materials that expand safely in hot weather.

Matter that expands may cause other problems. Tires get hot when a car is driven for a long time. What do you think happens to the air in the tires? What might happen if the rubber on the tires has worn thin?

Lesson Summary

- Physical changes take place in matter.
- Most matter expands when it is heated and contracts when it cools.
- Heat causes matter to expand because the particles of matter move farther apart from each other.

Lesson Review

Review the lesson to answer these questions.

1. What are some physical properties that can be changed?
2. What happens to most matter when it is heated? Cooled?
3. How does expansion of matter cause problems?

Activity 4-1 Expansion of Air

QUESTION Why does the dime move?

Materials
soft drink bottle dropper
freezer dime
safety goggles pencil and paper
water

What to do
1. Place the empty bottle in the freezer for 30 minutes.
2. Put on the safety goggles.
3. Put the cold bottle on a table. Using the dropper, place a few drops of water on the rim of the bottle.
4. Cover the mouth of the bottle with a dime.
5. Watch the dime and the bottle for a few minutes.

What did you learn?
1. What happened to the dime?
2. What happened to the air in the bottle?

Using what you learned
1. From the results of this activity how do you know that air is matter?
2. How is what happened to the air in the bottle similar to how a thermometer works?

4:2 Matter Changes State

LESSON GOALS

In this lesson you will learn
- heat may cause matter to change state.
- the difference between melting and freezing.
- the difference between evaporation and condensation.

Addition or loss of heat causes matter to expand or contract. Heat may also cause matter to change its state. What if you need juice for breakfast? You open a can of frozen juice but the juice does not pour. You leave the can on the counter for a while. Later, you try to pour the juice again. This time the juice pours easily. Why could you pour the juice the second time you tried?

Figure 4-5. Solids change to liquids when heat is added.

68

Figure 4-6. Warm temperatures cause the ice to melt.

Solid matter can change state. Solids melt when they change to the liquid state. Heat makes the particles in solids move faster. Heat also makes the particles move apart. The pattern formed by the particles breaks down. As the pattern breaks down, the solids change to liquids. You may have seen ice change to liquid water. Most solids melt if enough heat is added.

What word describes the change of matter from the solid to the liquid state?

Figure 4-7. High temperatures are necessary to melt some solids.

69

Activity 4-2 An Ice Cube Race

QUESTION How can you win the race?

Materials
ice cube   paper towels
various materials   pencil and paper
stopwatch

What to do
1. Think of ways to melt an ice cube.
2. Choose the way you think will melt the ice cube in the shortest time.
3. Wait for your teacher's starting signal. Try the way you chose.
4. Record how long it takes for your ice cube to melt.
5. Compare your results with those of classmates.

What did you learn?
1. What was the shortest time required to melt an ice cube?
2. What way was used to melt the ice cube in the shortest time?

Using what you learned
1. What could you do to keep an ice cube solid the longest time? Try it and record the results.
2. Why do some people put cold food in foam ice chests when they go on picnics?

Liquids can also change state. Liquids freeze when they change to the solid state. Liquids freeze when heat is removed from them. As heat is lost, the particles of matter move more slowly. They move closer together. The particles form a definite pattern and the liquid becomes a solid.

Figure 4-8. Warm temperatures speed the evaporation of water.

Liquids can also change to gases. Remember that particles of liquids move. They bump into each other. Particles on top of a liquid may be bumped away from the rest of the liquid. These particles become a gas. The change from a liquid to a gas is called **evaporation** (ih vap uh RAY shun).

After they wash clothes, people use dryers or hang the clothes outside to dry. Warm temperatures in the dryer or outdoors speed evaporation. Liquids can evaporate at any temperature. Heat makes them evaporate faster. Why do you think this is true?

Activity 4-3 Evaporation of Water

QUESTION What will happen to the water?

Materials

baking dish   plastic wrap
water   paper cup
tape   pencil and paper

What to do

1. Place the dish by a window.
2. Fill the dish half full of water.
3. Cover the dish tightly with plastic wrap.
4. Tape the plastic wrap to the dish.
5. Observe the dish each day for 2 days.
6. Record your observations.

What did you learn?

1. What happened to the total amount of water in the covered dish?
2. What happened to the plastic wrap?
3. What changes did you observe between the first and second day?

Using what you learned

1. What caused the changes?
2. What do you think would happen if you took the plastic wrap off the dish? Try it and find out.
3. How does this activity show why bathroom mirrors sometimes become foggy?

People and Science

Making Diamonds

Carol Lee makes diamonds. The diamonds are not used for jewelry. They are used in industries and research. Diamonds are made from carbon and normally take millions of years to form. Carol, however, makes diamonds every day in her lab.

Carbon is mixed with some metals. It is then heated to temperatures of about 1,300°C. The mixture is also put under great pressure. The mixture melts and the carbon becomes diamond. When it cools, the diamond is cleaned and unwanted material is removed.

These artificial diamonds are used in many ways. The size and quality of the diamonds determine how the diamonds are used. Large, high quality diamonds are used on saws that cut rocks and also on oil well drill bits.

Small, imperfect artifical diamonds are combined with other materials to produce polishing compounds. The edges of people's glasses and car windows are polished with artificial diamonds. Carol says that in many cases her diamonds are better than natural diamonds.

Chapter 4 Review

Summary

1. Properties of matter can be changed. 4:1
2. Matter can expand or contract. 4:1
3. Adding heat causes particles of matter to move faster and farther apart. 4:1
4. Matter may change state when heat is added or taken away. 4:2
5. Solids melt when they change to liquids. 4:2
6. Liquids freeze when they change to solids. 4:2
7. The change from a liquid to a gas is evaporation. 4:2
8. The change from a gas to a liquid is condensation. 4:2
9. Matter that is mixed together but keeps its own properties is called a mixture. 4:3
10. A compound is matter that has different properties than the elements from which it is made. 4:3
11. A chemical change takes place when a compound is formed. 4:3

Science Words

evaporation   condensation   mixture   compound

Understanding Science Words

Complete each of the following sentences with a word or words from the Science Words that will make the sentence correct.

1. The change from a liquid to a gas is called _____.
2. Matter that is mixed together without changing the properties of each type of matter is a _____.
3. The change from a gas to a liquid is called _____.
4. Matter that is formed when a chemical change takes place is a _____.

Questions

A. Recalling Facts

Choose the word or phrase that correctly completes each of the following sentences.

1. Mixtures can
   - (a) be separated.
   - (b) not be separated.
   - (c) only be formed with liquids.
   - (d) only be formed with solids.

2. When rust forms, the kind of change that takes place is
   - (a) state.
   - (b) physical.
   - (c) chemical.
   - (d) evaporation.

3. An example of a common mixture is
   - (a) oxygen.
   - (b) fruit salad.
   - (c) rust.
   - (d) salt.

4. Evaporation speeds up when liquids are exposed to
   - (a) heat.
   - (b) expansion.
   - (c) condensation.
   - (d) cold.

B. Understanding Concepts

Answer each of the following questions using complete sentences.

1. Name two ways that heat changes matter.
2. Name a solid, liquid, and gas and tell how the physical properties of each can be changed.
3. What causes matter to expand and contract?
4. What may happen to pavement in hot weather?

C. Applying Concepts

Think about what you have learned in this chapter. Answer each of the following questions using complete sentences.

1. Why would people pour hot water on tight jar lids?
2. You are cooking stew. There is too much liquid in the pan. Why do you take the cover off the pan?

UNIT 2 REVIEW

CHECKING YOURSELF

Answer these questions on a sheet of paper.
1. Name five properties that can be used to describe objects.
2. What units are used to measure the mass of an object?
3. Which unit is used to measure the mass of an automobile?
4. In what way are solids and liquids the same? Different?
5. What would happen to the gas particles in a balloon if the balloon was deflated in a large room?
6. Why does heat cause matter to expand?
7. What is an element?
8. Why are the properties of elements different from each other?
9. Name two compounds that are found in your home.
10. What is the difference between evaporation and condensation?
11. What is the difference between a mixture and a compound?
12. How does temperature affect evaporation and condensation?

RECALLING ACTIVITIES

Think about the activities you did in this unit. Answer the questions about these activities.
1. How can you use properties?   3-1
2. How do you measure mass?   3-2
3. How do you classify properties of matter?   3-3
4. How can you tell that air expands?   4-1
5. How did you experiment with an ice cube?   4-2
6. How can you observe evaporation of water?   4-3

IDEAS TO EXPLORE

1. Make a bulletin board display on changes of matter. Use magazine pictures or your own drawings. Tell whether each picture shows a physical or chemical change.
2. Write a story telling how it would feel to be made of snow. What changes would happen to you?
3. Make a display listing common elements and how they are used at home and school.

CHALLENGING PROJECT

Work with a partner to complete the following project. Use flat ice cream sticks and other materials to build a model of a bridge that is used for a highway. The bridge should be designed in such a way that it will prevent the breaking of pavement due to expansion during hot weather. Show your model to the class and explain how it is designed for expansion during hot weather.

BOOKS TO READ

Berenstain Bears' Science Fair by Jan Berenstain and Stan Berenstain, Random House: New York, © 1984.
   Get some ideas for great science fair projects.

Bet You Can! Science Possibilities to Fool You by Vicky Cobb and Kathy Darling, Avon Books: New York, © 1983.
   Try to figure out these science puzzles.

220 Easy-to-Do Science Experiments for Young People by Muriel Mandell, Dover Publications: Mineola, NY, © 1985.
   Learn about science by doing these experiments.

UNIT 3
Earth's Rocks

Years ago, Incas ruled one of the largest and richest empires in South America. These walls were built on mountain slopes by the Incas. Walls such as these enclosed areas within Inca cities. The Incas were skilled workers and shaped the rocks of these walls so the rocks fit together very closely. Today, rocks are also used to make buildings. Some buildings are also made so they blend into the surrounding area. How is the use of rocks in this building like their use in the Inca walls?

Walls of Inca city—1450

Modern building made with rocks

Chapter 5
How Are Rocks Formed?

Rocks form in different ways. Some rocks are formed when hot liquid material inside Earth cools. Other rocks form from solid Earth material that is stuck together. A third type of rock forms when heat and pressure change rocks that have already formed. Look at the picture of rock layers. How can you tell that pressure has changed the rocks?

Pressure inside Earth changes rocks.

Rocks and Earth Layers 5:1

LESSON GOALS

In this lesson you will learn

- rocks are made of minerals.
- rocks have different properties.
- Earth has layers.

Figure 5-1. Carla has two favorite rocks.

Carla likes to collect rocks. She often wonders how the rocks formed. Her favorite rocks are those shown in Figure 5-1. Each rock has different properties. How would you describe each rock?

What Are Rocks?

All rocks are made of one or more minerals (MIHN uh rulz). A **mineral** is solid matter that is found in nature but is not made by plants or animals. You can tell minerals apart by their properties. Minerals are different colors. They may be shiny, dull, or clear like glass. How many minerals can you see in the rock in Figure 5-2?

Figure 5-2. Different kinds of minerals are found in rocks.

85

A **rock** is a solid made of one or more minerals. Like minerals, rocks also have different properties. Some rocks are colorful. Others are plain. Some rocks are smooth and other rocks are rough. Some rocks are very hard while others are soft.

Figure 5-3. Rocks have different properties.

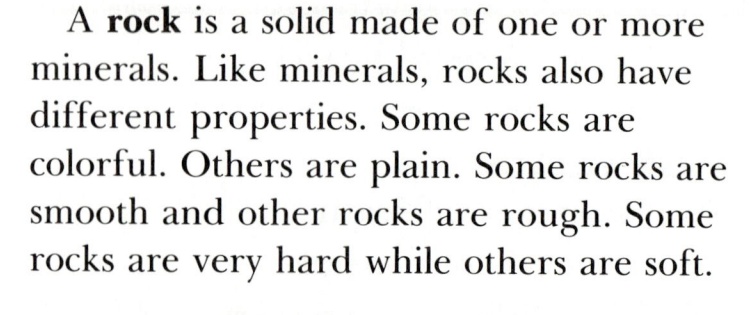

Where Are Rocks Found?

Earth has layers like a peach. When you slice a peach, you can see its layers. A thin skin is all around the outside. A thick layer is in the middle. A seed is in the center. Scientists cannot slice Earth. They know, however, that Earth has layers, too. Look at Figure 5-4. Compare the peach and Earth.

How are a peach and Earth similar?

Figure 5-4. The layers of a peach can be compared to those of Earth.

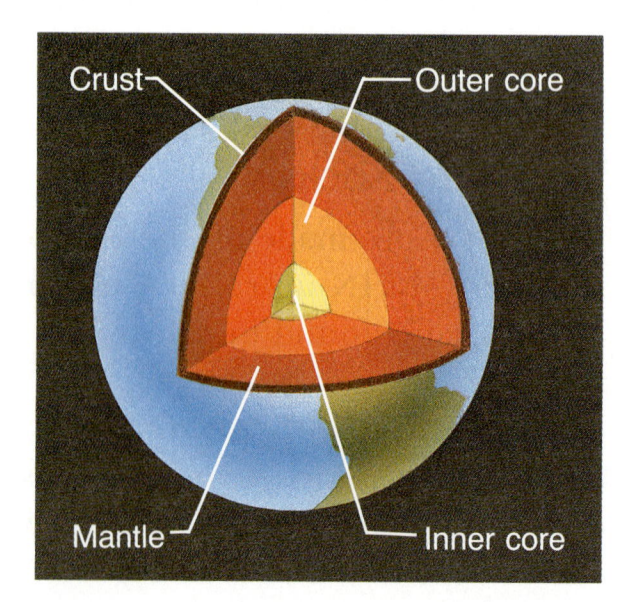

86

Figure 5-5. Much of Earth's crust is solid rock.

The top layer of Earth is called the **crust.** Mountains, valleys, and ocean floors are all part of Earth's crust. Most of the crust is solid rock. The small rocks you find on the ground come from larger rocks of the crust. Some areas of the crust are covered with soil.

The crust is thin like the skin of a peach. Earth's crust, however, is not even in thickness. It is thin in some places and thick in others. Ocean floor crust is thinner than the crust under land areas. The crust of the ocean floor is about 5 kilometers thick. The crust is about 35 kilometers thick under most land areas. It is even thicker under mountains.

How does the thickness of ocean floor crust compare to the crust under land areas?

Figure 5-6. Earth's crust is not even in thickness.

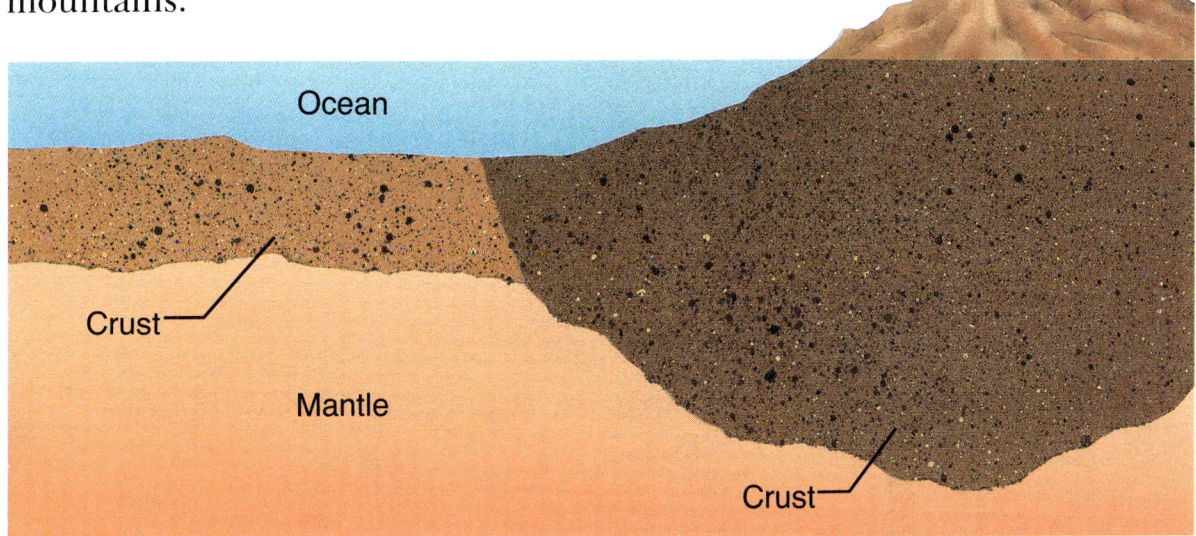

How are mantle rocks different from rocks found in Earth's crust?

Layers of rock beneath the crust make up the **mantle** (MANT ul). The mantle is Earth's middle layer. It can be compared to the middle part of the peach. Mantle rocks are different from rocks in the crust. Mantle rocks are more tightly packed. Some are partly melted.

Like a peach, Earth also has a center section. The **core** is the innermost part of Earth. It has two parts. The outer core is liquid. The inner core is solid. Both are very hot and made mostly of iron. The core is the hottest part of Earth.

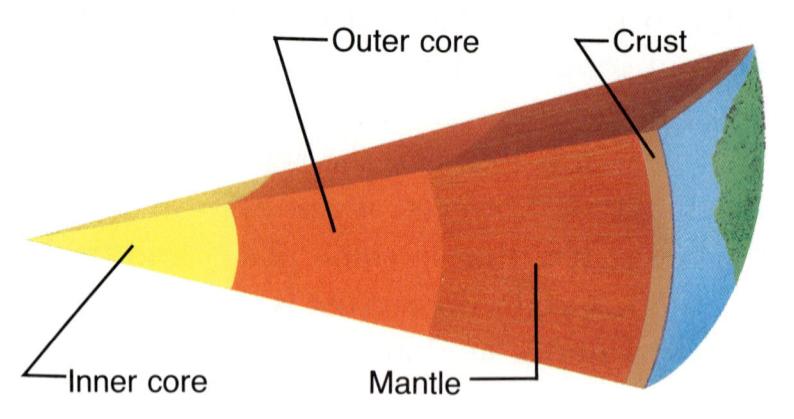

Figure 5-7. Earth's mantle and core are represented in this drawing.

Lesson Summary
- Rocks are made of one or more minerals.
- Rocks may be smooth, rough, colorful, or plain.
- The crust, mantle, and core are layers of Earth.

Lesson Review
Review the lesson to answer these questions.
1. What is a mineral?
2. What is the name of Earth's middle layer?

Science and Technology

Extinction of Dinosaurs

Sedimentary rocks contain clues to the history of Earth. Fossils are remains of animals and plants that are preserved in rocks. Scientists study these rocks to find out when the rocks were formed. Scientists can also find out about how long ago the plants and animals were alive.

Information about dinosaurs comes from fossils. About 65 million years ago, dinosaurs and many other living things became extinct. Scientists have studied sedimentary rocks to find out why this happened.

There are two major theories. According to one theory, an asteriod or other space object struck Earth. The impact might have added toxic material to the air and water, and also blocked out sunlight. As a result, many life forms became extinct.

The second theory suggests that erupting volcanoes changed Earth's climate. Dust from the volcanoes blocked sunlight, causing temperature changes on Earth. Dinosaurs and other animals and plants could not adapt and became extinct.

5:2 How Are Rocks Formed?

LESSON GOALS

In this lesson you will learn
- there are three types of rocks.
- fossils are found in some rocks.

Scientists study the properties of rocks. They compare the way rocks look and feel. Some rocks are made of pieces of different rocks. They feel rough. Others appear to be made of just one material. They have a smoother surface.

Rocks Formed from Magma

Some rocks form from melted Earth material. Hot liquid material that forms inside Earth is called **magma** (MAG muh). Magma rises in Earth. It becomes rock when it cools.

Sometimes magma flows onto the surface of Earth. This often takes place at a volcano. Magma at Earth's surface is called **lava** (LAHV uh). Lava flows over the ground and cools quickly. It forms rock when it cools.

What is magma?

Figure 5-8. Lava flows down sides of a volcano and hardens when it cools.

90

Figure 5-9. Igneous rocks may contain different sizes of minerals.

A rock that forms from cooled magma or lava is called an **igneous** (IHG nee uhs) **rock.** All igneous rocks do not look the same. Rocks that cool slowly have large minerals. Therefore, igneous rocks that form when magma cools slowly have large minerals. You can see them without a hand lens. Look at the rocks in Figure 5-9. Which rock cooled slowly? Why do you think so?

Lava cools quickly. Large minerals do not have time to form. Rocks formed from cooled lava have small minerals. The minerals may be so small you cannot see them. Which of the two rocks in Figure 5-10 cooled faster? How do you know?

Figure 5-10. Lava has much smaller minerals than rocks formed inside Earth.

91

a b

Figure 5-11. Conglomerate (a) and limestone (b) form from different kinds of sediments.

What are sediments?

Rocks Formed from Sediments

Water, wind, and ice break large rocks into smaller rocks. Small rocks can be broken into even smaller pieces. These pieces are called sediments (SED uh muhnts). **Sediments** are pieces of Earth material. They are carried by wind, ice, and water. When the wind or water slows down, or the ice melts, they are dropped. After a period of time, the sediments become pressed together to form rock. A **sedimentary** (sed uh MENT uh ree) **rock** is a rock made of sediments that are pressed together.

Some sedimentary rocks are made when minerals form in a lake or ocean. When the water evaporates, minerals are left behind. They become hardened into rocks. Figure 5-11 shows two sedimentary rocks. Which rock formed in moving water? Which rock formed in an ocean? Explain your answers.

Figure 5-12. Sedimentary rocks may form from sand.

Activity 5-1 Sedimentary Rocks

QUESTION How is sedimentary rock formed?

Materials
paper cup
cementing solution
sand
hand lens
pencil and paper

What to do
1. Fill the cup half full of sand. Pack the sand with your hand.
2. Slowly add cementing solution until all of the sand is wet.
3. Put the cup in a warm place until the sand dries completely.
4. Carefully tear away the paper cup.
5. Observe the "sandstone" with the hand lens.

What did you learn?
1. How did the sand change?
2. How is your "rock" like sedimentary rock?

Using what you learned
1. If you found clam shells in sedimentary rock, what could you say about the place where the rock formed?
2. Why is your "sandstone" not a rock?

Figure 5-13. Fossils are found in sedimentary rocks.

From what is coal made?

Figure 5-14. Heat and pressure can change sandstone (a) to quartzite (b).

a   b

Over a long period of time, plant and animal parts may become covered with sediments. These parts may become fossils. Some sedimentary rocks contain fossils. Coal is sedimentary rock. It is made from plants that lived long ago.

Rocks Formed from Other Rocks

Look at the two rocks in Figure 5-14. Both rocks contain many of the same minerals. Both rocks used to be the same. Now rock b is changed. How has it changed?

The temperature and pressure within Earth are not equal at each layer. The temperature and pressure increase in Earth from the crust to the core. Temperature and pressure can change rocks. A rock that is changed by heat and pressure is a **metamorphic** (met uh MOR fihk) **rock.** Igneous and sedimentary rocks can become metamorphic rocks. Metamorphic rocks can also become other metamorphic rocks.

94

Activity 5-2 Metamorphic Rocks

QUESTION How is metamorphic rock formed?

Materials
modeling clay
paper clips
waxed paper
heavy book
pencil and paper

What to do
1. Take 3 clay cakes. Each should be a different color.
2. Push paper clips into all parts of the cakes.
3. Stack the cakes on waxed paper.
4. Put waxed paper on top of the stack. Lay a book on top of the stack. Press down hard on the book.
5. Remove the book and waxed paper.
6. Observe any changes in the stack.

What did you learn?
1. How did the clay cakes change when they were pressed?
2. What happened to the paper clips?

Using what you learned
1. How is the pressed clay like a metamorphic rock?
2. What did you learn by looking at the position of the paper clips after the activity was finished?

What is one difference between two types of metamorphic rocks?

Metamorphic rocks can be grouped by the way they look. Some of them have bands. Pressure causes some minerals to form bands. Other metamorphic rocks are not banded. Which metamorphic rock in Figure 5-15 is banded?

Figure 5-15. Some metamorphic rocks have bands while others do not.

Lesson Summary

- Igneous, sedimentary, and metamorphic are the three types of rocks found on Earth.
- Fossils may be found in sedimentary rocks.

Lesson Review

Review the lesson to answer these questions.

1. What is lava?
2. Compare the sizes of minerals in igneous rocks that cool slowly with those that cool quickly.
3. Why would fossils probably not be found in metamorphic rocks?

People and Science

Looking for Clues in Rocks

Peter Schwans is a sedimentologist. A sedimentologist is a scientist who studies and describes sedimentary rocks. Peter studies the sedimentary rock called conglomerate (kun GLAHM rut). A conglomerate is made of pebbles that are cemented together by sand and mud.

Peter spends every summer collecting rock samples in central Utah. To begin a day's work, he drives a four-wheel drive van high into the mountains. There he uses a rock hammer to break off rock pieces that he takes back to the laboratory.

Peter also makes observations. He marks his location on a special kind of map that shows Earth's surface features. He also records the rocks that are above and below the conglomerates. Peter uses this information to find out what this part of Utah was like in the ancient past.

Peter discovered that Utah used to be much different than it is today. Millions of years ago, it was covered by a large seaway, and mountain ranges were eroded. This Earth material later formed the conglomerates that Peter studies today.

Chapter 5 Review

Summary

1. Rocks are made of one or more minerals. 5:1
2. Rocks may be smooth, rough, colorful, or plain. 5:1
3. Earth's layers are the crust, mantle, and core. 5:1
4. Three types of rocks are igneous, sedimentary, and metamorphic. 5:2
5. Fossils are found in sedimentary rocks. 5:2

Science Words

mineral	**core**	**sediments**
rock	**magma**	**sedimentary rock**
crust	**lava**	**metamorphic rock**
mantle	**igneous rock**	

Understanding Science Words

Complete each of the following sentences with a word or words from the Science Words that will make the sentence correct.

1. Cooled magma forms _____.
2. Pieces of Earth material are called _____.
3. Earth's top layer is called the _____.
4. Magma that flows onto the surface of Earth is called _____.
5. A rock formed from sediments that are pressed together is _____.
6. Earth's middle layer is the _____.
7. The innermost part of Earth is the _____.
8. A rock changed by heat and pressure is called _____.
9. Solid matter found in nature that is not made by plants or animals is a _____.

10. Liquid Earth material is called ―――――.
11. A solid made of minerals is a ―――――.

Questions

A. Recalling Facts

Choose the word or phrase that correctly completes each of the following sentences.

1. Rocks are placed into three groups because of
    (a) their color.   (c) their hardness.
    (b) their shape.   (d) the way they form.
2. Slow cooling magma forms igneous rocks with
    (a) large minerals.   (c) no minerals.
    (b) small minerals.   (d) only one mineral.
3. Coal is an example of
    (a) a mineral.   (c) a metamorphic rock.
    (b) an igneous rock.   (d) a sedimentary rock.
4. Earth's crust is thickest
    (a) under deserts.   (c) on the ocean floor.
    (b) under mountains. (d) along the sea shore.

B. Understanding Concepts

Answer each of the following questions using complete sentences.

1. How do sedimentary rocks form?
2. Tell about Earth's layers and the rocks in these layers.

C. Applying Concepts

Think about what you have learned in this chapter. Answer each of the following questions using complete sentences.

1. What could you do in order to decide whether a certain igneous rock formed near the surface of Earth or deeper inside Earth's crust?
2. Why would metamorphic rocks probably not contain fossils?

Chapter 6
Nature Changes Rocks

Rocks seem to last forever. They are, however, affected by forces in nature. Wind blown sand slowly changes rocks in a desert. Flowing water in streams carries small rocks and smoothes their surfaces. Cliffs, such as this one, are constantly hit by ocean waves. How have its rocks been changed by the water?

Ocean waves change rocks.

Weathering 6:1

LESSON GOALS

In this lesson you will learn
- weathering is always taking place.
- four forces in nature change rocks.

Water, wind, ice, and living things change rocks. The change often happens slowly. Over a long period of time, the rocks are broken into smaller parts. The breaking down or wearing away of rock is called **weathering.** Weathering is always taking place.

What is weathering?

Water and Wind Change Rocks

Water changes rocks in different ways. Fast moving water moves sediments and rocks downstream. As they move, the sediments and rocks bump into each other. Over a long time the sediments and rocks wear and change. The water itself smoothes the surfaces of rocks and some sediments. Look at Figure 6-1. How have the rocks in this river changed?

Figure 6-1. Rocks are changed by fast moving water.

Activity 6-1   Weathering

QUESTION   How can water break rocks?

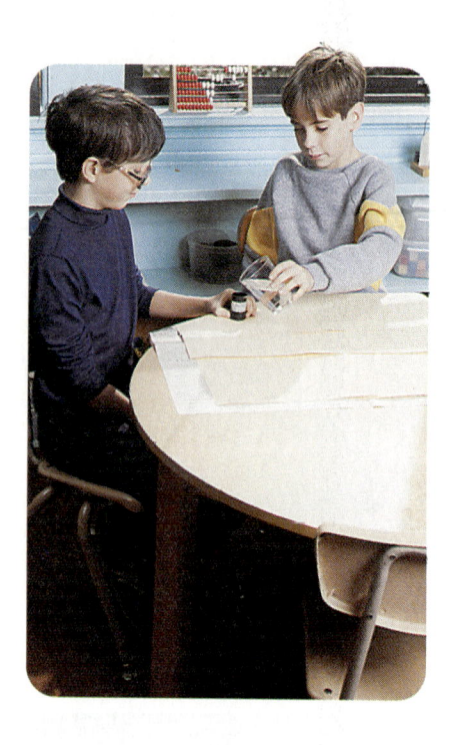

Materials
plastic film container with lid
water
masking tape
freezer
clear plastic glass
pencil and paper

What to do
1. Write your names on a piece of tape. Place it on a plastic film container.
2. Fill the container with water and snap the lid on tightly. Draw a picture of the container.
3. Place the container in a freezer for one day.
4. Remove your container and observe it. Draw another picture.

What did you learn?
1. How has the water changed?
2. What happened to the container?
3. What caused the change?

Using what you learned
1. Why is it not safe to put glass bottles of liquid in a freezer?
2. Suppose water freezes in empty spaces in a rock. What might happen to the rock?

Figure 6-2. Freezing water pushes cracks in rocks farther apart.

Water also changes rocks when the water freezes and thaws. During warm weather, water flows into cracks and spaces in rocks. When the temperature gets cold enough, the water freezes. When water freezes, it expands. The ice pushes cracks in the rock farther apart. Over many years, water in the cracks may melt and freeze many times. The cracks get bigger with time. Then, the rocks break.

Water can change rocks in another way. Rain and groundwater can soak into rocks. Some minerals in rocks dissolve in the water. The minerals are removed from the rocks and carried away by the water. Holes are left where the minerals used to be. Figure 6-3 shows this type of weathering.

How does freezing cause rocks to break?

Figure 6-3. Holes result when minerals are removed from rocks.

103

What is a glacier?

Water in the form of ice can also weather rocks. A **glacier** (GLAY shur) is a large mass of ice that moves. Frozen in the glacier are large rocks, sand, and other sediments. The rocks scratch the surfaces over which the glaciers move. Figure 6-4(a) is a rock weathered by glaciers.

Figure 6-4. Rocks (a) are weathered by glaciers (b).

a

b

Wind also weathers rocks. Strong winds pick up and carry dust and sand. These sediments are blown with much force. They scratch rocks and the rocks slowly wear away. Sometimes windblown sediments weather rocks into strange shapes.

Plants and Animals Change Rocks

How do plants change rocks?

Plants can change rocks. Some plants grow in soil that fills cracks in rocks. The roots push on the rocks as the plants grow. The rocks may break if the plants grow large enough. Tree roots can even break sidewalks and curbs. Look around your neighborhood. See if you can find places where plants are breaking sidewalks.

Some animals change rocks. They make places for weathering to happen. Some animals dig tunnels in the ground. They loosen rocks and soil. Air and water can then move deeper into the ground.

People change rocks, too. People use machines to break rocks. People dig tunnels and build roads through rocks. Some rocks are used to build houses or statues. Workers break the rocks into small pieces. The pieces are then put together to make walls or cover roofs. How are people changing rocks in Figure 6–5?

What is one way that people change rocks?

Figure 6–5. The girls (a, c) and man (b) are changing rocks.

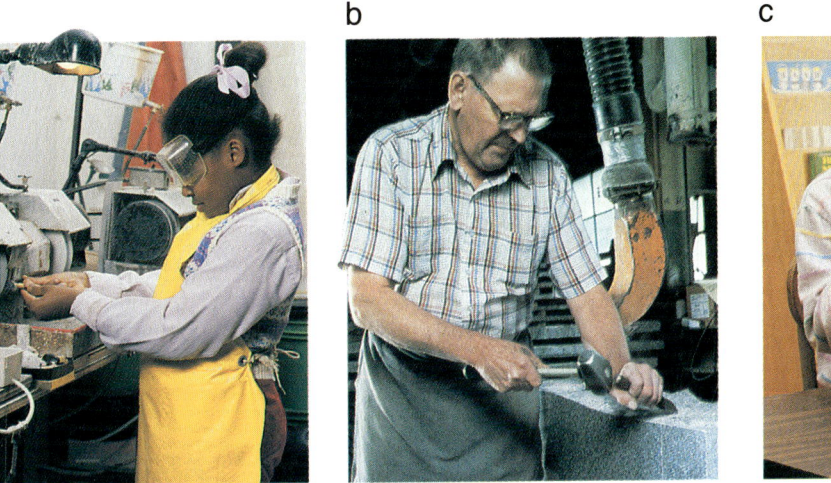

Lesson Summary

- Rocks are constantly worn away, or broken down by weathering.
- Water, wind, ice, and living things change rocks.

Lesson Review

Review the lesson to answer these questions.
1. What is weathering?
2. Describe how plants can change rock.

6:2 Soil Formation, Erosion, the Rock Cycle

LESSON GOALS

In this lesson you will learn

- soil is made of Earth materials.
- water, wind, ice, and living things cause erosion.
- changes take place in rocks as part of the rock cycle.

Figure 6-6. Soil forms as rocks weather.

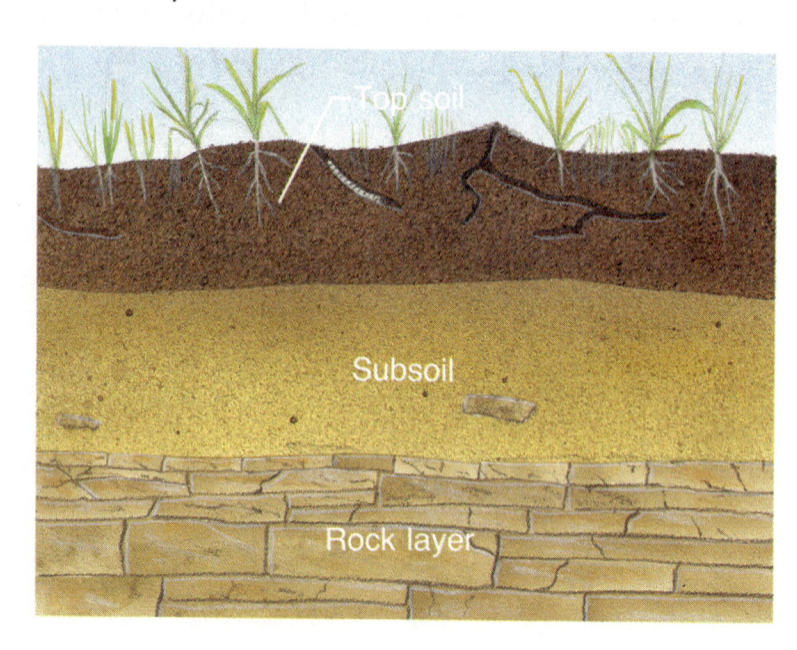

Why is soil important for plants?

Figure 6-7. Some soils are rich in decayed plants and animals.

Soil forms from the weathering of rocks. Rocks are broken into small pieces. Weathering over time makes the pieces even smaller. Slowly, rock changes to soil. The kind of soil formed depends on the kind of rock that weathers. Rocks rich in clay will produce soils with a lot of clay. Some soils are rich in decayed plants and animals. These soils are good for growing crops. Spaces between small pieces of soil hold water, air, and nutrients needed by plants.

Activity 6-2 Comparing Soils

QUESTION How do different soils compare?

Materials
soil samples   bean seeds   metric ruler
hand lens   water   labels
paper cups   pencil and paper

What to do
1. Use the hand lens and your fingers to observe soils **A**, **B**, and **C**. Record what you observe.
2. Place soil samples in different paper cups. Fill each cup and then pack down the soils.
3. Label each cup **A**, **B**, or **C**.
4. Plant 2 seeds in each cup.
5. Place the cups near each other at a window.
6. Add equal amounts of water until the soils are moist. Repeat this step as needed.
7. Measure and record plant growth after 1 week and after 2 weeks.

What did you learn?
1. How do the soil colors and feel compare?
2. In which soil did the plants grow best?

Using what you learned
1. Which soil is best in a garden? Why?
2. Why should each cup of soil get equal amounts of water and light?

107

Erosion

What is erosion?

You learned in Lesson 6:1 that water, wind, and ice weather rocks. They also cause erosion (ih ROH zhun). **Erosion** is the movement of sediments and rocks to new places. Water from heavy rains carries away loose rocks and sediments from hillsides. When the water slows down, these sediments and rocks are dropped in other places.

Fast moving water in rivers and streams also causes erosion. Rocks and sediments are carried downstream. Floods also can wash away rocks and sediments.

Wind causes erosion in dry areas. Strong winds pick up and carry loose dirt and sand. Where have you seen wind erosion?

As glaciers move, they weather Earth's surface. Pieces of rocks and sediments become frozen in the ice. The ice moves these rocks and sediments. When the ice melts, the rocks and sediments are dropped.

Figure 6-8. Water or wind can cause erosion.

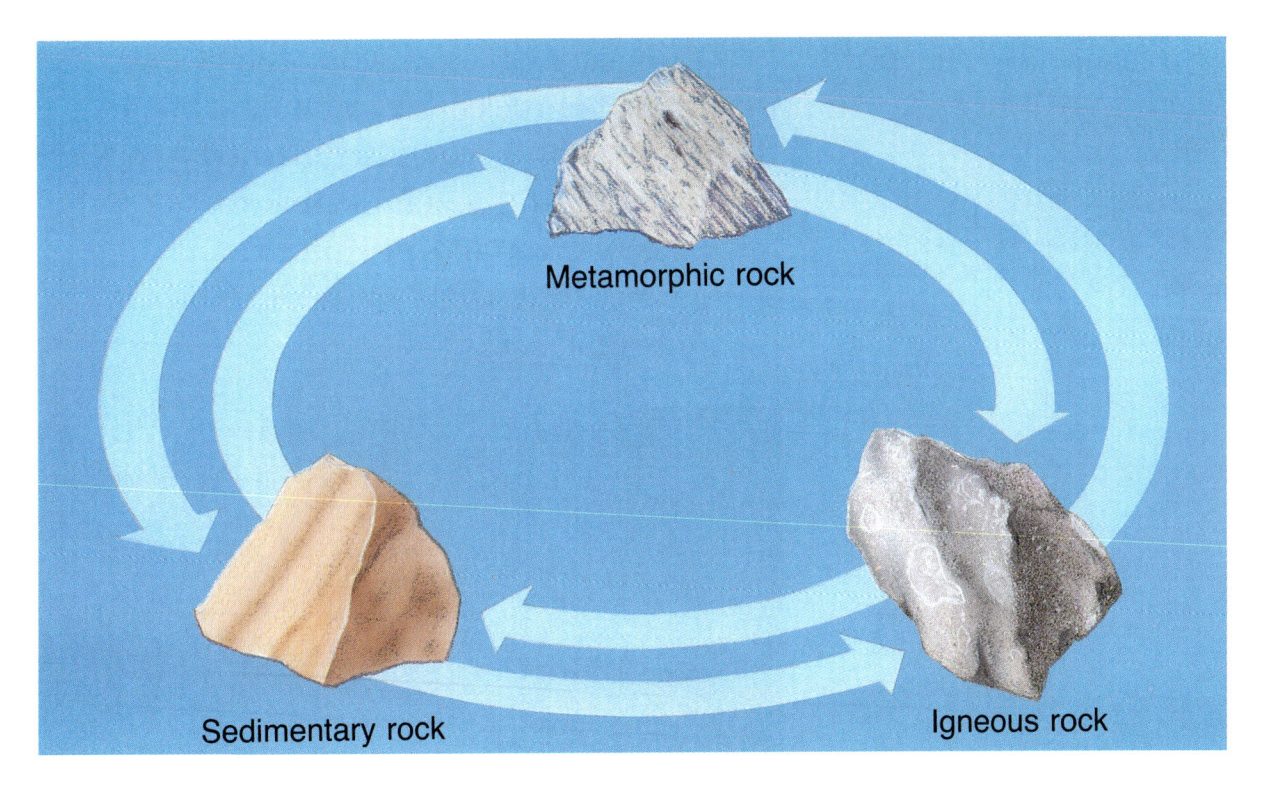

The Rock Cycle

Earth's rocks are always changing. One kind of rock changes into a different kind of rock. The changing of rocks into other rocks is the **rock cycle.**

Igneous rocks are made from magma. Weathering breaks these rocks into smaller rocks. These smaller rocks are also broken by weathering and sediments are formed. The sediments can become pressed together. Therefore, igneous rock can become sedimentary rock.

Some igneous rocks are buried deep in Earth. Heat and pressure in Earth change these rocks to metamorphic rocks. Sometimes igneous rocks are very deep in Earth. They are heated so much that they melt. They become magma again. What kind of rock will form when the magma cools?

Figure 6-9. The rock cycle is the changing of rocks into other rocks.

What is the rock cycle?

109

How can metamorphic rock become sedimentary rock?

Weathering changes sedimentary and metamorphic rocks also. Sediments from these rocks can become sedimentary rock. Sedimentary and metamorphic rocks can be buried too. Heat and pressure can change these rocks to igneous rocks or to other metamorphic rocks.

Figure 6-10. Weathering continually changes all rocks.

Lesson Summary
- Soil is made of pieces of rocks, plant and animal parts, water, and air.
- Water, wind, and ice move sediments and rocks, causing erosion.
- Each type of rock is changed to a different type of rock as part of the rock cycle.

Lesson Review
Review the lesson to answer these questions.
1. Why is soil important?
2. What is erosion? List three causes of erosion.
3. Describe how an igneous rock might be changed to a sedimentary rock.

Language Arts Skills

Fact and Opinion

A fact is a statement that can be proven. It is always true. An opinion is a person's viewpoint or feeling about something or someone.

Read the following sentences. One sentence tells a fact. The other sentence gives an opinion.

- This rock contains three minerals.
- This rock is pretty.

The first sentence is a fact. Tests can be run to prove that the rock contains three minerals. The second sentence is an opinion. Someone else may not think the rock is pretty.

Read the following paragraph. Find one fact in the paragraph. Also, find one opinion in the paragraph.

People use minerals in many ways. Some minerals are used in building materials such as cement and steel. Other minerals are used to make items such as fertilizer, talcum powder, and pencil lead. Minerals are often part of rocks. Rocks with a lot of minerals can be worth more than other rocks. Rocks with a lot of minerals are also prettier than other rocks.

111

Chapter 6 Review

Summary

1. Rocks are constantly worn away or broken down by weathering. 6:1
2. Water, wind, ice, and living things change rocks. 6:1
3. Soil is made of pieces of rocks, plant and animal parts, water, and air. 6:2
4. Water, wind, and ice move soil and rocks, causing erosion. 6:2
5. The changing of rocks from one type of rock to another type of rock is the rock cycle. 6:2

Science Words

weathering   glacier   erosion   rock cycle

Understanding Science Words

Complete each of the following sentences with a word or words from the Science Words that will make the sentence correct.
1. Wind, water, and ice move soil and rocks to cause _____.
2. Rocks change from one type to another in the _____.
3. The breaking down or wearing away of rocks is called _____.
4. A large, moving mass of ice is a _____.

Questions

A. Recalling Facts

Choose the word or phrase that correctly completes each of the following sentences.
1. Animals affect the weathering of Earth when they
   (a) sleep.   (c) dig tunnels.
   (b) drink water.   (d) eat food.

2. Earth's rocks are
   (a) never changing.
   (b) always changing.
   (c) always formed from magma.
   (d) never changed by pressure.
3. If igneous rocks are broken down into sediments, the type of rock that may form from the sediments is
   (a) sedimentary.   (c) metamorphic.
   (b) igneous.   (d) minerals.
4. Soils that are especially good for growing crops are rich in
   (a) clay.
   (b) sand.
   (c) clay and sand.
   (d) decayed plants and animals.

B. Understanding Concepts

Answer each of the following questions using complete sentences.
1. How can a metamorphic rock be changed into an igneous rock?
2. How is soil formed?
3. How does water change rocks?
4. How can glaciers cause weathering and erosion?

C. Applying Concepts

Think about what you have learned in this chapter. Answer each of the following questions using complete sentences.
1. Why do you never really see the "same" rocks from one year to the next even though you live in a limited area?
2. How do weathering and erosion affect the life of a farmer who grows crops?

UNIT 3 REVIEW

CHECKING YOURSELF

Answer these questions on a sheet of paper.
1. How can a glacier change rocks?
2. What type of rock is formed by heat and pressure?
3. Why do not all igneous rocks look the same?
4. What layer of Earth forms Earth's surface?
5. Give an example of the rock cycle.
6. How are minerals different?
7. What can carry sediments and cause erosion?
8. How does flooding cause erosion?
9. Why do people change rocks?
10. How does Earth's crust constantly change?
11. How are all rocks alike?
12. What kind of rock forms from sediments?
13. How is erosion different from weathering?
14. In what three ways can water change rocks?

RECALLING ACTIVITIES

Think about the activities you did in this unit. Answer the questions about these activities.
1. How is sedimentary rock formed? 5–1
2. How is metamorphic rock formed? 5–2
3. How can water break rocks? 6–1
4. How do different soils compare? 6–2

IDEAS TO EXPLORE

1. Using a hand lens, examine some soil that contains plant parts. Put this soil and three worms in a glass jar. Keep the jar in a dark place and keep the soil moist. Wait two weeks. Look at the soil again. How is it different?
2. Find out how to grow crystals from alum, salt, and sugar. Compare the structures of the crystals. Find out how crystals in rocks are formed.
3. Prepare a stream table. Measure the amount of soil eroded when one liter of water is poured over it. Try different methods to reduce soil erosion without changing the tray's slope or the amount of water used.

PROBLEM SOLVING

How does pressure affect the formation of sedimentary rocks? Stack ten slices of bread on a table. Lay books on top of the bread until it is flattened. Leave the bread under the books for a week. Examine the bread and record what you see and feel. How are the bread slices like sedimentary rock? Prepare a report for the class.

BOOKS TO READ

Earth by Keith Brandt, Troll Associates: Mahwah, NJ, © 1985.
Read this fascinating book about the planet you live on.

Earthquakes and Volcanoes by Laurence Santrey, Troll Associates: Mahwah, NJ, © 1985.
Learn about the nature of earthquakes and volcanoes.

Rock Collecting, 2nd Edition by Roma Gans, Crowell Junior Books: New York, © 1984.
This book makes rock collecting easy and fun.

UNIT 4
Forces, Work, and Machines

Bicycles are machines that have been popular for years. An early model of the bicycle was the high-wheeler. Its front wheel was very tall. This bicycle could travel a long distance on each turn of the pedals. Modern bicycles use a chain to turn the rear wheel. Some have gears which reduce the force needed to turn the rear wheel. Some modern bicycles are also made of lightweight metal. In what ways has the bicycle improved since the high-wheeler?

Man riding high-wheeler — 1872

Modern racing bikes are designed for speed.

Chapter 7
Forces and Work

We use forces every day. Force is used to lift a bag of groceries or to walk from one place to another. Machines also use force when they do work. This machine is called a grader. It pushes soil to make a smooth surface for a new road. How else is it using force when it does work?

A road grader uses force to do work.

Force 7:1

LESSON GOALS

In this lesson you will learn
- what is needed to move objects.
- the amount of force needed to move an object depends on the object's mass.

Figure 7-1. Workers use force to move the stove.

What is a force?

Figure 7-2. Pushes can be used to move objects.

We can move objects in different ways. Many objects will move if you push them. Other objects move when you pull them. A push or pull is a **force**. The workers in Figure 7-1 are moving furniture. They are using forces. They are using pushes and pulls.

An object will move when you lift it. Lifting is a force. Do you use a push or a pull to lift a chair off the floor? Some objects can be lifted by using a small force. Other objects need greater forces in order to be lifted. The amount of force needed to lift or move an object depends on how much matter the object has.

119

Activity 7-1 Forces

QUESTION How much pull does it take?

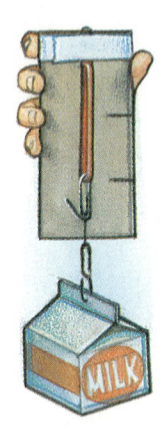

Materials
cardboard strip
large rubber band
masking tape
string (30 cm)
3 paper clips
5 small objects
pencil and paper

What to do
1. Make a "Puller Pal" like the one shown.
2. Make a pencil mark on the cardboard to show where the rubber band ends.
3. Hook an object to your Puller Pal. Lift the object.
4. Make a pencil mark on the cardboard to show how far the rubber band stretches. Write the name of the object by the mark.
5. Repeat steps 3 and 4 with all the objects.

What did you learn?
1. Which object took the most force to lift? How do you know?
2. Which object took the least force?

Using what you learned
1. Predict the force needed to lift 3 of the objects at once. Test your prediction.
2. Pull each object across the table with the Puller Pal. Compare these forces with those needed to lift the objects.

Figure 7-3. Equal sized objects may have different amounts of mass.

Imagine you and a friend are shopping in an antique store. You find two boxes like the ones in Figure 7-3. Both boxes are the same size. One box, however, is filled with old books. The other box is filled with postcards. The box of books takes more force to lift. This is because the box of books has more mass than the box of postcards.

More force is needed to lift an object with a large mass. Look at Figure 7-4. It would take more force to lift the bowling ball than the soccer ball. Which ball has more mass?

Figure 7-4. The force needed to lift an object depends on the object's mass.

Lesson Summary

- Force is needed to move objects.
- The greater an object's mass, the more force that is needed to move the object.

Lesson Review

Review the lesson to answer these questions.

1. What is a force?
2. What type of objects need large forces in order to be moved?

7:2 Gravity and Friction

LESSON GOALS

In this lesson you will learn
- there is a pulling force between objects.
- friction slows moving objects.
- physical properties affect friction.

What is gravity?

Earth pulls on objects. This pull brings you back to Earth when you jump into the air. The attraction or pulling force between objects is called **gravity** (GRAV ut ee). Gravity is a property of all matter. Gravity causes the grain in Figure 7-5 to fall. Gravity causes the rain to fall, too.

When is the pull of gravity greatest?

The pull of gravity is greatest when two objects are close together. The pulling force on each object gets less, however, as the two objects get farther apart. Think of the pulling force between two magnets. The pull is great just before the magnets touch. What happens to the pull on each magnet when the magnets get farther and farther apart?

Figure 7-5. Gravity causes matter to fall toward Earth.

Science and Technology

Super Skyscrapers

The Sears Tower in Chicago rises 443 meters into the sky. Engineers dream of building super skyscrapers as much as four times that height, one and a half kilometers high. However, first, they must solve a problem. Every day, a super skyscraper must withstand wind as strong as 150 kilometers per hour.

How can tall buildings withstand wind? Braces on the sides of skyscrapers provide stiffness. Linking neighboring buildings with cables would help support the buildings.

Steel-reinforced concrete might also be used to make super skyscrapers strong, but flexible. This type of concrete is made by letting concrete harden around steel rods. It permits some bending or flexing. Skyscrapers must bend or flex with the wind. If the building is too rigid, it could crack.

Taller and taller buildings are likely to be built. The force of wind against them will be strong. Holding them steady against this force will be an increasing challenge.

Figure 7-6. Friction slows the bicycle.

What is friction?

Figure 7-7. The sled slides easily down the hill.

Friction

Friction (FRIHK shun) is the force that slows down or stops objects in motion. Imagine that you are riding a bike on level ground. Think about what happens when you stop pedaling. Friction between the tires on your bike and the ground slows you.

Friction happens whenever one object moves over another. The amount of friction depends on the kind of surfaces that touch each other. There is more friction when an object moves over a rough surface than when it moves over a smooth surface. For example, you are able to ride a sled very fast down a hill covered with snow. You could not ride a sled as easily on a grassy hill. There is more friction because the grass is not as smooth as the snow.

Lesson Summary

- The attraction or pulling force between objects is called gravity.
- Friction causes moving objects to slow down or stop.
- Contact between rough objects causes more friction than contact between smooth objects.

Lesson Review

Review the lesson to answer these questions.
1. Why do rain drops fall toward Earth?
2. Why is it hard to ride a sled down a grassy hill?

Activity 7-2 Reducing Friction

QUESTION How can you make less friction?

Materials
hand lens   liquid soap
3 marbles   pencil and paper

What to do
1. Rub your hands together 20 times. Record what you feel.
2. Use the hand lens to look at your hands. Record what you see.
3. Put 3 marbles between your hands. Rub your hands together again. Record what you feel.
4. Put a little liquid soap in your hands. Repeat step 1.

What did you learn?
1. Tell about the surface of your hands after each step.
2. Why did your hands feel different each time you rubbed them together?
3. What caused the difference?

Using what you learned
1. How do marbles reduce friction?
2. How does soap reduce friction?
3. How could you make more friction? Why would you want to make more friction?

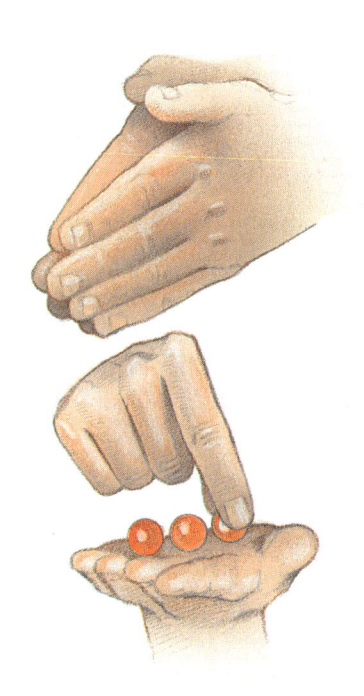

125

7:3 Work and Energy

LESSON GOALS

In this lesson you will learn
- work is done when a force moves an object.
- energy is used when work is done.
- there are different sources of energy.

Figure 7-8. Work is done when a force moves an object.

When is work done?

Figure 7-9. Force is used to lift the bricks.

Forces cause objects to move. Scientists say that **work** is done when a force moves an object. Where is work being done in Figure 7-8? How do you know?

To find the amount of work done on an object you need to know two things. You must know how much force is needed to move the object. You must also know how far the object is moved. The amount of work done depends on both force and distance. More work is done if a wagon is pulled uphill ten meters than if it is pulled five meters up the same hill.

Look at Figure 7-9. The workers are stacking bricks. The bricks move. They move because the workers use a force. Which worker is doing more work? Why?

Figure 7-10. Work is only done on the books when they are moved.

Remember that an object must be moved in order for work to be done on the object. You may push with all your might on a stalled car. However, if you do not move the car, you have not done work on the car. Likewise, imagine that you have picked up a pile of books. You do work when you lift the books. However, if you stand holding the books you have not done more work on the books. Why?

Each time a force moves an object, such as the wagon or bricks, work is done. When work is done, energy (EN ur jee) is used. **Energy** is the ability to do work. The more work you do the more energy you use.

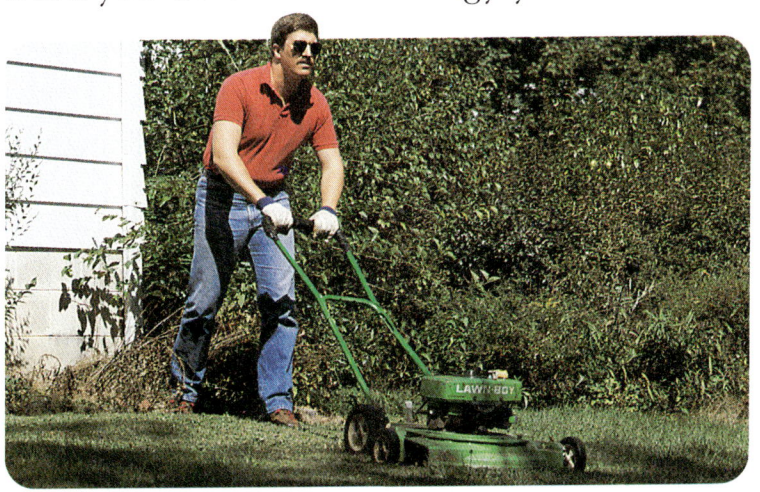

What is energy?

Figure 7-11. Energy is used when work is done.

127

Figure 7-12. Electricity supplies energy for some machines.

Figure 7-13. Forces in nature supply energy.

In order to do work, people need a source of energy. Food is important. It provides the energy people need to do work.

Machines also need a source of energy. Sometimes forces in nature supply this energy. Water flowing in a stream, for example, may turn a paddlewheel.

Most of the energy to run machines is supplied by fuel or electricity. Gasoline supplies the energy needed to run the engines of cars. Electricity runs machines such as computers.

Lesson Summary

- The amount of work done depends on both force and distance.
- The more work you do the more energy you use.
- Food and fuel are two sources of energy.

Lesson Review

Review the lesson to answer these questions.

1. When is work done on an object?
2. What is energy?
3. Name four different sources of energy.

Language Arts Skills

Taking Notes

A detective is a person who searches for information that is not easy to find. A detective must investigate or find out information. He or she must closely study facts already known, and ask questions to get all the information that is needed. A detective, while observing or asking questions, writes notes. These notes are important. They are the written record of what the detective has seen or heard.

A doctor is similar to a detective. The doctor observes or listens to a patient and records information. All information is then on hand when the doctor decides what is wrong with the health of the patient.

As a student, you should work in the same way as a detective or doctor. You should observe, study, ask questions, and take notes. When you get ready to review, the notes can help you remember what you have already read or observed.

Chapter 7 Review

Summary

1. Force is needed to move objects.   7:1
2. The amount of force needed to move an object depends on the object's mass.   7:1
3. Gravity is the pulling force between objects.   7:2
4. Friction causes moving objects to slow down or stop.   7:2
5. Rough surfaces cause more friction than smooth surfaces.   7:2
6. Work is done when a force moves an object.   7:3
7. Energy is the ability to do work.   7:3
8. Energy comes from many different sources.   7:3

Science Words

force   gravity   friction   work   energy

Understanding Science Words

Complete each of the following sentences with a word or words from the Science Words that will make the sentence correct.

1. When a force moves an object you have done _____.
2. The pulling force between objects is called _____.
3. The ability to do work is called _____.
4. A force that slows down moving objects is called _____.
5. A push or a pull is a _____.

Questions

A. Recalling Facts

Choose the word or phrase that correctly completes each of the following sentences.

1. A ball falls when it is thrown because of
    (a) pressure.   (c) friction.
    (b) gravity.   (d) air.

2. You may move an object when you use
   - (a) air.
   - (b) friction.
   - (c) mass.
   - (d) force.
3. The force needed to lift an object depends on the object's
   - (a) mass.
   - (b) energy.
   - (c) friction.
   - (d) shape.
4. Work is being done when a person is
   - (a) reading.
   - (b) sitting.
   - (c) holding a chair.
   - (d) lifting a pencil.

B. Understanding Concepts

Answer each of the following questions using complete sentences.

1. Which will take more force to lift, (a) a wooden block the size of a chalkboard eraser or (b) a block of the same kind of wood the size of a shoe box? Why?
2. Why are different amounts of force needed to move different objects?

C. Applying Concepts

Think about what you have learned in this chapter. Answer each of the following questions using complete sentences.

1. You and a friend each pull a wagon up a hill. Both wagons are the same except yours is filled with books. Who does more work? How do you know?
2. Why are most playground slides made with smooth surfaces?

Chapter 8
Simple and Compound Machines

There are many different kinds of machines. Some machines have few moving parts. Other machines have many moving parts. This machine was used to peel apples. The apple was placed on the spike and the blade moved around the apple to peel it. How many movable parts do you see on the machine?

Machine used for peeling apples

Simple Machines, Levers   8:1

LESSON GOALS

In this lesson you will learn
- why simple machines are important.
- a lever is a simple machine.
- not all levers are the same.

Imagine that you need to move a barrel but it is too heavy. A friend says to place one end of a long board under the barrel and rest the board on a log. Now, when you push down on the other end of the board the barrel moves. The board and log were used as a type of machine.

People can use many kinds of machines to do work. A machine with few or no moving parts is called a **simple machine.** Simple machines can be used to make work easier to do. They can change the amount of force needed to do work. Simple machines can also change the direction of the force. However, they do not decrease the amount of work that is done. Figure 8-1 shows the six kinds of simple machines.

Figure 8-1. The lever (a), inclined plane (b), wedge (c), screw (d), wheel and axle (e), and pulley (f) are six kinds of simple machines.

133

Activity 8-1 Levers

QUESTION   How much push does it take?

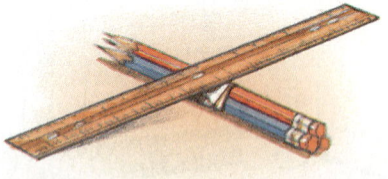

Materials
3 pencils   small ball of clay
masking tape   5-8 metal washers
metric ruler   pencil and paper

What to do
1. Tape the pencils together as shown. Put them under the middle of the ruler.
2. Put the clay at one end of the ruler.
3. Add washers one at a time to the other end of the ruler until the ball of clay is lifted.
4. Record how many washers it took to lift the ball of clay.

What did you learn?
1. What simple machine did you make?
2. What was the force?
3. What was the load?
4. How many washers lifted the load?

Using what you learned
1. What happens to the force needed if you move the pencils? How can you find out?
2. Where do you put the pencils to use the smallest force? The largest force?

Lever

The man in Figure 8-2 is lifting an object. In Figure 8-2(b) he is using a lever. A **lever** is a simple machine that is used to move objects.

All levers have three parts. The object to be moved by the lever is called the **load.** The point where the lever rocks back and forth is called the **fulcrum** (FUL krum). The push or pull that moves the lever is the force. Find the load, fulcrum, and force in Figure 8-2(b).

Levers can be used to change the direction of the force needed to lift an object. Think about a seesaw. When you push down on one end, the person on the other end goes up.

What are the three parts of a lever?

Figure 8-2. Moving an object by hand (a) takes more force than using a lever (b).

a
b

Figure 8-3. The force needed to lift a load depends on the position of the fulcrum.

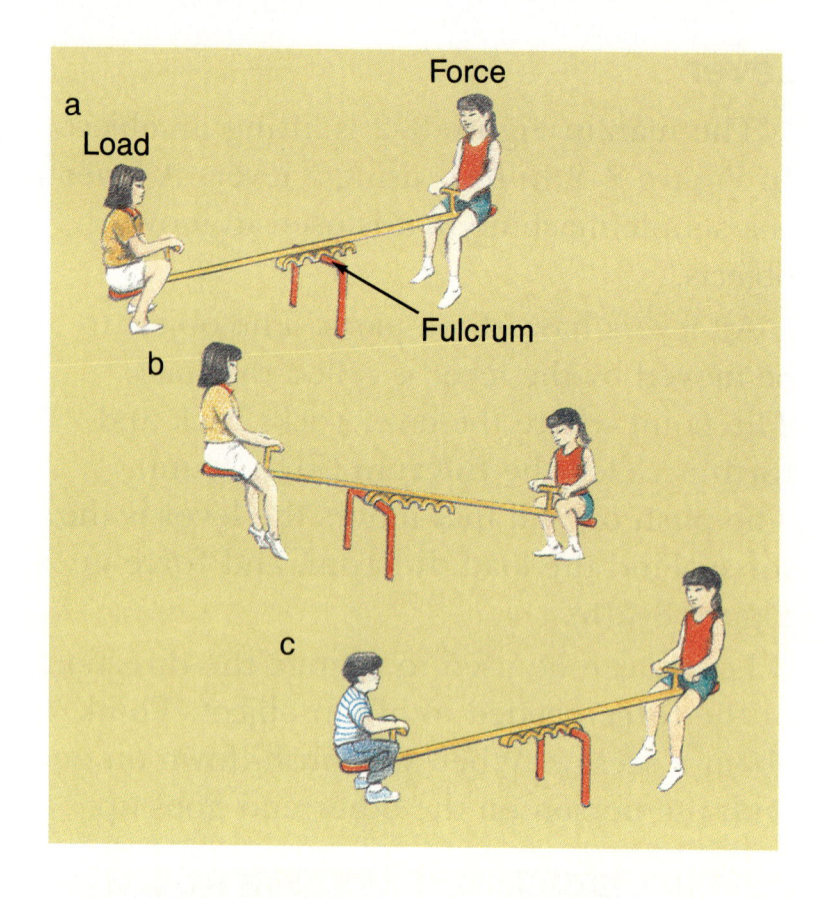

What can we say about the force needed to lift a load if the fulcrum is near the load?

Levers can also be used to change the amount of force. Think about the seesaw again. The girl in Figure 8-3(a) wants to play on the seesaw with her older sister. She cannot lift her older sister if the fulcrum is in the middle. If the fulcrum is moved closer to her sister, as in Figure 8-3(b), she is able to lift her sister. Look at Figure 8-3(c). Her younger brother wants to ride on the seesaw. She is now the heavier one. Therefore, she must move the fulcrum closer to herself. The amount of force needed to lift a load depends on where the fulcrum is. The closer the fulcrum is to the load, the less force needed to lift the load.

Not all levers are the same. Some levers do not have the fulcrum between the force and the load. The nutcracker is a lever with the fulcrum at one end. The force is applied at the other end. The load is in the middle.

Figure 8–5 shows a person doing work. This machine is a lever, too. Find the fulcrum of the lever. Find the force and the load. Why do we call this machine a lever?

Figure 8-4. A nutcracker is a lever with the fulcrum at one end.

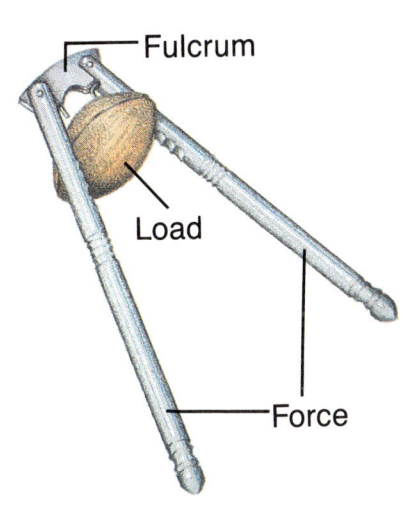

Figure 8-5. This machine is also a kind of lever.

Lesson Summary

- Simple machines can be used to change the amount of force needed to do work or to change the direction of a force.
- A lever is a simple machine that is used to move objects.
- The position of the fulcrum is not the same on all levers.

Lesson Review

Review the lesson to answer these questions.
1. What is a simple machine?
2. What are the three parts of a lever?
3. What does a lever do?

8:2 Inclined Plane, Wedge, and Screw

LESSON GOALS

In this lesson you will learn
- an inclined plane is a simple machine used to move objects.
- a wedge has two important uses.
- a screw is a type of inclined plane.

What is an inclined plane?

An **inclined plane** is a simple machine used to move objects to a higher or lower place. A ramp and a path going up a hill are examples of inclined planes. In Figure 8-6 both children want to go to the top of the hill. The girl on the steeper path goes a shorter distance. She uses more force to get to the top. The boy goes a longer distance. He uses less force to get to the top. The longer the distance moved on an inclined plane, the less force needed.

Figure 8-6. More force is needed on the steeper path.

138

Activity 8-2 Inclined Planes

QUESTION How do inclined planes make work easier?

Materials
4 books
"Puller Pal"
milk carton
8 marbles
ramp (board)
pencil and paper

What to do
1. Pile 4 books on top of each other.
2. Put 8 marbles into the milk carton.
3. Lift the milk carton with the Puller Pal until the bottom of the carton is even with the top book.
4. Mark how far the rubber band stretches.
5. Set up the ramp, milk carton, and Puller Pal as shown.
6. Pull the carton up the ramp. Mark how far the rubber band stretches.

What did you learn?
1. Which way took more force to move the carton?
2. Which way took a longer distance?

Using what you learned
1. Find out what happens to the force needed if the ramp is made higher.
2. Why are roads built around mountains instead of straight up the sides?

139

In what two ways is a wedge useful?

A **wedge** (WEJ) is a simple machine made of two inclined planes. Knife blades, chisels, pins, and the blade of a hatchet or axe are all examples of wedges. Work is done when the wedge presses against two objects. Sometimes a wedge is used to raise objects a short distance. A heavy object such as a stove might be raised over a crack in a floor by using a wedge. Other times a wedge is used to push objects apart. Logs are split by using axes and hatchets. The blade of the hatchet or axe is forced into the log. It pushes the pieces of log apart. How can you use each wedge shown in Figure 8-7?

Figure 8-7. Wedges may be used to raise objects (c) or to push objects apart (a, b, d).

The force needed to raise an object with an inclined plane depends on the distance moved. A longer distance is covered when an inclined plane is wrapped around a post. This can be shown by cutting an inclined plane out of paper. When this paper is wrapped around a cardboard tube the resulting object is a screw. A **screw** is an inclined plane wrapped around a post. Each time the screw makes a complete turn it moves a load a certain distance along the screw. This distance depends on the amount of space between each overlap of the inclined plane on the post. Screws, drill bits, and other objects commonly found in the home make use of the screw. The force needed to turn a screw is less than that needed to pound a nail of equal size. A longer distance is covered when you turn a screw. Therefore, less force is needed.

Figure 8–8. A screw is an inclined plane wrapped around a post.

Why is less force needed to turn a screw than to pound a nail of equal size?

Lesson Summary

- An inclined plane is a simple machine used to move objects to higher or lower places.
- A wedge is a simple machine used to raise objects or to push them apart.
- A screw is an inclined plane wrapped around a post.

Lesson Review

Review the lesson to answer these questions.
1. Name three examples of inclined planes.
2. Why is less force needed to turn a screw than to pound a nail of equal size?

8:3 Wheel and Axle, Pulley

LESSON GOALS

In this lesson you will learn
- a wheel and axle is a simple machine.
- a pulley is a simple machine with two different uses.

Figure 8-9. A doorknob makes it easier to unlatch the door.

Figure 8-10. The large wheels and axles are used to control the flow of water.

Look at Figure 8-9. Which door would you want to try to turn open? Why? The doorknob is a wheel and axle. A **wheel and axle** is a simple machine with a wheel that turns a post. The post is called an axle. Wheels and axles are commonly seen on cars, trains, trucks, and bicycles. The crank on some fruit presses, which crush fruit, is also a wheel and axle.

Compare the sizes of the wheels and axles in Figure 8-10. The distance around the wheel is greater than the distance around the axle. Therefore, less force is needed to turn the wheel than to turn the axle.

142

Pulley

A **pulley** is a simple machine that changes the direction or amount of a force. A pulley is a wheel on a post with a rope around the wheel. A pulley may be fixed or movable. One fixed pulley is shown in Figure 8-11. It can make work easier to do by changing the direction of a force. This type of pulley is used to raise a flag on a flagpole. You pull down on the rope. As you pull down, the flag moves up the pole.

A movable pulley is shown in Figure 8-12. It is helpful in a different way. Using it can decrease the force needed to lift a load. The force can be reduced by one-half if one movable pulley is used to lift the load.

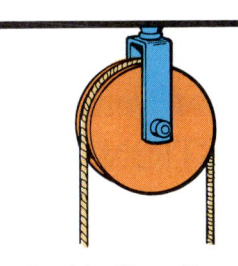

Figure 8-11. One fixed pulley can be used to change the direction of a force.

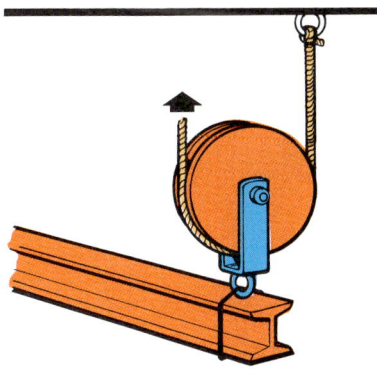

Figure 8-12. A movable pulley reduces the force needed to lift a load.

Figure 8-13. A fixed pulley can be used to raise a flag on a flagpole.

Activity 8-3 Pulleys

QUESTION   How do you use a pulley?

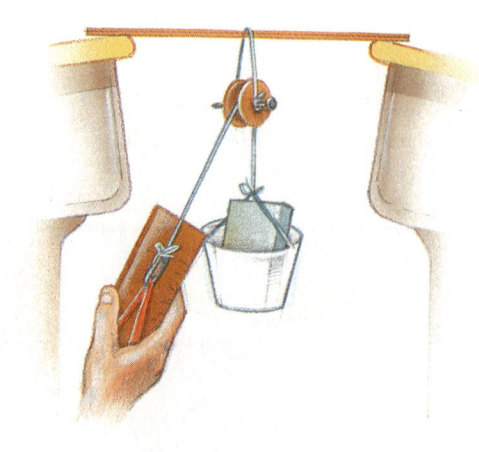

Materials
paper cup   nail
string   meter stick
small object   spool
Puller Pal   pencil and paper

What to do
1. Make three holes in the top of the cup. Use string to make a handle.
2. Put an object into the cup. Use the Puller Pal. Record how much force is needed to lift the cup.
3. Use a nail, spool, and short piece of string to make a pulley.
4. Set up the pulley as shown. Record the force needed to lift the cup.

What did you learn?
1. What did you notice about the force needed in steps 2 and 4?
2. How did the direction of the force change?

Using what you learned
1. When might you use a pulley to lift a heavy object?
2. When might you use a pulley to change the direction of a force?

Figure 8-14. Pulleys can be joined together to decrease the force needed to lift a heavy object.

Two or more pulleys joined together may also be used to decrease the force needed to lift a load. Each part of the rope that is wrapped around the pulleys supports a part of the load. Look at Figure 8-14. The pulleys are being used to lift a heavy object. A person would not be able to lift it without the pulleys. The pulleys decrease the force needed to lift the object.

Why are two or more pulleys joined together useful?

Lesson Summary

- A wheel and axle is a simple machine with a wheel that turns a post.
- A pulley is a simple machine that changes the direction or amount of force.

Lesson Review

Review the lesson to answer these questions.

1. Why is it easier to open a door with the doorknob than with the doorknob axle?
2. What is the advantage of using several pulleys?

8:4 Compound Machines

LESSON GOALS

In this lesson you will learn
- the difference between simple and compound machines.
- people use compound machines for many reasons.
- safety is important when using a machine.

Figure 8-15. Can openers have three kinds of simple machines.

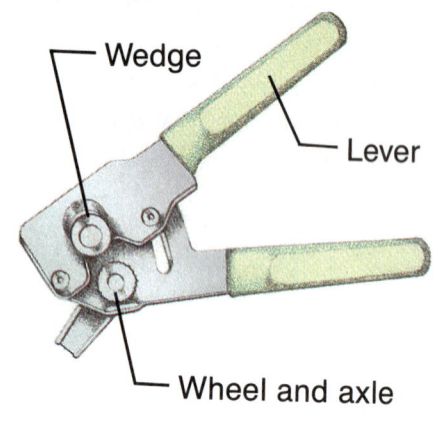

What is a compound machine?

Some simple machines have few moving parts. Some have no moving parts. Most machines people use, however, have many moving parts. Most machines are compound machines. A **compound machine** is a machine made of two or more simple machines. In a compound machine the simple machines are connected. The work each does is combined to do the job of the compound machine. A can opener has three simple machines. The blade of the opener is a wedge. A lever forces the blade into the can. The force used to open the can is applied to a wheel and axle.

Figure 8-16. Most machines have many moving parts.

The woman in Figure 8-17 is using an axe. The axe is a compound machine. It is made of two simple machines. The cutting end of the axe is a wedge. The handle of the axe is a lever. A hatchet is like an axe. The hatchet has a shorter handle or lever. Hatchets and axes are both used to chop wood. Axes are often used to chop larger pieces of wood. Why do you think this is so?

Figure 8-17. An axe is a compound machine.

People Use Machines

How did you get to school today? If you rode your bicycle or rode in a bus or a car, you used a compound machine. People can use compound machines to move or to transport objects from place to place. Machines used to carry people and objects are kinds of transportation. Trucks, trains, boats, and planes are compound machines that are kinds of transportation.

Figure 8-18. Compound machines such as boats are kinds of transportation.

Figure 8-19. Machines are used on farms.

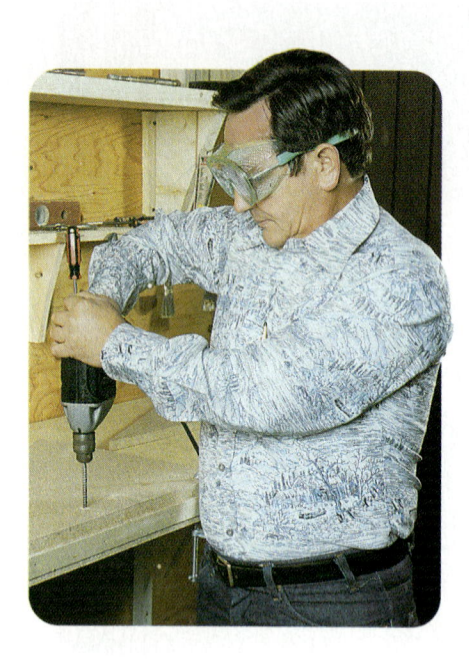

Figure 8-20. Safety glasses should be worn when using some machines.

People use machines for other reasons. Machines are used in factories. People also use machines in growing food. Machines can do some work more quickly than people. Machines can also be used to do work that may be dangerous or harmful to people.

Machines are helpful when used the right way. They can cause problems when they are not used the right way. Some machines make very loud noises. It is important to wear earplugs when working with these machines. What are some machines that make harmful noises? Other machines throw out sparks. Safety glasses should be worn when people use machines such as power saws. It is important for people to use all machines safely.

Lesson Summary

- A compound machine is made of two or more simple machines.
- People may use compound machines to move from place to place, to do work quickly, or to do work that is dangerous.
- People should use all machines carefully and wear proper safety equipment.

Lesson Review

Review the lesson to answer these questions.
1. What is the difference between a simple and a compound machine?
2. Name two compound machines found in the home.

People and Science

Pedal Power

Joseph Pérex is a bicycle racer who also test rides bicycles. Some of the racing bikes he tests look very unusual. Some bikes require that Joseph lie on his back in order to pedal them. These bikes are designed to get the most speed for the racer. Another bike that Joseph has been testing is enclosed. A canopy, or cover, is placed over the frame and the rider. Scientists hope the canopy will lower wind resistance without adding much weight.

Joseph enjoys testing bicycles, but he also has plans for the future. Some day, he wants to compete in the Olympics. After the Olympics, Joseph hopes to test pedal-powered aircraft and boats.

Improvements to test cars, aircraft, and other experimental products often find their way to the general public. The same is true in regard to bicycles. In a few years your new bike may look like one Joseph has been testing.

Chapter 8 Review

Summary

1. Simple machines can be used to change the amount or direction of a force.   8:1
2. A lever is a simple machine used to move objects.   8:1
3. The position of the fulcrum varies on levers.   8:1
4. Inclined planes are used to move objects to a higher or lower place.   8:2
5. A wedge is used to raise objects or push them apart.   8:2
6. A screw is an inclined plane wrapped around a post.   8:2
7. A wheel and axle is a simple machine with a wheel that turns a post.   8:3
8. A pulley changes the direction or amount of a force.   8:3
9. Compound machines contain two or more simple machines.   8:4
10. There are many useful compound machines.   8:4
11. People need to be careful when using machines.   8:4

Science Words

simple machine	**inclined plane**	**wheel and axle**
lever	**wedge**	**pulley**
load	**screw**	**compound machine**
fulcrum		

Understanding Science Words

Complete each of the following sentences with a word or words from the Science Words that will make the sentence correct.

1. A machine made of two or more simple machines is called a _____.
2. A doorknob is an example of a _____.
3. An inclined plane wrapped around a post is a _____.
4. A ramp is an example of an _____.

5. A lever rocks back and forth at its _____.
6. A knife blade is an example of a _____.
7. The object to be moved by a lever is the _____.
8. A machine with few or no moving parts is a _____.
9. A simple machine that uses a rope and a wheel is a _____.
10. A seesaw is an example of a _____.

Questions

A. Recalling Facts

Choose the word or phrase that correctly completes each of the following sentences.
1. Simple machines can change the direction or the amount of
   (a) work.   (b) force.   (c) energy.   (d) mass.
2. The simple machine formed from two inclined planes is a
   (a) wedge.   (b) screw.   (c) lever.   (d) wheel and axle.
3. The simple machine used to attach a hose to a faucet is a
   (a) screw.   (b) wedge.   (c) lever.   (d) pulley.
4. A can opener is a compound machine containing a wedge, lever, and
   (a) screw.   (b) pulley.   (c) inclined plane.   (d) wheel and axle.

B. Understanding Concepts

Answer each of the following questions using complete sentences.
1. Give two reasons why a pulley is used to lift an object.
2. How is work easier to do when an inclined plane is used?

C. Applying Concepts

Think about what you have learned in this chapter. Answer each of the following questions using complete sentences.
1. Why are machines often used to paint cars in factories?
2. How do you change the position of the fulcrum on a lever in order to move a heavier load?

UNIT 4 REVIEW

CHECKING YOURSELF

Answer these questions on a sheet of paper.
1. Why is more force used to lift a bowling ball than a soccer ball?
2. Name three forces that can be used to move objects.
3. Why is it difficult for a bicycle to stop on an icy street?
4. Why is reading a book not considered work, while turning the pages of a book is work?
5. If you push on a large crate but it does not move, why have you not done work on the crate?
6. Describe the difference between work and energy.
7. Name several sources of energy used in machines.
8. How are a wedge and a screw alike? Different?
9. Name several uses for a wheel and axle.
10. Compare compound machines and simple machines.
11. How are compound machines used outside the home?
12. Why is safety important when using compound machines?

RECALLING ACTIVITIES

Think about the activities you did in this unit. Answer the questions about these activities.
1. How can you tell in an experiment the amount of force needed to lift an object?   7-1
2. How can you reduce friction when rubbing your hands?   7-2
3. How do you measure the force used in a lever?   8-1
4. How do inclined planes make work easier?   8-2
5. How do you use a pulley?   8-3

IDEAS TO EXPLORE

1. Collect pictures from magazines that show the six simple machines. Make a bulletin board display.
2. Build one or more of the six simple machines or a compound machine. You may use building toys and other old materials from home.
3. Use resource books to gather information about an invention and its inventor. Write a report and share this information with the class.

CHALLENGING PROJECT

Invent a special machine that can perform a household task. Write a story or draw a picture of the machine. Tell how this machine helps people in their daily lives.

BOOKS TO READ

How Things Work edited by Donald J. Crump, National Geographic Society: Washington, DC, © 1983.
  What is inside a clock? Read this book to find out.

Simple Machines by Rae Bains, Troll Associates: Mahwah, NJ, © 1985.
  This book will introduce you to all kinds of simple machines.

Tractors: From Yesterday's Steam Wagons to Today's Turbocharged Giants by Jim Murphy, Lippincott Junior Books: New York, © 1984.
  Learn about the history of tractors.

UNIT 5
Water Around Us

Irrigation is the watering of land by people. Years ago, Egyptians used irrigation. They enclosed land near the Nile River with banks of soil. Water from the river was brought to this land by canals dug in the ground. Today, irrigation is used in many areas. One type of irrigation uses sprinklers that spray the water over crops. Water is pumped to the sprinklers through pipes from a place where water is stored. How does this irrigation compare with that used by Egyptians years ago?

Egyptian irrigation—3000 B.C.

Modern sprinkler irrigation

Weather and Climate

Weather is important to everyone. Farmers depend on the correct amount of moisture for their crops. People who fish depend on calm seas so they can use their boats. Pilots check weather maps before flying their planes. How is weather important to them?

Pilots check weather maps.

Evaporation and Condensation 9:1

LESSON GOALS

In this lesson you will learn
- water changes from a liquid to a gas during evaporation.
- two factors affect the speed of evaporation.
- condensation may take place when water as a gas cools.

Figure 9-1. Weather may change quickly.

Friday morning was clear, sunny, and warm. Jon was excited about the field trip to the zoo. He left his coat at home and hurried to school. At noon, Jon and his classmates ate their lunches. It was getting cloudy and began to rain. Jon was cold and wished he had brought his coat. The weather had changed quickly.

The weather affects everyone. We wear certain clothes to keep us warm. We wear other clothes to help us stay cool. Weather changes affect both work and play. These weather changes take place in Earth's atmosphere (AT muh sfihr). The **atmosphere** is all the air that surrounds Earth.

What is the atmosphere?

157

Evaporation

Remember from Lesson 4:2 that evaporation is the change of matter from a liquid to a gas. Water evaporates to form water vapor. **Water vapor** is water as a gas. Water vapor is one gas in the air. It is formed when water evaporates from oceans, lakes, and streams. It is also released by plants and animals while they live.

We cannot see water vapor. However, after a storm, we see that puddles on a street disappear. How does the drying of puddles show that water vapor forms?

The amount of water vapor in the air changes. It depends on what the air is like. Sometimes water evaporates quickly. For example, suppose you spilled water on a piece of clothing. What could you do to make it dry faster?

Water evaporates only where it meets the air. The larger the surface that meets the air, the more water that can evaporate.

How does surface area affect evaporation?

Figure 9-2. Liquid water can change to water vapor.

Activity 9-1 Water Vapor

QUESTION When does water evaporate faster?

Materials
water
2 washcloths
small paper cup
clock or watch

What to do
1. Pour a cup of water on each washcloth.
2. Fold one washcloth in half. Fold it in half again.
3. Let the second washcloth lie flat.
4. Put both washcloths in a warm, dry place.
5. Observe how long it takes for each washcloth to dry.

What did you learn?
1. Which washcloth dried faster?
2. Why did it dry faster?

Using what you learned
1. How could waving the washcloth in the air change evaporation?
2. How would you hang clothes so they dry quickly?
3. What could you do to slow down evaporation? When would this be useful?

159

Both containers in Figure 9–3 hold the same amount of water. In which one does more water meet the air? From which one will water evaporate faster?

Figure 9–3. Evaporation takes place faster from one of the containers.

Warm air speeds evaporation. In Lesson 4:2 you learned that particles of liquids bump into each other. When the particles of the liquid are heated, they move faster. Some of them are bumped away from the liquid. They become a gas.

Suppose that the amounts of water vapor in the air are similar on two days. On one day the weather is sunny and warm. On the other day the weather is cooler. Wet clothes will dry faster on the warmer day.

Figure 9–4. Moving air speeds evaporation.

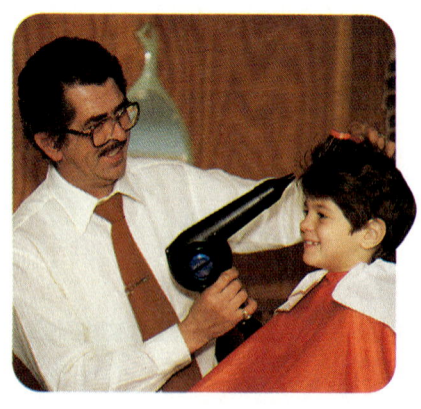

Moving air speeds evaporation too. Suppose you just washed your hands. You find that there are no towels. How could you dry your hands? Wet hair and clothes dry faster on windy days. Warm, dry, windy days are better than dry, still days for drying clothes. How is a clothes dryer like a warm, dry, windy day?

Condensation

Water vapor can change back to a liquid. In Lesson 4:2 you learned that the change of matter from a gas to a liquid is condensation. Condensation changes water vapor to liquid water. Water vapor changes to a liquid when it cools. This change can take place in the air or on the ground.

Figure 9–5. Condensation takes place when water vapor cools.

When does water vapor condense to liquid water?

Lesson Summary

- Evaporation is the change of matter from a liquid to a gas.
- Air temperature and air speed affect the speed of evaporation.
- Condensation is the change of matter from a gas to a liquid.

Lesson Review

Review the lesson to answer these questions.

1. What is water vapor?
2. Suppose equal amounts of water are outdoors in two open containers. One is tipped over and spilled. The other is not. Which water will evaporate faster? Why?

9:2 Clouds and Precipitation

LESSON GOALS

In this lesson you will learn
- how clouds form.
- the names of types of clouds.
- precipitation falls from the atmosphere.

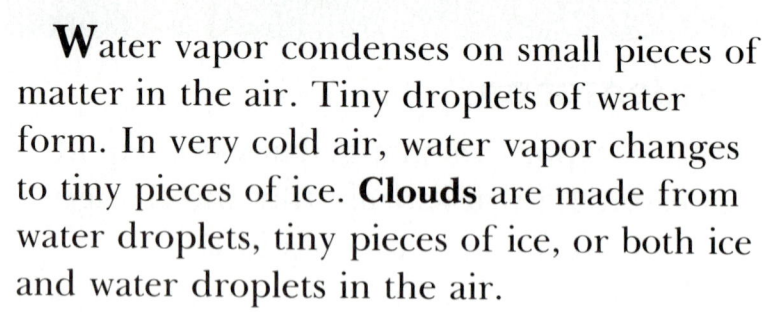

Water vapor condenses on small pieces of matter in the air. Tiny droplets of water form. In very cold air, water vapor changes to tiny pieces of ice. **Clouds** are made from water droplets, tiny pieces of ice, or both ice and water droplets in the air.

Some clouds are high above the ground. Others are lower. One kind of cloud even forms near the ground.

Cirrus (SIHR uhs) clouds are thin white clouds. They have fuzzy edges and look like feathers. Cirrus clouds are made of ice. They form high above the ground. We often see these clouds during nice weather.

Figure 9-6. Some clouds have interesting shapes.

Of what are cirrus clouds made?

Figure 9-7. Cirrus clouds form high above the ground.

Science and Technology

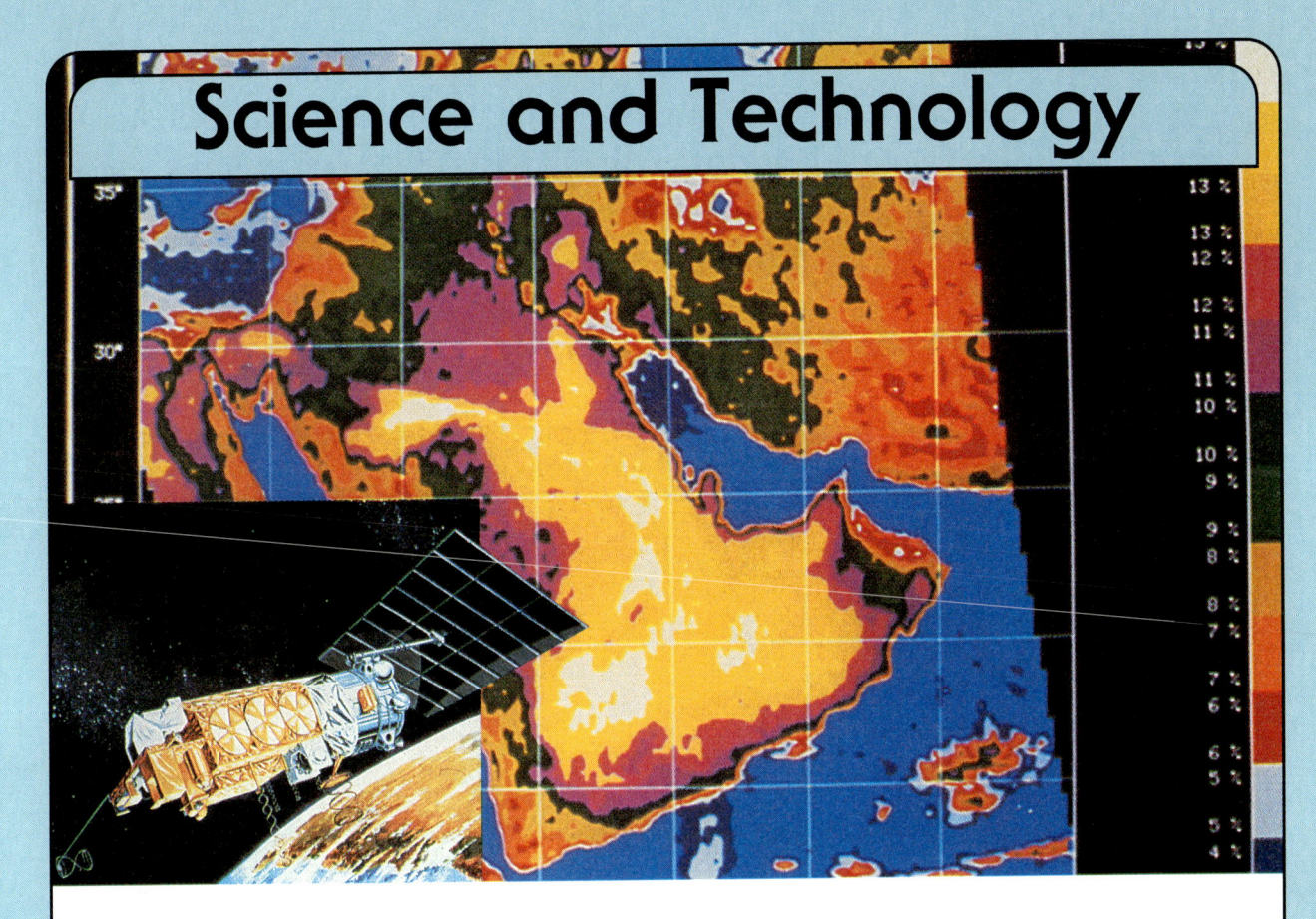

Weather Pictures

Imagine that it is Monday. Your teacher tells you that you will be going on a class picnic on Friday, if it does not rain. How can you plan for your picnic? The weather forecast can help. It tells you the weather today and what the weather may be in the near future.

Where do weather forecasters get their information? Weather satellites send weather information to receiving stations around the world. Computers at the stations organize and store the information.

A weather satellite sends information about clouds, temperatures, wind speed, and wind direction. It also has equipment to take many kinds of pictures of Earth and its weather. This infrared photograph was taken by a satellite. The different colored areas show differences in temperature in the atmosphere.

Weather satellites are useful instruments. They provide us with much important information. We can even use some of this information to plan a picnic!

In what kind of weather do we see scattered cumulus clouds?

Cumulus (KYEW myuh luhs) clouds are large, puffy clouds. They are much thicker and lower than cirrus clouds. Cumulus clouds may change their shape. Scattered, puffy cumulus clouds are seen during nice weather. Low, dark gray cumulus clouds can bring rain showers.

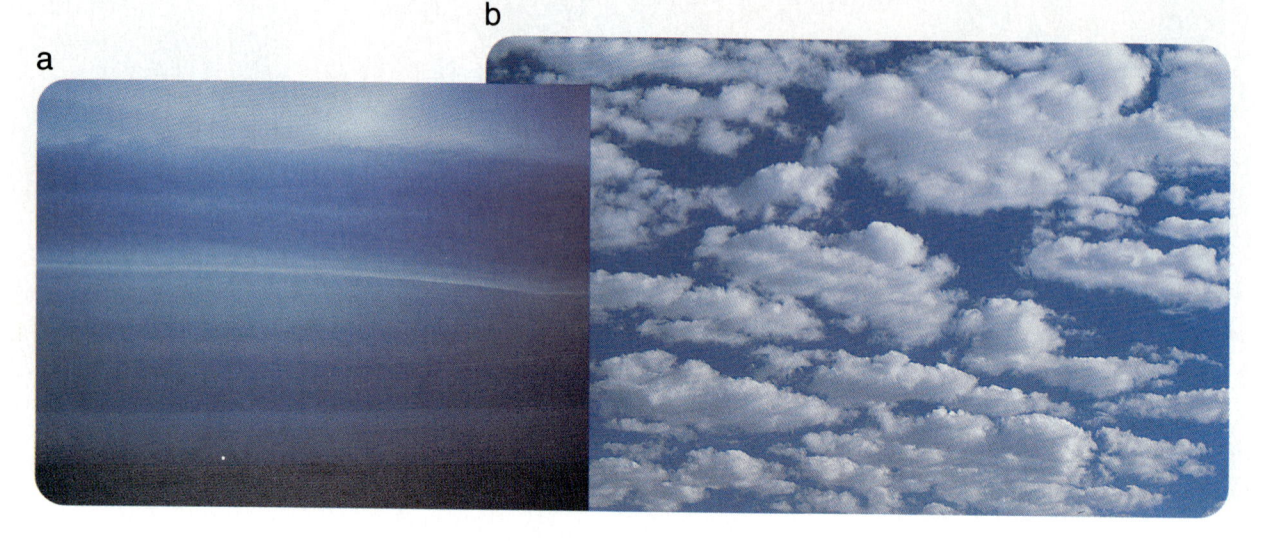

Figure 9-8. Stratus clouds (a) cover the sky completely. Cumulus clouds (b) are thick and puffy.

Clouds that cover all the sky are **stratus** clouds. Low, thick stratus clouds may cause rain or snow. **Fog** is a stratus cloud close to the ground. Why could fog be dangerous for people who are traveling?

Water vapor may condense on objects on the ground. **Dew** is a form of condensation. Dew may form on objects when air cools at night. You may see it as drops of liquid on cars and grass in the morning. Water vapor may also change to a solid without first becoming a liquid. This may happen when the air temperature is below 0°C. The water vapor changes to frost. **Frost** is ice that forms from water vapor. In what seasons would you see frost?

Precipitation

Water droplets and ice in clouds are so small they stay in the air. Sometimes droplets or pieces of ice become large very quickly. Then water drops or ice fall to the ground. Moisture that falls from the atmosphere is called **precipitation** (prih sihp uh TAY shun).

Figure 9-9. No two snowflakes have exactly the same shape.

Rain and snow are two kinds of precipitation. Rain is liquid water that falls when the air is warmer than 0°C. Snow is ice particles formed from water vapor in the air. It forms when the air is 0°C or colder.

Sleet and hail are two other kinds of precipitation. Sleet is frozen rain. Hail is ice chunks made of many layers. Notice the different-sized hailstones in Figure 9-10. Why might it be dangerous to be in a hailstorm?

Lesson Summary

- Water vapor condenses on very small particles to form clouds.
- Cirrus, cumulus, and stratus are three types of clouds.
- Rain, snow, sleet, and hail are four kinds of precipitation.

Figure 9-10. Hailstones may be different sizes.

Lesson Review

Review the lesson to answer these questions.
1. How are cirrus clouds different from cumulus clouds?
2. What is fog?
3. How are dew and frost similar? Different?

165

9:3 Climate

LESSON GOALS

In this lesson you will learn
- there are three climate zones.
- climate is affected by three factors.

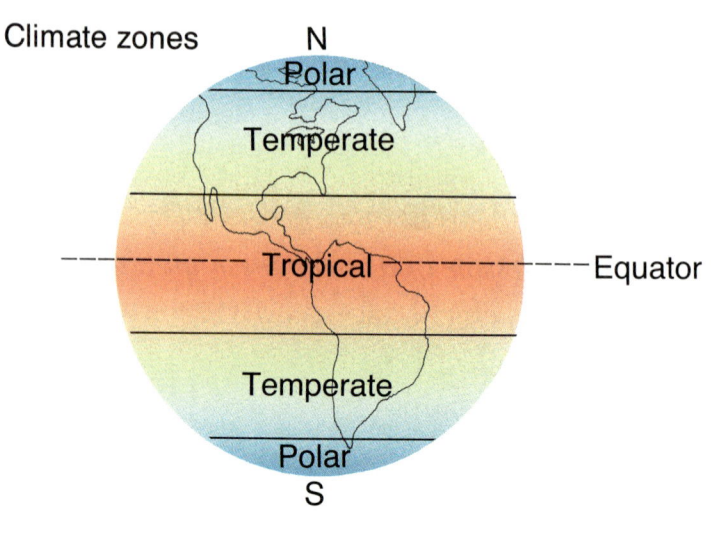

Figure 9-11. Temperatures in the tropics are hot year round.

What are the three major climate zones?

The weather in an area is similar from one year to the next. Scientists study weather over long periods of time. These weather conditions are called climates (KLI muts). **Climate** is the usual weather in an area year after year.

There are three climate zones in the world. These are shown in Figure 9-12. The two polar zones are in the far northern and southern parts of Earth. The climate here is always cold. The tropics is a climate zone centered over the middle of Earth. Here the temperatures are hot year round except on high mountains. The two temperate zones have weather that changes during four seasons of the year.

Figure 9-12. There are three climate zones in the world.

166

Climates have different temperatures and amounts of moisture. The temperatures and amounts of moisture are affected by three factors. One of these factors is large bodies of water. Places near oceans or large lakes often receive much rain or snow. These places also are likely to have more even temperatures during the year. Large bodies of water stay cooler in summer and warmer in winter than nearby land areas. Air moving across the water toward land makes the summers cooler and the winters warmer. Temperatures year round are more even. Places far from oceans or large lakes change greatly in temperature from season to season.

How do large bodies of water affect temperature?

Figure 9-13. Temperature graph for Des Moines, Iowa

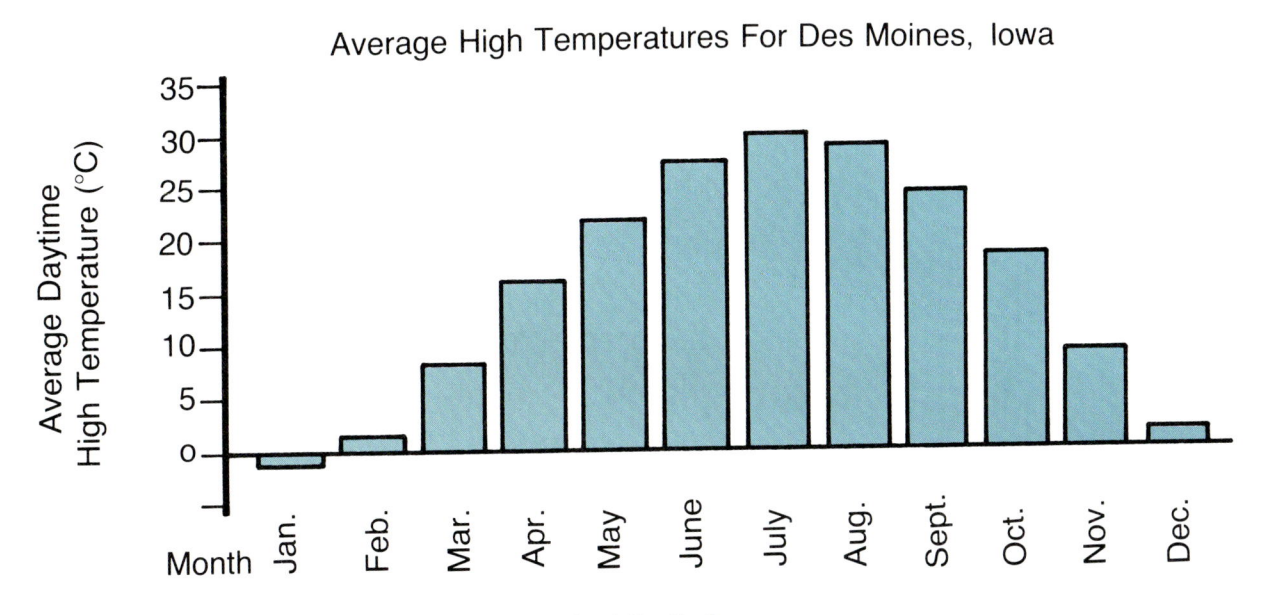

Average High Temperatures For Des Moines, Iowa

Look at the graph in Figure 9-13. It has temperature information about Des Moines, Iowa. Study the graph carefully. Notice the change in high temperatures during the year. From this information would you say that Des Moines is located near a body of water or inland? Why?

167

Activity 9-2 Climate

QUESTION How do amounts of precipitation compare?

Materials
precipitation graphs
pencil and paper

What to do
1. Look at the graphs.
2. Compare the monthly amounts of precipitation for Denver and Honolulu.

What did you learn?
1. Which city has the most precipitation during summer (June, July, August)? What summer month has the most precipitation?
2. Which city has the most precipitation during winter (December, January, February)? What winter month has the most precipitation?
3. During what month is Denver driest? Honolulu driest?
4. Which city has the greatest change in amount of precipitation from one month to the next?

Using what you learned
1. What season of the year could be called Honolulu's "wet season?"
2. What other information besides amount of precipitation is important when comparing climates?

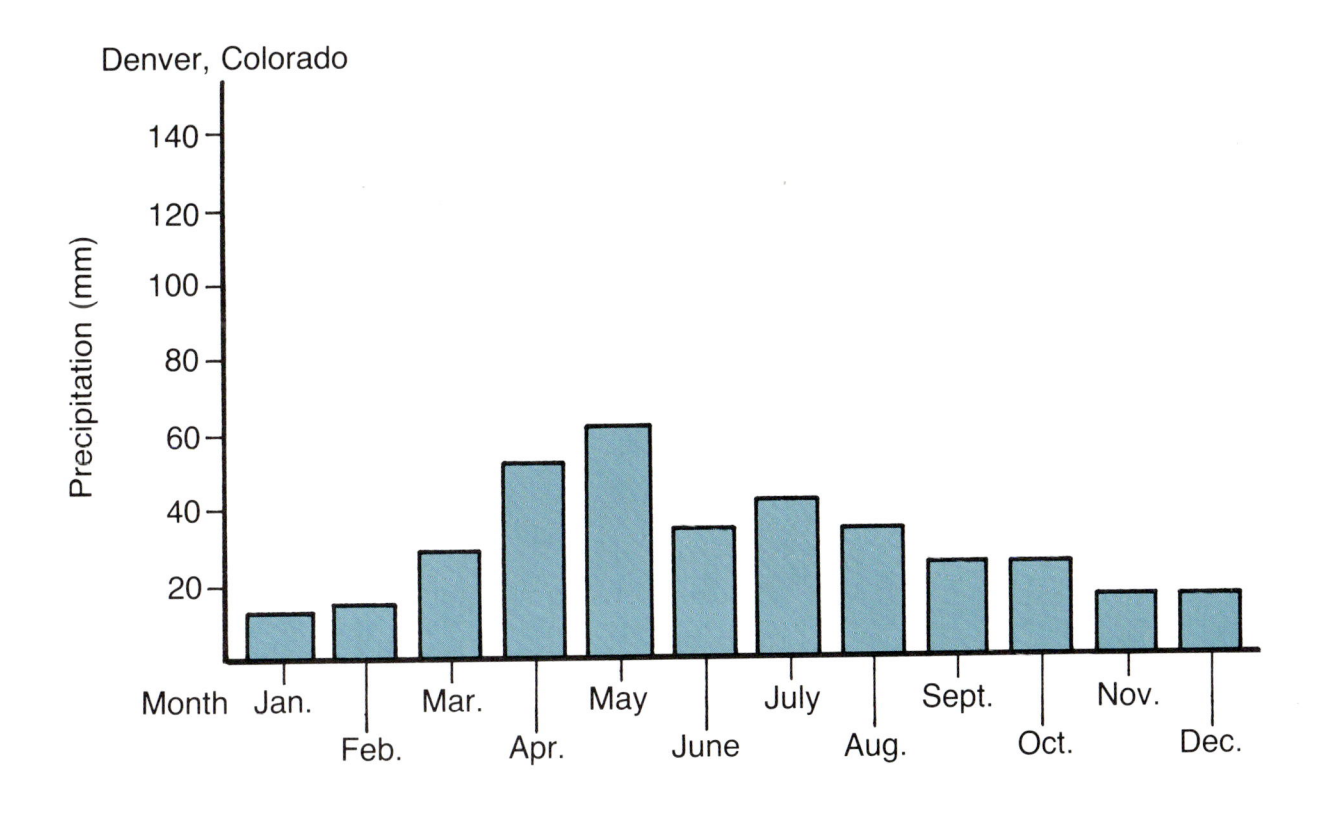

Denver, Colorado

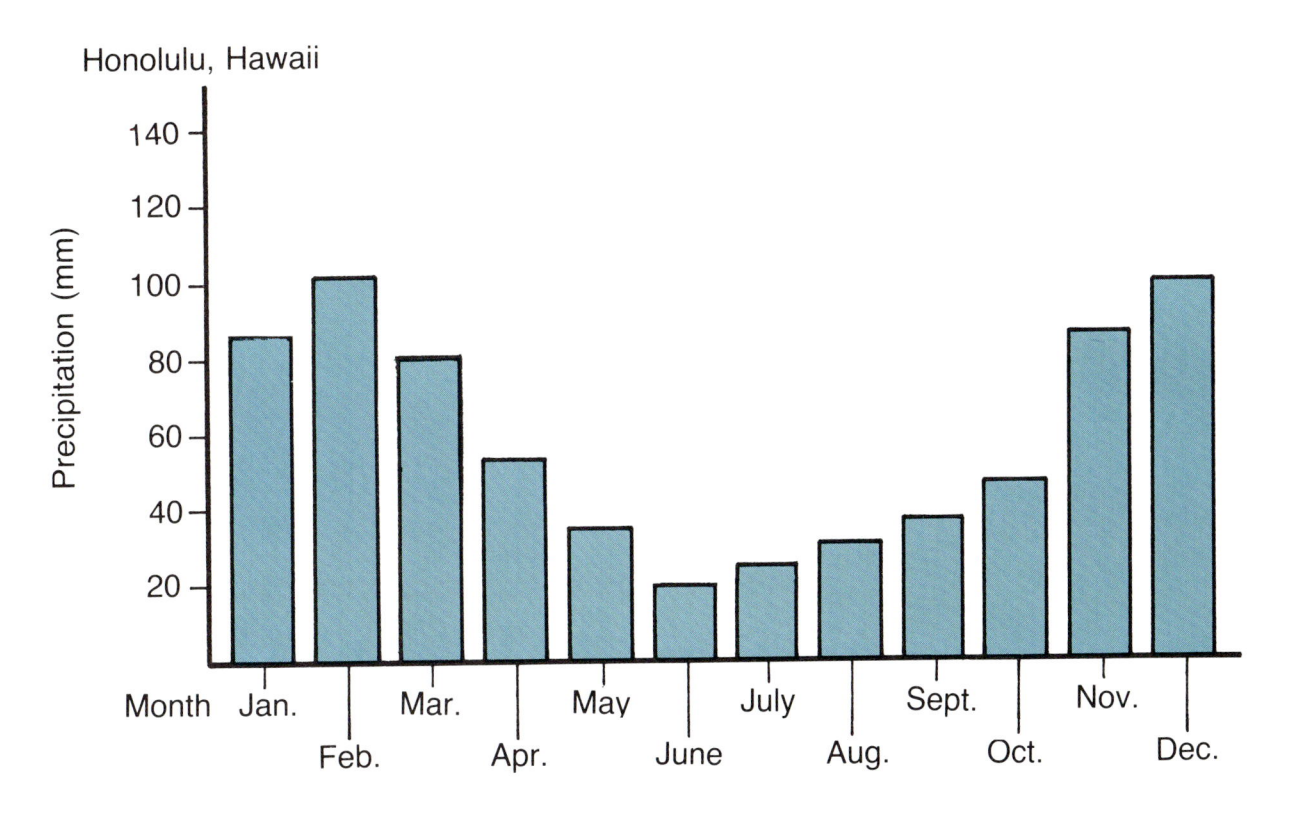

Precipitation (mm) by Month

Month	Jan.	Feb.	Mar.	Apr.	May	June	July	Aug.	Sept.	Oct.	Nov.	Dec.
Precipitation (mm)	13	15	30	53	63	36	44	36	28	28	19	19

Honolulu, Hawaii

Precipitation (mm) by Month

Month	Jan.	Feb.	Mar.	Apr.	May	June	July	Aug.	Sept.	Oct.	Nov.	Dec.
Precipitation (mm)	86	102	81	54	36	21	26	33	39	49	89	102

Figure 9-14. Mountain ranges can affect climate.

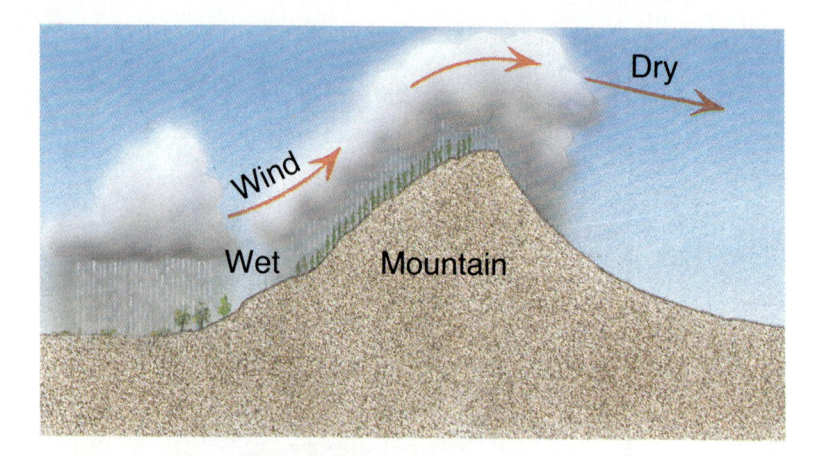

How can mountains affect climate?

Mountains can also affect climate. They change the pattern of the winds. One side of the mountains may get much rain or snow. The other may have much less precipitation.

Large cities can affect climate. The large areas of concrete in cities absorb more energy from the sun than the open areas of country. Cities become warmer during the day than less crowded areas. Buildings in cities also change wind patterns. These changes affect the climate of the area.

Figure 9-15. Large cities can affect climate.

Lesson Summary

- The polar zones, tropics zone, and temperate zones are three climate zones in the world.
- Water, mountains, and large cities can affect climate.

Lesson Review

Review the lesson to answer these questions.

1. What is climate?
2. In what ways do large cities affect climate?

People and Science

Drying Up the Great Salt Lake

Dan Taylor works for the Department of Public Works near Salt Lake City, Utah. His job is to patch potholes, maintain signs, and keep roads repaired. Some of the roads Dan has worked on are now under water! The Great Salt Lake has flooded the roads near it. The lake has not been this high since 1873.

In 1986, there was a lot of rainfall. The summer was cloudy, causing little evaporation from the lake. For a while, Dan's department used sandbags to try to stop the flooding of roads and other areas.

They also dug ditches to help the water run off. The lake, however, kept rising. It covered some railroad tracks, highways, and farms. Even the airport was threatened.

Because of the flooding, Dan's department has begun to pump water from the lake into a nearby desert. By creating a second lake, the evaporation of water should speed up. Dan hopes the level of Great Salt Lake will drop by 40 centimeters. After the new lake is made, it will be up to the weather to dry up the extra water.

Chapter 9 Review

Summary

1. Evaporation is the change of matter from a liquid to a gas.   9:1
2. Air temperature and air speed affect the speed of evaporation.   9:1
3. Condensation is the change of matter from a gas to a liquid.   9:1
4. Water vapor condenses on very small particles to form clouds.   9:2
5. Three types of clouds are cirrus, cumulus, and stratus.   9:2
6. Rain, snow, sleet, and hail are four kinds of precipitation.   9:2
7. The three climate zones are the polar zones, tropics, and temperate zones.   9:3
8. Water, mountains, and large cities affect climate.   9:3

Science Words

atmosphere	**cumulus**	**frost**
water vapor	**stratus**	**precipitation**
clouds	**fog**	**climate**
cirrus	**dew**	

Understanding Science Words

Complete each of the following sentences with a word or words from the Science Words that will make the sentence correct.

1. The usual weather in an area year after year is called _____.
2. High, thin clouds made of ice are _____.
3. Ice from water vapor that forms on objects on the ground is called _____.
4. Thick, puffy clouds are called _____.
5. Water as a gas is called _____.
6. Millions of tiny water droplets, tiny pieces of ice, or both ice and water droplets form _____.
7. Clouds that cover all the sky are called _____.

8. Moisture that falls from the atmosphere is called _____.
9. Drops of condensed liquid water on grass is called _____.
10. A stratus cloud close to the ground is _____.
11. All the air that surrounds Earth is the _____.

Questions

A. Recalling Facts

Choose the word or phrase that correctly completes each of the following sentences.
1. The change of matter from a gas to a liquid is
    (a) precipitation.   (c) evaporation.
    (b) condensation.   (d) water vapor.
2. Compared to a large open area of land, a large city near this open land has a climate which
    (a) is warmer.   (c) has more rainfall.
    (b) is colder.   (d) has less rainfall.
3. Precipitation that is made of layers of ice is
    (a) rain.   (b) snow.   (c) sleet.   (d) hail.
4. The climate zone centered over the middle of Earth is the
    (a) polar zone.   (c) tropics.
    (b) temperate zone.   (d) Antarctic.

B. Understanding Concepts

Answer each of the following questions using complete sentences.
1. How do mountains and large bodies of water affect climate?
2. Compare the different forms of precipitation.

C. Applying Concepts

Think about what you have learned in this chapter. Answer each of the following questions using complete sentences.
1. On what kind of day will clothes dry fastest? Why?
2. How do weather changes affect our lives?

Chapter 10
The Water Cycle

Evaporation, condensation, precipitation, and storage are repeated as stages of the water cycle. Water is stored in a lake. It evaporates from the lake. Later the water condenses and falls as precipitation. How does this cycle show the importance of water as both a liquid and a gas?

Storage is a stage of the water cycle.

Runoff, Groundwater, and Storage   10:1

LESSON GOALS

In this lesson you will learn
- water is important to living things.
- water flows across the ground.
- water moves through the ground.
- there are many kinds of water reservoirs.

Figure 10-1. Every living thing needs water.

 Each living thing on Earth needs water. Think of all the plants and pets at home and near your home. How do they get water to meet their needs?

 How much water do you use each day? Most people do not think about how important water is to their lives. They forget how often they use water each day. Suppose the water in your home were turned off for one day. How would your life change?

Figure 10-2. We use water every day.

 Water that gets to our homes was first water that fell to Earth. Then the water may have flowed across the ground or soaked into the ground. Finally it was stored and cleaned for use in our homes.

175

Figure 10-3. Runoff flows across the ground.

Where does runoff water finally collect?

Figure 10-4. Flood waters cause damage on land.

Runoff

Precipitation brings water from the air back to Earth. Much of the water from rain and melted snow soaks into the ground. Some water flows across the ground instead of soaking in. Water that flows across the ground is called **runoff.**

Gravity causes runoff to flow downhill. It flows into small streams or ponds. The streams flow into rivers. Rivers become bigger as more streams flow into them. Finally the rivers flow into oceans.

Runoff may be great after rain storms. Melting snow also increases runoff. The increased runoff may damage the land. Sometimes rain fills streams and rivers. Floods happen when water flows over banks of rivers and streams. Floods can carry away soil, trees, and even houses.

Groundwater

Not all precipitation becomes runoff. Some soaks into the ground. Water that soaks into the ground is called **groundwater.** Groundwater moves down into soil and rock. Water can soak into rock layers under the soil. Some rocks have small holes or spaces. Sometimes the spaces are joined. Then the water can move into and through them.

Some of the groundwater is trapped in spaces in the rocks. However, much of it does not stop moving. Gravity causes groundwater to move down and through soil and rocks. Groundwater moves. It moves until it reaches places where it can flow back onto Earth's surface. There it may evaporate back into the air. Lakes, rivers, springs, and swamps are places where groundwater flows onto Earth's surface.

At what places does groundwater reach the surface?

Figure 10-5. Groundwater moves through soil and rock layers.

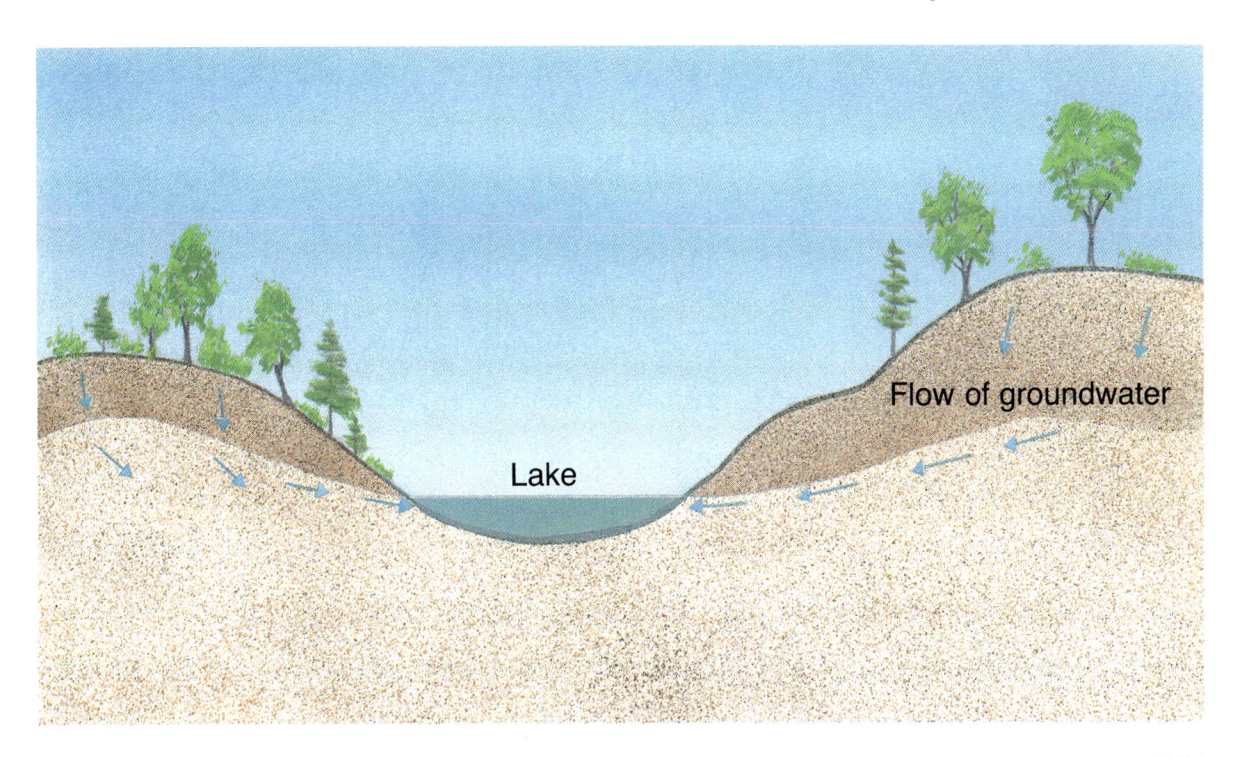

Activity 10-1 Water Storage

QUESTION What kind of soil soaks up more water?

Materials
2 different kinds of soil
2 large clear jars
masking tape
marking pen
water
small paper cup
stopwatch
pencil and paper

What to do
1. Fill each jar half full with a soil. Pack down the soil.
2. Label each jar with type of soil.
3. Pour a cup of water on each soil. Record how long it takes for the water to soak into the soil.
4. Add cups of water until the soil cannot soak up any more. Record the number of cups.

What did you learn?
1. Which soil soaks up water faster?
2. Which soil soaks up the most water?

Using what you learned
1. Which soil would have the least amount of runoff during a heavy rain? Why?
2. Which kind of soil would have the biggest mud puddles after a heavy rain? Why?

Water storage

It is easy to pour a glass of water. It is easy to take a drink from a fountain. Where does this water come from? Water for people in cities is stored in lakes or other places until it is used. A place where water is stored is called a **reservoir** (REZ urv wor).

There are different kinds of reservoirs. Rock layers holding groundwater are reservoirs. Wells are drilled to get the stored water. Some ponds, rivers, and lakes are used as reservoirs. Lake water is run through large pipes to towns and cities. There it is stored again in large tanks called water towers. Some tall buildings have water towers on their roofs. Why do you think these towers are placed on roof tops?

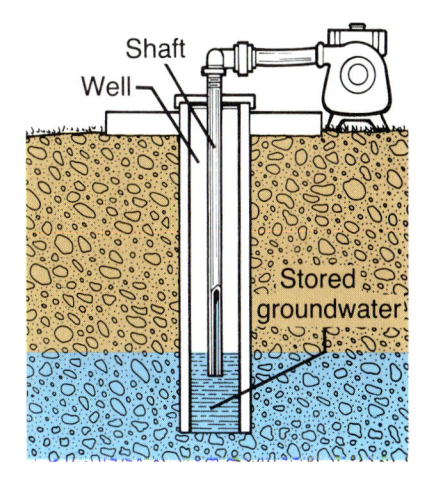

Figure 10-6. Wells are drilled down to stored groundwater.

Figure 10-7. Water towers are reservoirs for water in some cities.

Lesson Summary

- Living things must have water to live.
- Water that flows across the ground is called runoff.
- Water that moves through the ground is called groundwater.
- Lakes, wells, and water towers are examples of reservoirs.

Lesson Review

Review the lesson to answer these questions.
1. Give an example of runoff that is harmful.
2. Give two examples of places where groundwater flows onto Earth's surface.

10:2 The Water Cycle

LESSON GOALS

In this lesson you will learn
- there are four stages in the water cycle.
- energy from the sun is important in the water cycle.
- Earth has a limited supply of water.
- careful use of water is important.

What are the four stages of the water cycle?

Earth's water is always moving. It changes from solid to liquid to gas and back again. Each of these changes is part of a cycle. The cycle has different parts, or stages. Evaporation, condensation, precipitation, and storage are all parts of the **water cycle.**

Energy from the sun is important in the water cycle. Heat from the sun provides energy for evaporation. Water evaporates from oceans, lakes, and streams to form water vapor. Plants and animals are also a part of the water cycle. Both add water vapor to air.

Figure 10-8. Plants release water vapor into the air.

Figure 10-9. Sunlight provides the energy for evaporation.

180

Water vapor rises into the air. It cools as it rises. Cooling causes it to condense. Condensation changes water vapor to liquid droplets. These droplets join together to form rain. When rain falls, water is returned to the ground.

What changes water vapor to liquid droplets?

Part of this water from precipitation becomes groundwater. The rest becomes runoff. It flows into streams, lakes, and oceans. The cycle is ready to start again. It repeats itself over and over.

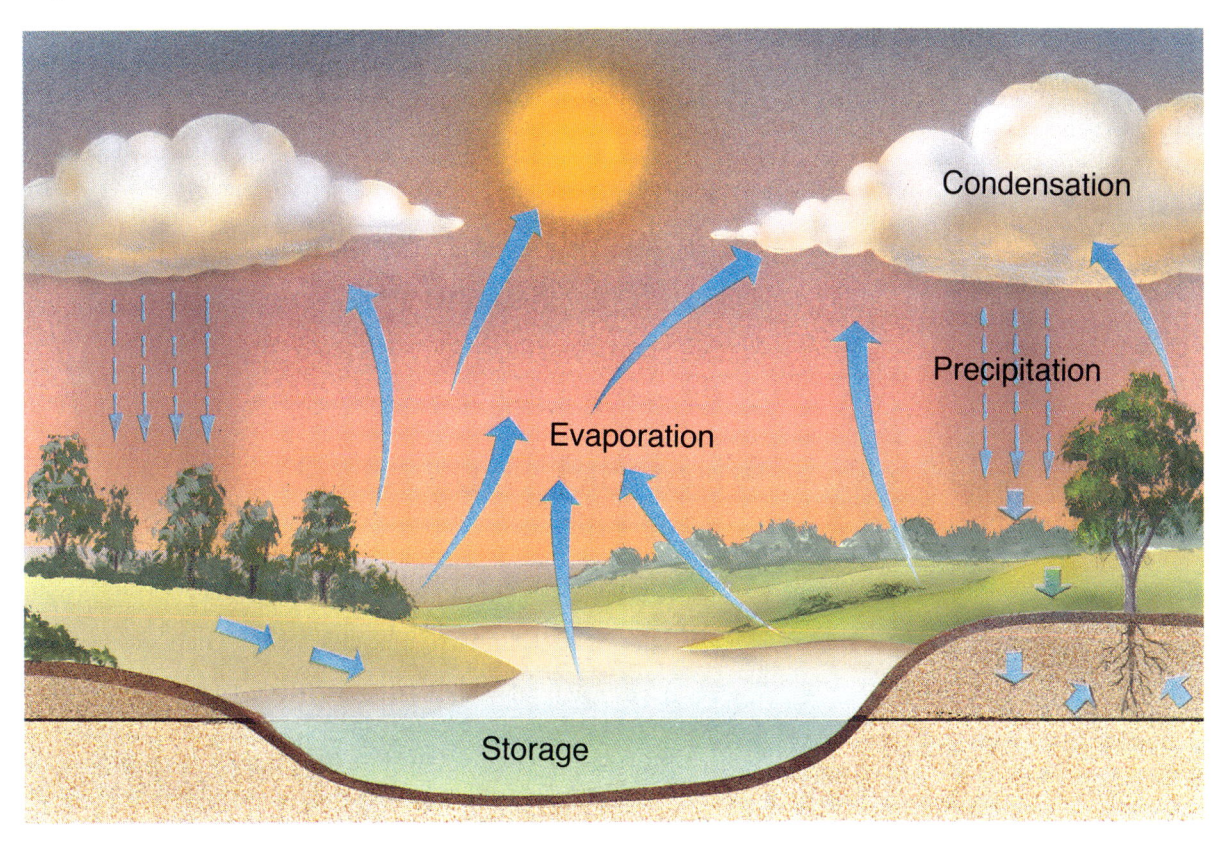

Figure 10-10 shows the water cycle. Tell about each stage of the water cycle. Where is each stage taking place in Figure 10-10? Why are all of these stages together called a water cycle?

Figure 10-10. Water moves in the water cycle.

181

Activity 10-2 Water Cycle

QUESTION What is the water cycle?

Materials
clear plastic glass
oven mitt
hot water
plastic dish
4 to 5 ice cubes
pencil and paper

What to do
1. Hold the glass with the oven mitt. Fill the glass two-thirds full of hot water.
2. Tilt the glass to wet the sides to the top.
3. Put some ice in a dish.
4. Set the dish on top of the glass.
5. Observe what happens.

What did you learn?
1. What happened in the glass?
2. Where did evaporation take place?
3. Where did condensation take place?
4. Where did precipitation take place?

Using what you learned
1. How does this activity show what happens to some lake water?
2. How does the activity show how clouds form?
3. How does the activity show a water cycle?

Figure 10-11. Pollution of water in any of the water cycle stages affects living things.

Earth's supply of water is limited. It must be used wisely. Each one of the four steps of the water cycle is important. Problems for living things happen when pollution of any of these stages takes place. For example, water vapor may condense on particles found in some smoke. Then the droplets join and fall to Earth as precipitation. These particles mix with water on Earth and are harmful to plants and animals.

Drinking water is often stored in reservoirs. Pollution of these reservoirs is also a problem for living things. When substances, such as oil or sewage, enter these reservoirs, the supply of clean water is affected.

Why is the water cycle so important?

183

When water is polluted the amount of healthful water is decreased. The normal supply of clean water cannot be replaced without the pollution first causing harm to living things. It is important that our water remain clean. What can you do to keep water clean and use it wisely?

Figure 10-12. Water conservation should be everyone's concern.

Lesson Summary

- Evaporation, condensation, precipitation, and storage are stages of the water cycle.
- Heat from the sun provides energy for the evaporation of water.
- Earth's supply of water is used over and over again in the water cycle.
- Water in any stage of the cycle should remain unpolluted.

Lesson Review

Review the lesson to answer these questions.

1. How is energy from the sun important in the water cycle?
2. How are plants and animals a part of the water cycle?

Language Arts Skills

Creating a Graphic Picture

A picture may show information and help readers understand written information. *Read the following paragraphs. They explain how people get drinking water.*

Drinking water may come from reservoirs above ground. The water in these reservoirs is dirty. It must be cleaned before it is safe to drink.

Large pipes carry the water to a water treatment plant. There it is purified. The water is sent through tubes of sand and charcoal that remove dirt. Chemicals are also added to kill harmful germs.

Next, the water travels to a storage area. Pipes then carry the water from the storage area to other parts of the town. Smaller pipes branch off from the large pipes and carry water to buildings. Pipes inside the buildings bring water to faucets. When people open faucets, water flows and is ready to be used.

Now, look at the picture. It shows the same information and the steps water goes through as it is cleaned. Using the picture, explain to a friend the route that water takes while it is cleaned.

Chapter 10 Review

Summary

1. Living things need water to live. 10:1
2. Water that flows across the ground is called runoff. 10:1
3. Water that moves through the ground is called groundwater. 10:1
4. Lakes, wells, and water towers are examples of reservoirs. 10:1
5. Evaporation, condensation, precipitation, and storage are stages of the water cycle. 10:2
6. Sunlight provides energy for evaporation. 10:2
7. Earth's water supply is used over and over in the water cycle. 10:2
8. Water should remain unpolluted. 10:2

Science Words

runoff

groundwater

reservoir

water cycle

Understanding Science Words

Complete each of the following sentences with a word or words from the Science Words that will make the sentence correct.

1. A place where water is stored is called a _____.
2. Water that soaks into the ground is _____.
3. Water that flows across the ground is _____.
4. Evaporation, condensation, precipitation, and storage are parts of the _____.

Questions

A. Recalling Facts

Choose the word or phrase that correctly completes each of the following sentences.

1. Water returns to the ground as
    (a) evaporation.   (c) storage.
    (b) reservoir.   (d) precipitation.
2. Liquid water becomes water vapor through
    (a) precipitation. (c) storage.
    (b) evaporation.   (d) condensation.
3. Water vapor changes to liquid droplets through
    (a) evaporation.   (c) precipitation.
    (b) condensation. (d) storage.
4. Lakes, wells, and water towers are kinds of
    (a) reservoirs.   (c) groundwater.
    (b) runoff.   (d) tanks.

B. Understanding Concepts

Answer each of the following questions using complete sentences.

1. Trace the flow of runoff as it is affected by gravity.
2. Describe the possible movement(s) of water that soaks into the ground as groundwater.
3. How are plants and animals part of the water cycle?
4. How does pollution affect the water cycle?

C. Applying Concepts

Think about what you have learned in this chapter. Answer each of the following questions using complete sentences.

1. How is water important to you?
2. Draw a picture to show the water cycle. Label each stage of the water cycle.

UNIT 5 REVIEW

CHECKING YOURSELF

Answer these questions on a sheet of paper.
1. Describe the stages of the water cycle.
2. What are two forms of condensation?
3. How do water, mountains, and large cities affect climate?
4. How is water stored for future use?
5. What is the difference between runoff and groundwater?
6. Where do weather changes take place?
7. How are clouds formed?
8. Why does moisture fall from the atmosphere?
9. How can runoff cause damage on land?
10. What factors affect the speed of evaporation?
11. What are the differences among snow, sleet, and hail?
12. What is climate?
13. What climate zones are found on Earth?
14. What are three examples of reservoirs?

RECALLING ACTIVITIES

Think about the activities you did in this unit. Answer these questions about the activities.
1. When does water evaporate faster? 9-1
2. How do amounts of precipitation compare? 9-2
3. What kind of soil soaks up more water? 10-1
4. What is the water cycle? 10-2

IDEAS TO EXPLORE

1. Make a book of clouds in which each type is drawn and labeled. Also tell the kind of weather when each type of cloud is seen.
2. Form a committee to find out about folk methods of predicting the weather. Give a report in class.
3. Find out what is being done to combat water pollution in your state. Give a report to your class.

CHALLENGING PROJECT

Create a mini-weather station for your school. Obtain an outdoor thermometer and construct an anemometer, barometer, rain gauge, and weather vane. Record the readings from your instruments and the kind of clouds you see. Record the information at the same time each day. Compare this information with a newspaper's weather report. If possible, visit a weather station and prepare a report about other tools that scientists use to study the weather.

BOOKS TO READ

Rain and Hail by Franklyn M. Branley, Crowell Junior Books: New York, © 1983.
   Learn about the water cycle and the different forms of water.

Water by Rae Bains, Troll Associates: Mahwah, NJ, © 1985.
   Read this interesting book to learn more about water.

Wonders of Water by Jane Dickinson, Troll Associates: Mahwah, NJ, © 1983.
   A fascinating question and answer book about water.

UNIT 6
Life Around Us

Charles Darwin was a British scientist. From 1831 to 1836, he sailed around the world studying plants and animals. During the trip, Darwin observed how animals are adapted to the places in which they live. Today, scientists still study animals where they live. Jane Goodall is a British scientist. She has studied chimpanzees in Africa. One discovery she made is that chimpanzees use blades of grass as tools to get insects for food. Why is it important for scientists to study animals where they live?

Charles Darwin—1854

Jane Goodall studying chimpanzees

Chapter 11
Living Things Have Needs

All living things have needs, such as air, food, water, and space. These lion cubs find space in this large plain. They are protected by other lions and also find food and water here. Why is a regular supply of food important to small animals such as lion cubs?

Lion cubs have needs.

Living Things Need Food 11:1

LESSON GOALS

In this lesson you will learn
- living things need food.
- green plants are food producers.

All living things have needs. Food and water are two needs of living things. The right amount of space and proper temperature are also needs. If these needs are not met, an animal or plant cannot live.

Food is a very important need for living things. Food provides energy for plants and animals. The energy is used to keep the parts of each plant and animal working.

Green plants make or produce their own food. A living thing that makes its own food is called a **producer** (proh DEW sur). Plants are producers.

Figure 11-1. Living things need food, water, and space.

193

Figure 11-2. Food is stored in many plant parts.

What do green plants use to make food?

Food is made in the green leaves of plants. Plants use sunlight, water, and the gas carbon dioxide to make this food. What would happen to a plant if light from the sun no longer reached it?

Plants often make more food than they use. The food that is not used right away is stored in many plant parts. Food is stored in roots, stems, leaves, fruits, and seeds. Many of the foods we eat are roots, stems, leaves, fruits, or seeds of plants.

Lesson Summary

- Food provides energy for plants and animals.
- Green plants use sunlight, water, and carbon dioxide to produce food.

Lesson Review

Review the lesson to answer these questions.

1. Why do plants and animals need food?
2. What name is given to plants that make food?
3. Name the plant parts where food is stored.

Science and Technology

Artificial Reefs

People who fish are like farmers. They harvest seafood for people to eat. Because seafood is popular, people who fish need to find new ways to catch shrimp, crabs, lobsters, and fish.

Scientists know that most animals in the ocean live in reefs. These scientists think that if similar reefs are built, there will be more seafood for people to eat. To make such a reef, objects are sunk in the ocean. Old ships, tires, buses, cars, and even playground equipment have been lowered into the ocean.

More than 400 reefs have been built along the coasts of the United States. Small animals and plants begin to grow on the sunken objects within a few weeks. Soon, crabs and other animals move in. The new reefs give shelter and a place for these animals to find food.

Sometimes the new reefs replace natural reefs that were damaged by pollution. However, in most cases, the new reefs are made to create better fishing grounds closer to shore. Then people who fish may have a more plentiful harvest.

11:2 Animals Are Consumers

LESSON GOALS

In this lesson you will learn
- animals are consumers.
- some animals are predators and some are prey.
- animals can be grouped as plant eaters or predators by the shapes of their teeth.

Animals cannot make their own food. They get their food from other living things. Animals are consumers (kuhn SEW murz). A **consumer** is a living thing that cannot make its own food.

Some animals eat only plants or plant parts. Plant eaters may be small or large. Many insects eat leaves, stems, or seeds. Mice and some birds eat seeds. Elephants eat stems and leaves. What plant parts are the animals in Figure 11-3 eating?

Figure 11-3. Some animals eat only plants.

Activity 11-1 Green Plants

QUESTION What plant part is eaten?

Materials
glass or wire cage
animal bedding
mixed seeds
lettuce
carrot
water
jar or dish
small plant-eating
   animal
pencil and paper

What to do
1. Prepare a cage for the animal.
2. Place plant parts in the cage.
3. Gently put the animal in the cage.
4. Observe what, when, and how the animal eats for two or three days.
5. Clean the cage each day and add fresh food and water.

What did you learn?
1. What did the animal eat?
2. When did the animal eat? How did it hold its food?

Using what you learned
1. Suppose your animal got out of its cage. How could information in this activity help you catch the animal?
2. Some animals eat only one kind of plant. If your animal eats many kinds of plants, why is it able to live in more areas than an animal that eats only one kind of plant?

Figure 11-4. Predators hunt other animals.

What is a predator?

Some animals eat only other animals. An animal that hunts and eats other animals is called a **predator** (PRED ut ur). Weasels, hawks, and bobcats are predators. They may eat rabbits, mice, or birds.

Predators are an important part of nature. Suppose coyotes were the only animals that ate ground squirrels. What would happen to the number of ground squirrels if all the coyotes died? How could killing all the coyotes hurt the ground squirrels?

Animals eaten by predators are called **prey.** Look at the animals in Figure 11-4. Which animals are prey? How can an animal be both predator and prey?

Some animals eat both plants and animals. Bears may eat fish, nuts, and berries. Raccoons eat fruits and meat. Robins eat insects, worms, and berries. Opossums eat fruits, vegetables, meat, and insects.

Scientists can group some animals as plant eaters or predators by their teeth. The teeth of plant eaters are broad and flat. They mash the grasses and grains that are eaten.

Predators have pointed teeth. These teeth are sharp and are used to tear prey. Figure 11-5(a) shows the skull of a dinosaur. Was this dinosaur a plant eater or a predator? How do you know?

How are the teeth of plant eaters and predators different?

Figure 11-5. Scientists study dinosaur teeth (a) to learn what they ate. Present-day plant eaters (b) and predators (c) have different types of teeth.

Lesson Summary

- Animals are consumers because they cannot make their own food.
- Some animals are hunted and eaten by other animals.
- Plant eaters have broad, flat teeth while predators have teeth that are pointed.

Lesson Review

Review the lesson to answer these questions.
1. What is a consumer?
2. Explain the meaning of predator and prey.
3. Imagine that only spiders eat flies. If all spiders die, what will happen to the number of flies? Why?

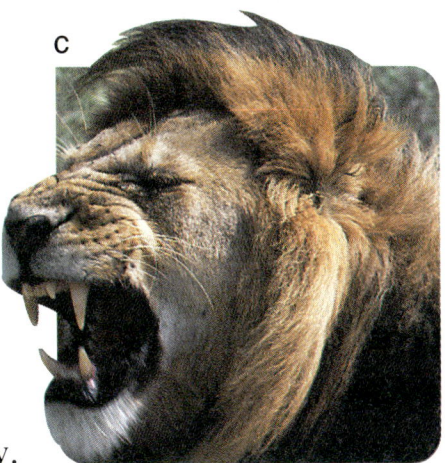

11:3 Scavengers and Decomposers

LESSON GOALS

In this lesson you will learn
- some animals are scavengers.
- some living things are decomposers.

Figure 11-6. Scavengers eat dead animals.

Why are scavengers important?

You have learned that green plants are producers. Remember also that plant eaters and predators are consumers. Two other kinds of living things are also consumers. Scavengers (SKAV un jurs) are consumers. A **scavenger** is an animal that feeds on dead plants and animals. Many animals, such as the hyena, crab, and crow, are scavengers. They help remove dead matter from Earth's surface.

Decomposers (dee kum POH zurz) are also consumers. A **decomposer** is a living thing that breaks down dead plants and animals into simpler matter. Molds are decomposers. They change the color and smell of dead plants or animals as decay takes place.

Figure 11-7. Molds live on dead plants and animals.

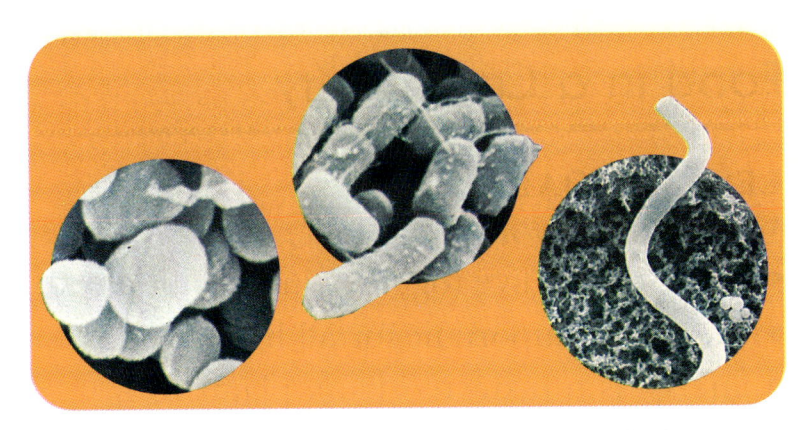

Figure 11-8. Bacteria are very small decomposers.

Some very small decomposers called bacteria cannot be seen by the eye alone. People use microscopes (MI kruh skohps) to see bacteria. A **microscope** is an instrument used to make small objects appear larger. A microscope magnifies objects. Bacteria break down dead matter into very small parts. Bacteria in the soil break down dead matter so that it becomes part of the soil.

Scavengers and decomposers get energy by feeding on dead matter. Decomposers put chemicals that were in living things back into the soil. Plants use these chemicals as they grow.

Why are decomposers important to plants?

Lesson Summary

- Scavengers eat dead plants and animals.
- Decomposers break dead plants and animals into simpler matter.

Lesson Review

Review the lesson to answer these questions.

1. Name two kinds of animals that are scavengers.
2. Name two decomposers.
3. Why are decomposers important?

11:4 Food in a Community

LESSON GOALS

In this lesson you will learn
- living things live together in a community.
- the sun is important for all living things.
- energy is transferred from plants to animals.

Figure 11-9. A pond community is producers and consumers living in a watery area.

What is a community?

A community is a group of producers and consumers living together in one area. Every living thing in a community is important. A pond community may have green plants, insects, fish, frogs, snakes, and bacteria. The green plants grow and make food. They are the producers in the community. Some insects eat parts of the plants. Frogs and fish eat the insects. Snakes eat the fish and frogs. When a snake dies, bacteria break down the snake's body. The insects, fish, frogs, snakes, and bacteria are all consumers in the community.

Remember that food supplies energy for living things. Where does this energy come from in the first place? If you said, "the sun!" you named the major source of energy on Earth. Plants use energy from the sun to grow. They use it to make food. This energy is passed on to animals when they eat the plants.

Why is energy from the sun important?

Think about the pond community. The green plants used energy from the sun. They made food. Some of the energy was passed on to an insect when it ate the plants. Some of the energy was passed on to the frog when it ate the insect. Some of the energy was passed on to the snake when it ate the frog. Later the snake died. Bacteria broke down the body of the dead snake. They got some of the energy.

The energy was moved or transferred from one living thing to another. The plant, insect, fish, frog, snake, and bacteria are part of a food chain. A **food chain** is the transfer of energy from the sun to producers and then to consumers. Look at the food chain in Figure 11-10. What is the producer? What are the consumers?

Figure 11-10. Energy is transferred from one living thing to another.

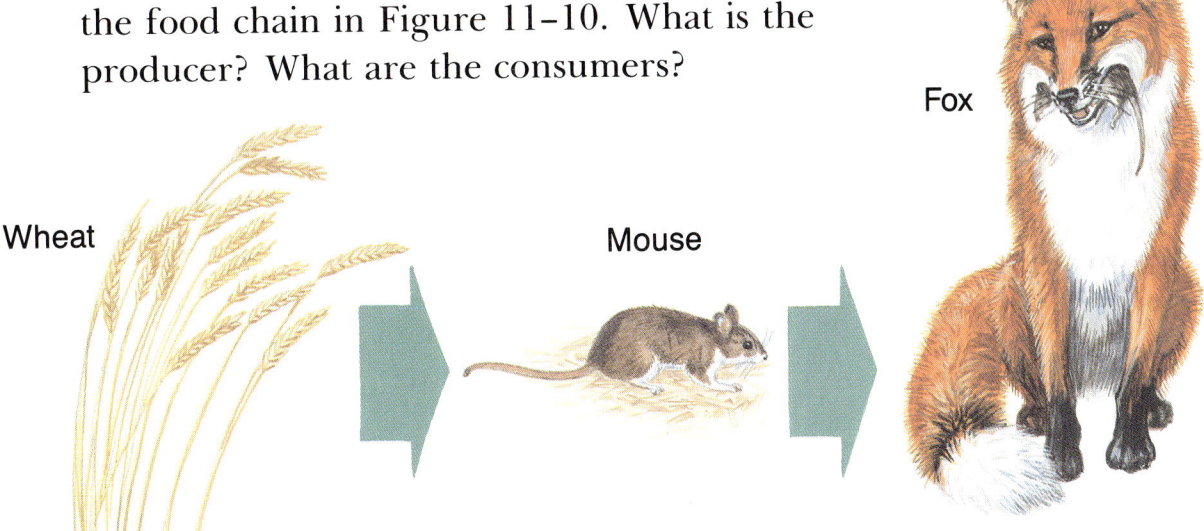

Wheat → Mouse → Fox

203

Activity 11-2 Food Chains

QUESTION How many food chains can you make?

Coyote
Grass
Sparrow hawk
Crayfish
Sunflower seeds
Deer
Cardinal
Horse
Cat
Caterpillar
Slime mold
Person
Leaves
Fungi

Materials
small cards
paper punch
yarn
crayons
pencil and paper

What to do
1. Look at each plant and animal.
2. Write the name of a plant or animal on each card. Write only one name on each card.
3. Punch a hole in each end of the cards.
4. Join each card or link with yarn. Make as many food chains as you can.
5. Hang your food chains in the classroom.

What did you learn?
1. How many links were on your longest food chain?
2. What was first on each chain?
3. Which animals were part of more than one food chain?

Using what you learned
1. How can a plant or animal be part of more than one food chain?
2. Describe the flow of energy through the food chain.

Figure 11-11. A person eating food is part of a food chain.

The producer and each consumer are links within the food chain. Each living thing is food for the next link in the food chain. Energy, in the form of food, is passed on through the food chain.

What is passed on through a food chain?

Food chains can have few or many links. A girl eating tomatoes and lettuce in a salad is part of a short food chain. A longer food chain might start with a mouse eating grain. The mouse is then eaten by a weasel. Later, the weasel dies. It is then eaten by a vulture. How long do you think a food chain can be?

Lesson Summary

- A community is a group of producers and consumers living together in one area.
- The sun is the major source of energy.
- Living things are parts of food chains.

Lesson Review

Review the lesson to answer these questions.

1. What is passed through a food chain?
2. What is Earth's major source of energy?
3. If a boy eating a strawberry is part of a food chain, what is the producer within this part of the food chain?

11:5 Food Webs

LESSON GOALS

In this lesson you will learn
- plants and animals are parts of different food chains.
- a food web is made of food chains.
- there is a flow of energy within food webs.

In a forest community, mice eat the seeds of many plants. The mice in turn are eaten by owls, snakes, and foxes. Each of these three predators may then be eaten by other predators.

Figure 11-12. Plants and animals may be part of more than one food chain.

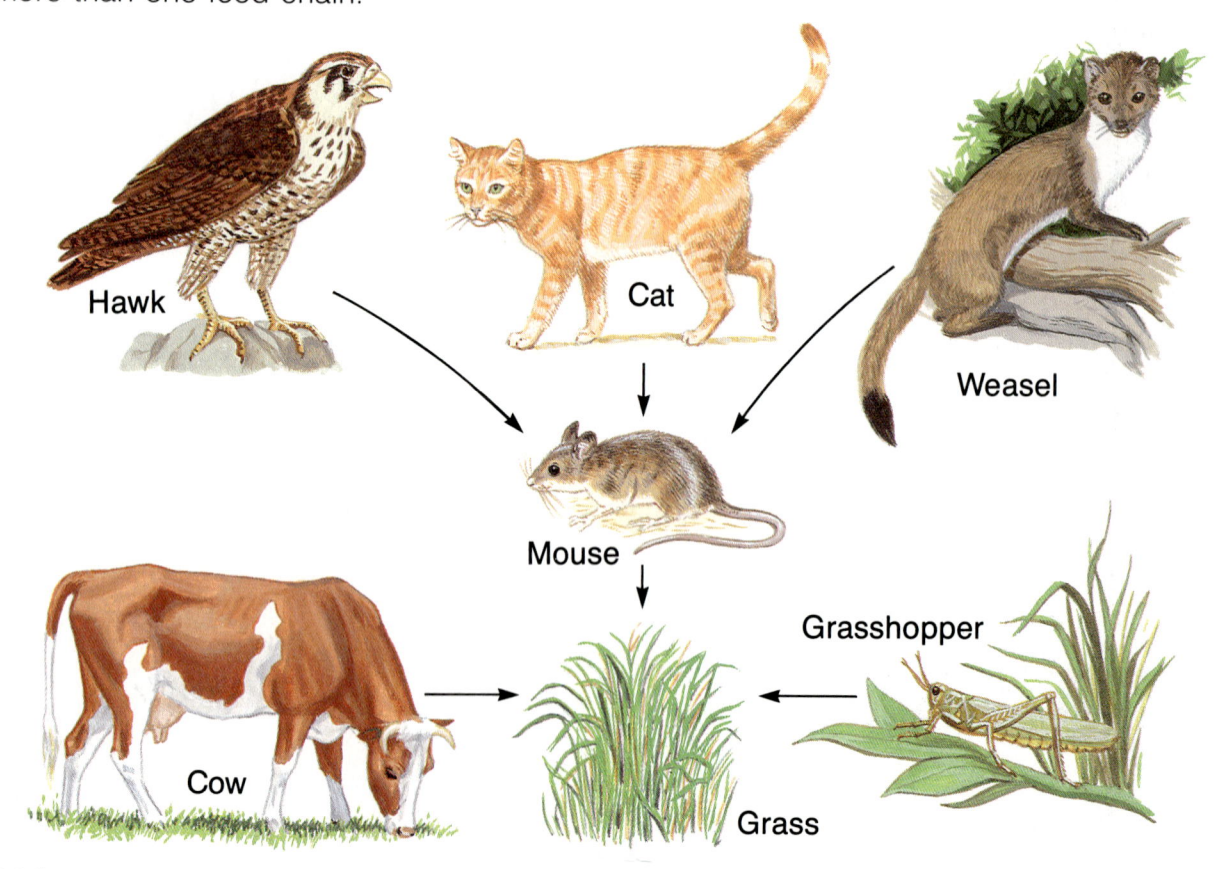

Suppose you looked at all the food chains in a community. You would see that a plant is eaten by many animals. You would also see that a mouse is chased by many predators. A plant is part of more than one food chain. An animal is also part of more than one food chain.

Imagine that you put together all the food chains in a community. You would create what is called a food web. A **food web** is all the feeding relationships in a community. A food web shows which animals are predators and which are prey.

What is a food web?

Figure 11-13. Large prey allows some predators to get much food without using a lot of energy.

In each food chain within a food web, food is produced by green plants. However, the total amount of energy in the food is not passed on to consumers. Part of the energy is used by the plant as it grows. Part of the energy in the plant is used by the consumer that eats the plant. Less of the energy from the plant is then available to other consumers in the food chain.

Figure 11-14. Less and less energy is passed from one consumer to another.

What happens to energy that is passed through a food web?

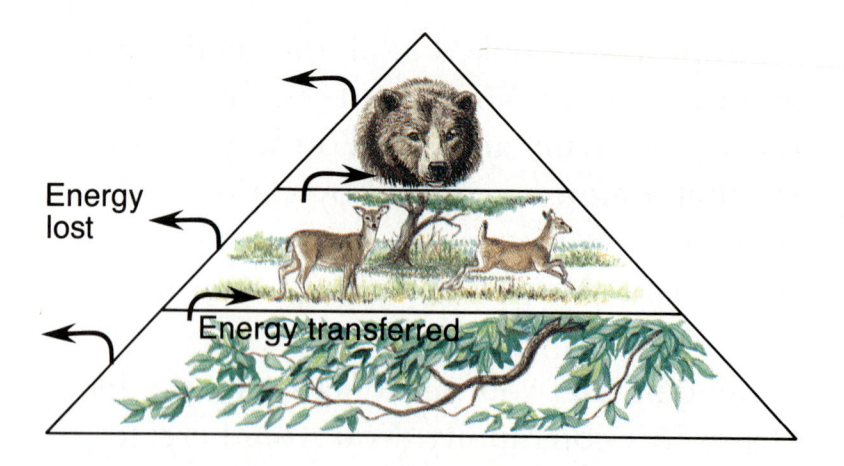

In a forest community, for example, energy is stored in food made by a green plant. Only some of that energy becomes stored in the body of a deer that eats the green plant. An even smaller part of the plant's energy is then available to a bear that eats the deer. As energy is passed through the food web, a large part of it is used by living things.

Lesson Summary

- Plants and animals are usually parts of more than one food chain.
- A food web is made of all the food chains within a community.
- The amount of energy available from producers decreases as it is passed from one consumer to another.

Lesson Review

Review the lesson to answer these questions.
1. What is a food web?
2. What happens to the amount of energy available in a plant when that plant is eaten by a consumer?

People and Science

Save the Condor

Bill Toone takes care of birds at a large zoo. He is working with California condors, which are seriously endangered. The last wild condors are being captured to try to save them.

Condors are birds that feed on dead animals. Some have died from eating poisoned animal bodies set out to kill predators such as coyotes. Others have died from lead poisoning. Adult condors become sick when they feed on bodies of birds killed by lead gunshot. The sick adults cannot care for their young. Therefore, people are trying to help.

Great care is taken with the condor eggs. After being taken from nests, the eggs are carefully packed and flown by helicopter to the zoo. When a chick hatches, Bill makes sure that it is cared for properly.

Loss of their habitat to humans and lead poisoning have caused the condor population to shrink to below 30. Biologists like Bill are working hard to save the largest flying bird in the United States. Bill wants to increase the number of condors at the zoo. These birds can then be released to the wild in a few years.

Chapter 11 Review

Summary

1. All living things need food for energy. 11:1
2. Green plants make or produce food. 11:1
3. Consumers are living things that cannot make food. 11:2
4. Some animals are eaten by other animals. 11:2
5. Plant eaters and predators have different types of teeth. 11:2
6. Scavengers eat dead plants and animals. 11:3
7. Decomposers break down dead plants and animals into simpler matter. 11:3
8. A community is a group of producers and consumers living together in an area. 11:4
9. The sun is the major source of energy. 11:4
10. Living things are parts of food chains. 11:4
11. A food web is all the food chains in a community. 11:5
12. The amount of available energy decreases as it passes from one consumer to another. 11:5

Science Words

producer	prey	microscope	food web
consumer	scavenger	community	
predator	decomposer	food chain	

Understanding Science Words

Complete each of the following sentences with a word or words from the Science Words that will make the sentence correct.

1. All the feeding relationships in a community are a _____.
2. A living thing that makes its own food is a _____.
3. Dead plants and animals are broken down by a _____.
4. An instrument that magnifies small objects is a _____.
5. A living thing that cannot make its own food is a _____.

6. An animal that eats dead plants and animals is a _____.
7. Other animals are hunted and eaten by a _____.
8. The transfer of energy from the sun to producers and then to consumers is a _____.
9. Plants and animals live together in a _____.
10. Animals eaten by predators are called _____.

Questions

A. Recalling Facts

Choose the word or phrase that correctly completes each of the following sentences.

1. When a polar bear eats a seal, the polar bear is a
    (a) producer.   (b) prey.   (c) predator.   (d) decomposer.
2. An example of a decomposer is a
    (a) root.   (b) mold.   (c) nutrient.   (d) prey.
3. Producers make food with energy from the
    (a) air.   (b) water.   (c) soil.   (d) sun.
4. All living things need
    (a) light.   (b) food.   (c) exercise.   (d) carbon dioxide.

B. Understanding Concepts

Answer each of the following questions using complete sentences.

1. Tell about the flow of energy through a food web.
2. How do plants make food? Where is the food stored?

C. Applying Concepts

Think about what you have learned in this chapter. Answer each of the following questions using complete sentences.

1. Tell about a food web that includes people.
2. Plant → insect → frog → snake is an example of a food chain. Which is the producer and which are consumers?

211

Chapter 12
Habitats

Animals and plants live in areas where their needs are met. A cactus, for example, needs a dry climate. Cacti are found in desert areas. This salamander has moist skin. It needs to live in a wet area. How does the area shown here meet this need?

Salamanders live in wet areas.

Habitats Are Important 12:1

LESSON GOALS

In this lesson you will learn
- each plant or animal lives in a habitat.
- all living things have special needs.
- animals can find protection in habitats.

Plants and animals live in all parts of the world. They live on high mountains and in deep oceans. Living things are found in hot as well as cold places. They live in areas that have dry or wet climates. Each living thing lives in a **habitat** (HAB uh tat) or place where its needs are met. A habitat provides the food, temperature, and living space that are needed by each plant or animal.

There are many kinds of habitats. A bird may have a nest in a tree. An octopus may live in part of a sunken ship. A beach pea plant may grow near an ocean. The nest and tree are part of the bird's habitat. The ship is part of the octopus's habitat. The sandy soil is part of the pea plant's habitat. The habitats, though different, meet the needs of these living things.

Each living thing is adapted to live in a certain place. The water lily and mole in Figure 12-1 are adapted to their habitats. How is the water lily adapted to where it lives? How is the mole adapted to where it lives?

What does a habitat provide?

Figure 12-1. Every living thing is adapted to live in a certain place.

213

Activity 12-1 A Land Habitat

QUESTION How can you make a land habitat?

Materials

large jar	plants
lid with holes	water
metric ruler	water dish
gravel	small animal
potting soil	animal food
paper cups	pencil and paper
rocks	

What to do

1. Add a 3 cm layer of gravel to the jar. Add an 8 cm layer of soil on top of the gravel Set a few small rocks on the soil.
2. Place the plants in the soil and add water.
3. Add food to the jar.
4. Put the animal in the jar. Replace the lid.
5. Add food as needed and keep the soil moist for two weeks.

What did you learn?

1. What was the animal's shelter?
2. How do you know if the needs of the plants and animal were met?

Using what you learned

1. How is this habitat the same or different from the animal's natural habitat?
2. What would happen if you planted these plants in an aquarium? Why?

All living things need air, food, and water. They also need space. If too many plants or animals are in one place, their needs cannot be met.

Suppose you planted vegetables in a garden. You put fifty seeds in a small area. All of the seeds sprouted. At first all the seedlings grew well. The next week, some of the plants began to yellow and wilt. Soon those plants died. The other plants did not look healthy. Too many plants were in one small area. They did not have enough water, food, and light.

The same thing would be true if too many foxes were in one habitat. There would not be enough water and food in the space. All of the foxes could not live there.

What do living things need in addition to air, food, and water?

Figure 12-2. Plants need space in order to grow.

215

Figure 12-3. Animals use shelters for protection.

Why do animals use shelters?

Within each living space, animals find shelters. A **shelter** is a place or object that protects an animal. Animals use shelters for protection from wind, rain, and hot or cold weather. They also use shelters to hide from predators. Think about different kinds of prey. What shelters could protect prey from predators? List as many shelters as you can.

Some animals may use caves as shelters. Bats, for example, hang from walls inside caves during the daytime. Other animals may use holes in trees or rocks, or ledges under the water. Some animals, such as insects and spiders, hide among plants. Other animals may dig burrows or tunnels. All of these shelters are a part of these animals' habitats.

Some animals are protected from predators by living in groups. Herds, flocks, packs, prides, pods, and schools are some names for animal groups. Most predators do not attack animals in a group. They look for prey that is alone. The group, therefore, is like a shelter for each animal.

A group can also protect some animals from storms. The wind and precipitation have less effect on each animal when the animals are huddled together.

How can a group be protection for an animal during bad weather?

Figure 12-4. Groups protect animals from predators.

Lesson Summary

- Each plant or animal lives in a habitat or place where its needs are met.
- Air, food, water, and space are life needs.
- Shelters in habitats protect animals from predators and hot or cold weather.

Lesson Review

Review the lesson to answer these questions.

1. What is a habitat?
2. Why would sixty seeds planted in a small area probably not grow well?
3. How are animals protected by a group?

12:2 Polar, Tundra, Desert, and Grassland Habitats

LESSON GOALS

In this lesson you will learn
- the names of four different types of habitats.
- each type of habitat has a variety of plants and animals.

Figure 12-5. Polar regions are located near the North and South Poles.

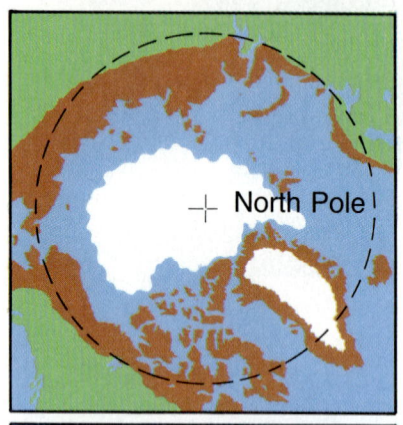

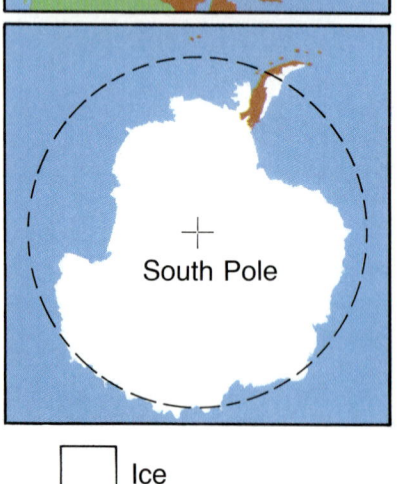

Ice

Tundra

Scientists group habitats into types. Each type of habitat has living things that are adapted to that habitat. Imagine a cactus plant living in the Arctic. Its needs would not be met there. Neither could a polar bear meet its needs if it lived in a hot desert. Plants and animals whose needs are alike live together in the same type of habitat.

Polar and Tundra Habitats

Two areas in the far northern and southern parts of the world have very cold climates and are called polar regions. A **polar region** is an area of ice and snow located near the North or South Pole. The ice of the northern region is a habitat for animals such as seals, walruses, and polar bears.

The southern region contains a large landmass covered with ice. Few plants are found here because of unfavorable growing conditions. Animals, however, are found in greater number and include seals, penguins, and other birds. Fish and whales are also found in salt water within both regions.

Many kinds of animal life and some plant life are found on frozen land surrounding the center of the northern polar region. This habitat is called the Arctic tundra (TUN druh). **Tundra** is a cold, dry habitat with a layer of soil that is frozen. The tundra is covered with snow more than half the year. Trees are not found in the tundra. The climate is too cold for them to grow. However, small plants, such as grasses and mosses, do grow in the tundra.

Why are trees not found in the tundra?

The tundra does contain animal life. There is a great variety. Caribou, musk oxen, lemmings, and golden plovers are some animals that live in the tundra.

Figure 12-6. Different kinds of animals live in the Arctic tundra.

Some animals living in the tundra look different during the year. Many grow thick fur in winter and then shed much of this fur in summer. Some animals are adapted to seasonal changes in other ways. Animals such as the Arctic hare have lighter-colored fur in winter than in summer. How is this color change important to the Arctic hare?

Desert Habitat

Another type of habitat is the desert. A **desert** is a habitat that has little moisture. Some deserts are hot and dry. Other deserts are cold and dry. Living things are adapted to life with little water. Some animals, such as the rattlesnake, get water from their food. Other animals, such as the camel, drink a lot of water at one time. They can live many days without drinking again.

Figure 12-7. Some desert plants have small leaves.

Figure 12-8. The desert tortoise stores moisture in its body.

How are cacti adapted to living in a dry climate?

Desert plants are also adapted to a dry climate. Some plants, such as cacti, store water in their stems or roots. Many desert plants have small leaves that lose very little water. These plants are able to live for a long time without absorbing water.

Small size is an important adaptation to desert living. Small living things find it easier to escape desert heat than do large animals. Why is this true?

Living underground is another way animals stay cool in the desert. Also, many animals hunt at night. It is cooler. Animals in the desert have adapted to a dry habitat.

Figure 12-9. Animals such as pronghorn antelope live on grassland.

Grassland Habitat

Another type of habitat is the grassland. A **grassland** is a habitat where most of the plants are grasses. Some animals that live on grasslands are prairie dogs, pronghorn antelope, foxes, hawks, kudu, and kangaroos. Some of the fastest animals on Earth live there. The grasslands are usually large open spaces. Speed is necessary to escape from predators or to catch prey. How is the animal shown in Figure 12-9 adapted to a grassland habitat?

Lesson Summary

- The polar regions, tundra, desert, and grassland are four types of habitats.
- Each type of habitat contains a variety of plants and animals that are adapted to that habitat.

Lesson Review

Review the lesson to answer these questions.

1. Describe a plant or animal that lives in a tundra habitat. How is it adapted?
2. Describe a plant or animal that lives in a desert habitat. How is it adapted?

12:3 Forest and Water Habitats

LESSON GOALS

In this lesson you will learn
- there are three kinds of forest habitats.
- there are two kinds of water habitats.

There are three kinds of forest habitats. Each kind of forest contains certain plants and animals. These living things have adapted to life in that kind of forest.

A **coniferous** (kuh NIHF rus) **forest** is a habitat in northern regions of the world. The growing season is short and the weather is very cold. Trees with needle-shaped leaves are found in these forests. The leaves stay green all year. Spruce and fir are two kinds of evergreens found in coniferous forests. What kinds of evergreen trees have you seen?

A variety of animals live in the coniferous forest. Some are large and some are small in size. Mice, beavers, moose, owls, wolves, and woodpeckers are examples of these animals.

Figure 12-10. Moose live in coniferous forests.

Figure 12-11. Trees with needle-shaped leaves grow in coniferous forests.

What is a temperate forest?

The **temperate** (TEM prut) **forest** is a habitat that has four seasons—spring, summer, autumn, and winter. Temperate forests contain many broad-leaf trees that lose their leaves in autumn. New leaf growth does not take place until spring. In spring, buds swell where new leaves will form. Oak, maple, and hickory trees are examples of broad-leaf trees. They are common in many temperate forests. Smaller plants, such as wildflowers and ferns, are also found in these forests.

Figure 12-12. Many broad-leaf trees grow in temperate forests.

Figure 12-13. Bears find food in temperate forests.

Animals living in temperate forests are adapted to four seasons. Most of the year they have a good supply of food. In winter there is less food. Deer, rabbits, mice, and some birds find food under the snow. Other birds fly, or migrate, to warmer places where they can find food. Some forest animals, such as insects, salamanders, chipmunks, and bears, sleep or rest through most of the winter.

Activity 12-2   Animal Habitats

QUESTION   What animals live in the ground?

Materials
rake
mixed birdseed
bread crumbs
peanuts
carrots
flour
metric ruler
resource book on animal tracks
pencil and paper

What to do
1. Select a hole in the ground where you think an animal lives.
2. Rake leaves away from the hole.
3. Spread flour around the hole.
4. Place food near the hole.
5. Return to the hole the next day. Observe any tracks in the flour and record which food was eaten.

What did you learn?
1. How many different types of tracks did you find?
2. From where did the animal come? How do you know?
3. Which food did the animal eat?

Using what you learned
1. What animals made tracks in the flour?
2. How could you use this activity to find out if an animal has made a home in your yard?

Rain forests are the third kind of forest habitat. A **rain forest** is a forest habitat that receives about 250 cm of rain a year. Rain forests are found in South America, Malaysia, and Africa, and are hot and wet.

Where are rain forests found?

Figure 12–14. A variety of plants and animals live in rain forests.

Plants grow quickly in rain forests. They are adapted to daily rainfall and heat. Many evergreen plants with broad leaves grow close together. Tall trees grow high above shrubs and vines.

Animals in rain forests are adapted to life among tall plants. Monkeys use their long tails and arms to swing from tree to tree. Large predators have body colors that help them hide when they hunt prey. Look at each animal in Figure 12–14. How is each animal adapted to life in a rain forest?

225

Water Habitats

Much of Earth is covered with water. On Earth there is more water than land. There are two types of water habitats. Each has different kinds of plants and animals living in it.

Freshwater habitats are found in ponds, bogs, swamps, lakes, and rivers. Each freshwater habitat has special kinds of plants and animals that live there. Some plants and animals live in waters that are very cold. Others live in waters that are warm. Some plants and animals adapt to waters that flow fast. Others adapt to still water.

What are the two types of water habitats?

Figure 12-15. Freshwater habitats contain many plants and animals.

The larger of the two types of water habitats is the **ocean** or saltwater habitat. There are large numbers of plants and animals living in the ocean. Some, such as jellyfish, sea bass, and whales, move freely through the ocean. Others, such as kelp and sea anemones, are attached to objects and do not move away.

Ocean habitat

Whale · Kelp · Jellyfish · Sea bass · Lookdown · Sea turtle · Coral · Starfish · Blue crab · Sea anemone

Figure 12-16. Many forms of life live in Earth's oceans.

Lesson Summary

- Northern coniferous forests, temperate forests, and rain forests are three kinds of forest habitats.
- Freshwater and ocean habitats are two kinds of water habitats.

Lesson Review

Review the lesson to answer these questions.

1. Compare the types of trees that grow in northern coniferous and temperate forests.
2. Tell about an animal that lives in the temperate forest.
3. How is a monkey adapted to living in a rain forest?
4. Describe two types of animals found in oceans. Give an example of each type of animal.

12:4 People Adapt to Many Habitats

LESSON GOALS

In this lesson you will learn
- people adapt to different habitats.
- wildlife conservation is important.

Figure 12-17. People live in urban (a), rural (b), and natural habitats (c).

Most plants and animals live in only one kind of habitat. People can adapt to different kinds of habitats. They can also make major changes in habitats.

People can build the shelters they need. They can change the food they eat. They can use food that is grown in other habitats. People, like some other animals, can also move from one habitat to another.

Figure 12-17 shows different habitats where people live. What is each habitat like?

Figure 12-18. Wildlife conservation is important.

Although people can change habitats, they need to be careful. A habitat should remain a healthy place for plants and animals. Some people work to protect habitats. The efforts people make to protect habitats and their living things is called **wildlife conservation.**

Wildlife conservation should be a concern for everyone. People need to make sure that food chains are not destroyed. They must remember that producers are the basis of every food chain in the world.

What is wildlife conservation?

Why are producers especially important parts of food chains?

Lesson Summary

- People can build shelters, grow food, and travel to different habitats.
- Wildlife conservation concerns the protection of habitats.

Lesson Review

Review the lesson to answer these questions.

1. What are some examples of changes that people can make to habitats?
2. Why is the conservation of producers especially important?

Did You Know . . . ?

The world of animals is a world full of mysteries and surprises. Sometimes these mysteries of the animal world cannot be solved. They just have to be accepted as a part of nature.

Here are some interesting and little-known facts about animals. Some of these facts may not be found in resource books. Some of them are strange as well as interesting.

A camel can walk 30 miles in a day and do this without eating or drinking. It can go without food or water for many days.

Cows moo. Lions roar. However, did you know that a giraffe seldom makes a sound?

A male lion sleeps or rests about 20 hours a day.

Some seahorses are only two inches long.

Most pouched animals live in Australia and nearby islands.

When a mole is hungry, it can dig up to five and one-half meters an hour looking for food.

Although lobsters walk forward, they swim backward.

An elephant can run as fast as 40 kilometers per hour.

The blue whale is the largest animal in the world. It is as big as 17 elephants.

The Arctic tern makes the longest regular journeys of any known animal. It travels 22,000 miles from the Arctic to the Antarctic and back. Each journey takes two months.

The three-toed sloth spends most of its time hanging upside-down from a branch. This sloth may spend its entire life in one tree.

Unlike most birds, the owl has both eyes in front of its head.

The kiwi has nostrils at the tip of its bill.

Now, it's your turn! See how many "little-known" facts you can find about animals and test them on a friend.

Chapter 12 Review

Summary

1. Each living thing lives in a habitat. 12:1
2. Living things need air, food, water, and space. 12:1
3. Animals use shelters for protection. 12:1
4. The polar regions, tundra, desert, and grassland are four types of habitats. 12:2
5. A variety of plants and animals are adapted to each habitat. 12:2
6. Three types of forest habitats are coniferous, temperate, and rain forest. 12:3
7. Freshwater and ocean habitats are two kinds of water habitats. 12:3
8. People can adapt to different habitats. 12:4
9. Wildlife conservation concerns the protection of habitats. 12:4

Science Words

habitat	**desert**	**rain forest**
shelter	**grassland**	**fresh water**
polar region	**coniferous forest**	**ocean**
tundra	**temperate forest**	**wildlife conservation**

Understanding Science Words

Complete each of the following sentences with a word or words from the Science Words that will make the sentence correct.

1. A kind of forest that has four seasons is called a _____.
2. A place where a plant or animal lives is a _____.
3. The efforts people make to protect living things and their habitats is called _____.
4. A kind of forest with a hot, wet climate is a _____.
5. A place or object that protects an animal is a _____.
6. A habitat with a layer of soil that is frozen is _____.
7. The habitat found in lakes is called _____.

8. A habitat with large, open spaces covered with grass is _____.
9. A dry habitat that receives little moisture is a _____.
10. A saltwater habitat is an _____.
11. A habitat that is covered by snow and ice all year is a _____.
12. A forest habitat in northern regions is the _____.

Questions

A. Recalling Facts

Choose the word or phrase that correctly completes each of the following sentences.

1. An animal living in a polar region must be able to
    (a) move rapidly.   (c) adjust to dryness.
    (b) keep warm.   (d) change with the seasons.
2. Animals live in groups to
    (a) attract predators.   (c) build shelters.
    (b) protect themselves. (d) have more space.
3. The tundra is a habitat that does NOT have
    (a) snow.   (b) trees.   (c) soil.   (d) animals.
4. A rain forest is a habitat that is
    (a) cold.   (b) dry.   (c) hot and dry.   (d) hot and wet.

B. Understanding Concepts

Answer each of the following questions using complete sentences.

1. Why do living things need space?
2. How are the two water habitats the same? Different?

C. Applying Concepts

Think about what you have learned in this chapter. Answer each of the following questions using complete sentences.

1. Describe a plant or animal that lives in each of the land habitats and tell how it is adapted to that habitat.
2. Why should people be concerned about wildlife conservation?

UNIT 6 REVIEW

CHECKING YOURSELF

Answer these questions on a sheet of paper.
1. List four needs of all living things.
2. How are producers and consumers different?
3. What kind of animal is a predator? Prey? Give an example of each.
4. Why are predators an important part of nature?
5. How do scavengers get energy? Name two scavengers.
6. How do decomposers change dead plants and animals?
7. What is the difference between a food chain and a food web?
8. What happens to energy as it is passed from the producer to the consumers in a food chain?
9. Name ways in which the following animals are adapted to life in their habitats: camel, polar bear, antelope, monkey.
10. How are tundra and grassland habitats alike? Different?
11. How are ocean and freshwater habitats alike? Different?
12. How can people help to conserve their habitats?

RECALLING ACTIVITIES

Think about the activities you did in this unit. Answer the questions about these activities.
1. What plant part is eaten? 11-1
2. How many food chains can you make? 11-2
3. How can you make a land habitat? 12-1
4. What animals live in the ground? 12-2

IDEAS TO EXPLORE

1. Make a drawing or collect pictures of animals that live in the (a) rain forest, (b) desert, and (c) ocean.
2. Invent an animal that is adapted to a certain habitat. Draw the habitat and animal on a sheet of paper. Tell how the animal is adapted to the habitat.
3. Exchange letters with a science class from another part of the country. Compare habitats.

CHALLENGING PROJECT

Watch a television program about a habitat. Choose three facts mentioned on the program. Write these facts or illustrate them so they can be shared with your classmates.

Observe a place where you find plants and animals. Write a report or give a talk about what you observe. (This can be done with a partner or in small groups.)

BOOKS TO READ

Amazing World of Animals by Lawrence Jeffries, Troll Associates: Mahwah, NJ, © 1983.
    This book tells about animals from all over the world.

Jungles by Edward R. Ricciuti, Western Publishing Co.: Racine, WI, © 1984.
    This colorful book describes many different jungles and tropical forests of the world.

Who Knows This Nose by Marlene M. Robinson, Dodd Mead & Co.: New York, © 1983.
    Learn how noses help animals live in their habitats.

UNIT 7
Comparing Earth and the Moon

In 1513, a Spanish explorer named Balboa discovered the Pacific Ocean. This discovery opened the western coast of South America to exploration by Europeans. It also renewed the search by Europeans for a western route to Asia. Saturn rockets have launched modern explorers on their way to the moon. In what way is their travel to the moon similar in importance to Balboa's discovery of the Pacific Ocean?

Balboa discovers Pacific Ocean—1513

Saturn V rocket launching astronauts toward moon

Chapter 13
Study of Earth and the Moon

People have made footprints on both Earth and the moon. This footprint on the moon will stay like this. It will not change. There is no atmosphere on the moon. Weathering does not take place. Think of footprints made on Earth. How do they compare to those made on the moon?

Astronaut's footprint on the moon

Earth and Moon Sizes

13:1

LESSON GOALS

In this lesson you will learn
- the difference in size between Earth and the moon.
- the size of an object may seem to change.

People have been interested in the moon for thousands of years. They were amazed at how it changed shape. These people made up stories about the moon. Today, scientists are interested in the moon. They know many facts about the moon. They use these facts to compare the moon to Earth.

Figure 13-1. People have been interested in the moon for many years.

Figure 13-2. Sometimes Earth looks smaller than the moon.

The moon looks very large in Figure 13-2. Earth looks much smaller but is really more than 3½ times wider than the moon. Why does the moon appear so much larger than Earth?

How much wider is Earth than the moon?

239

Activity 13-1 Spatial Relationships

QUESTION How large are the circles?

Materials
cardboard
circle patterns
scissors
modeling clay

meter stick
long table
pencil and paper

What to do
1. Trace the circle patterns on the sheet of cardboard. Cut out the circles.
2. Press the edge of each circle in a piece of clay.
3. Place the circles at the following distances from the table's edge: small circle—60 cm, middle-sized circle—90 cm, large circle—120 cm.
4. Kneel at the table's edge. Close one eye. Look at all the circles at the same time.

What did you learn?
1. Which circle was the closest to you? Farthest from you?
2. What size did all of the circles seem to be in step 4?

Using what you learned
1. Why does the sun sometimes look the same size as the moon?
2. When can a real airplane look the same size as a toy plane?

240

The red and blue balls in Figure 13–3 are not the same size. Which ball is smaller? Look at the second picture. The distance between the balls has changed. The large ball is farther away so it looks small. Objects look smaller when they are far away from you.

From Earth, the moon seems to be just as big as the sun. The moon, however, is much smaller than the sun. It would take almost 400 moons edge to edge to reach across the sun.

Figure 13-3. Objects look smaller when they are far away.

How many moons would it take to reach across the sun?

Lesson Summary

- Earth is over 3 times wider than the moon.
- Large objects look smaller when they are far away.

Lesson Review

Review the lesson to answer these questions.

1. How many moons edge to edge would it take to reach across the sun?
2. Why does the moon look as large as the sun?

241

13:2 Gravity

LESSON GOALS

In this lesson you will learn
- the difference in gravity between Earth and the moon.
- why Earth has an atmosphere.
- why the moon does not have an atmosphere.
- temperatures on the moon change quickly.

Why does Earth have more gravity than the moon?

Gravity pulls you back to Earth if you jump in the air. Earth has more gravity than the moon because it has more mass than the moon. Earth's gravity is six times greater than that of the moon. You weigh six times more on Earth than you would on the moon because of this difference in gravity. For example, if you weigh 60 pounds on Earth, you would weigh 10 pounds on the moon.

What keeps the atmosphere at Earth's surface?

Earth has an atmosphere because of gravity. This force keeps the atmosphere from moving away from Earth. Earth's atmosphere is very important. It contains the air which plants and animals need to live. The atmosphere also keeps heat at Earth's surface. Warm and cold air mix in the atmosphere. This mixing of air causes Earth's temperatures to remain somewhat even from place to place. Weather, climate, and seasons take place on Earth within the atmosphere. Look at Figure 13-4. How can you tell Earth has an atmosphere?

Figure 13-4. Warm and cold air mix within Earth's atmosphere.

242

The moon's gravity is too weak to "hold" an atmosphere. Because there is no air, temperatures change very quickly. The moon is very hot where the sun shines on it. It is much hotter than any place on Earth. Where it is dark, the moon is colder than any place on Earth.

Why is there no atmosphere on the moon?

Figure 13-5. Temperatures on the moon change quickly.

Lesson Summary

- Earth's gravity is six times greater than the moon's gravity.
- Gravity keeps an atmosphere at Earth's surface.
- The moon's gravity is too weak to "hold" an atmosphere.
- Temperatures on the moon may be very hot or very cold.

Lesson Review

Review the lesson to answer these questions.

1. Why would you weigh less on the moon than on Earth?
2. Tell why Earth's atmosphere is important.

13:3 Earth and Moon Surfaces

LESSON GOALS

In this lesson you will learn
- why Earth's surface changes.
- mountains, valleys, plains, craters, and rocks are found on Earth and the moon.
- the moon is covered with regolith.

Figure 13-6. Mountains were formed on both Earth and the moon.

What has caused changes on some Earth mountains?

In some ways the surfaces of Earth and the moon are alike. In other ways they are different. Since there is no atmosphere on the moon, there is no wind, rain, or snow to cause changes on the moon's surface. Mountains and hills on the moon are very sharp and rough. Land surfaces on Earth are affected by an atmosphere. Wind and running water carry away soil. They also smooth down the surfaces of mountains.

Moon mountains are made of bare rocks. Earth's mountains are made of rocks and soil. They also have trees, bushes, and other plants. Think about what plants need to grow. Why do plants not grow on the moon?

244

Both Earth and the moon have valleys. A long, narrow moon valley is called a **rill.** Some moon rills look like cracks in the surface. Some look like winding paths. Some rills may have been formed by flowing lava.

Most Earth valleys were formed by streams or rivers. Moving water and ice cut paths through soil and rocks.

Plains and Maria

Dark areas on the moon's surface are large, flat plains called **maria** (MAR ee uh). *Maria* is a Latin word that means *seas*. Long ago, people thought these areas were filled with water. Scientists now know the moon's maria are very bare, dry plains made of dark rocks.

Earth has plains, too. They are large, flat areas. Earth plains, however, are covered by thick, rich soil. Many people grow crops in this soil.

How were rills formed?

Figure 13-7. People grow crops on the Great Plains.

Figure 13-8. Maria look like dark seas on the moon's surface.

245

Figure 13-9. The moon has many craters.

What is a crater?

Figure 13-10. Some large craters are found on Earth.

Craters

Scientists think the moon had volcanoes a very long time ago. There are no active volcanoes on the moon now. Some of the moon's craters may have been formed by volcanoes. A **crater** is a hollow area in the ground. Most moon craters were made by objects hitting the moon.

Earth's atmosphere prevents small objects from hitting Earth. The objects burn up in the atmosphere before they can hit Earth. The area beyond Earth's atmosphere is called **space.** Some large objects from space do hit Earth and form craters. One such crater is in Arizona. Scientists believe it was made by an object that hit Earth very long ago. Why do Earth craters look different than moon craters after a long time?

Rocks, Soil, and Regolith

Igneous rocks are found on the moon. Igneous rocks on Earth form when magma or lava cools. Scientists think that the rocks on the moon were formed the same way.

Soil does not form on the moon. Rocks are broken into small pieces when objects hit the moon. This outer layer of the moon is called regolith (REG uh lihth). **Regolith** is dust and rock pieces that form when objects hit the moon.

You learned in Lesson 6:2 that not all soil on Earth is the same. Some soil is wet. Other soil is dry and sandy. Most soil contains pieces of plant and animal parts.

Figure 13-11. Igneous rocks are found on the moon.

Lesson Summary

- Wind, ice, and flowing water cause changes on Earth's surface.
- Moon rills, mountains, maria, craters, and rocks can be compared to Earth's valleys, mountains, plains, craters, and rocks.
- Regolith is a soil-like layer on the moon.

Lesson Review

Review the lesson to answer these questions.

1. How are rills and maria different from valleys and plains on Earth?
2. Footprints can be found on Earth and the moon. Which will last longer?
3. What is a crater?
4. How does regolith form?

Activity 13-2 Moon Craters

QUESTION How can you make moon craters?

Materials
newspaper
plastic dishpan
sand
metric ruler
talcum powder
marble
safety goggles
string
masking tape
flashlight
pencil and paper

What to do

Part A

1. Cover a square meter area with newspaper. Place the dishpan in the center of the paper.
2. Pour sand into the dishpan until it is 5 cm deep. Sprinkle a thin layer of powder on top of the sand. Put on the safety goggles.
3. Tape one end of the string to the marble.
4. Hold the other end of the string in one hand. With the other hand, hold the marble a little less than 1 meter above the pan.
5. Drop the marble into the sand. With the string, carefully lift the marble straight out of the sand.

248

6. Observe the crater in the sand.
7. Measure the sizes of the marble and the crater. Record your measurements.

Part B
1. Shine a flashlight straight down on the crater. Draw what you observe.
2. Shine the light on the crater from one side. Draw what you observe.

What did you learn?
1. What happened to the sand when the marble hit?
2. What is the shape of the crater?
3. What is the distance across the marble?
4. What is the distance across the crater?
5. What does the crater look like when you shine the flashlight straight down?
6. What does the crater look like when you shine the flashlight from one side?

Using what you learned
1. How does the size of the marble compare to the size of the crater it makes?
2. Why did you put a layer of powder on top of the sand?
3. What does the marble represent?
4. What does the flashlight represent?
5. How would crater size and shape change if you drop the marble from different heights? Try it.

13:4 Equipment For Studying the Moon

LESSON GOALS

In this lesson you will learn
- a special tool is used to study the moon.
- spacecraft are used to travel to the moon.
- astronauts have special needs on the moon.

Figure 13-12. Scientists use telescopes to study the moon.

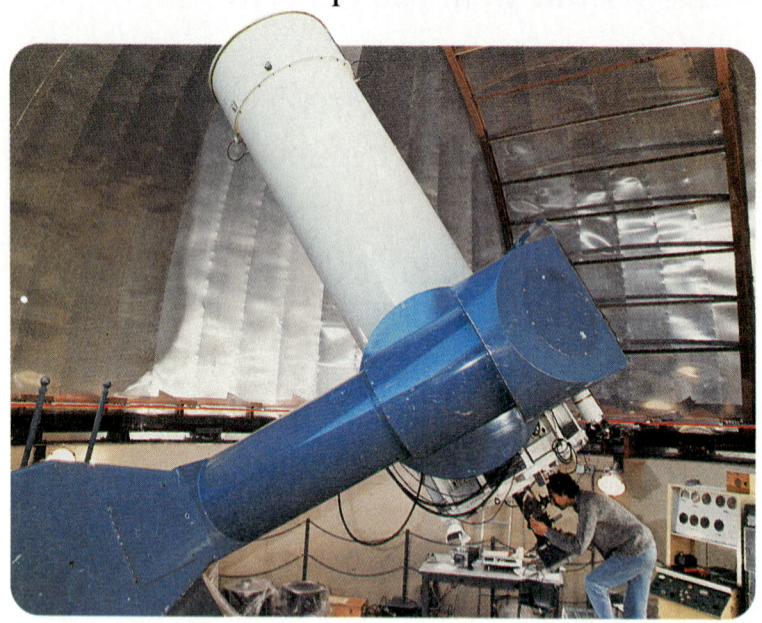

What are spacecraft?

Figure 13-13. Some spacecraft have been sent deep into space.

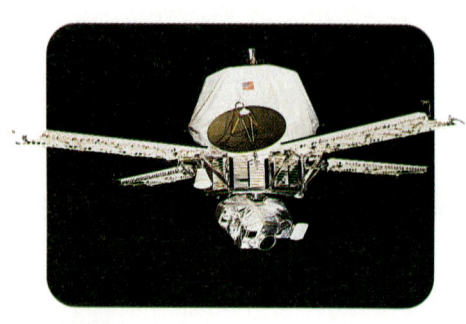

A telescope is a tool used to make distant objects look bigger. Some of the first telescopes were made by Galileo Galilei. In 1609 he made a telescope with which he could see mountains on the moon.

Today, scientists use modern telescopes to look at the moon. They can make maps of the moon. How is a map of the moon useful?

Some people have gone to the moon in spacecraft. A **spacecraft** is a machine that travels to the moon or to other space objects. Some spacecraft have taken pictures of the moon. Others have landed on the moon.

250

Many of the spacecraft that landed on the moon carried astronauts (AS truh nawts). An **astronaut** is a person who travels and works in space. Astronauts first landed on the moon in 1969. They have collected rocks and regolith from the moon's surface. Astronauts have found out what it is like in a place that has less gravity than Earth.

People need special clothing to live on the moon. The clothing protects the astronauts when they are out of their spacecraft. The clothing must protect astronauts from both very hot and very cold temperatures.

The moon has no atmosphere. The astronauts had to carry their own air. They carried the air in tanks on their backs when they went out of the spacecraft.

What is an astronaut?

Figure 13-14. Some spacecraft have taken astronauts to the moon.

Figure 13-15. The lunar rover can be driven over the moon's surface.

How is a lunar rover useful?

Figure 13-16. Food for astronauts is stored in special containers.

Astronauts used special tools on the moon. One tool was the lunar rover. The rover is a vehicle that can be driven over the moon's surface.

Foods and liquids for astronauts are prepared and stored in special ways. Much of the food is freeze-dried. Figure 13-16 shows food for astronauts traveling to the moon.

Lesson Summary

- Scientists use telescopes to study the moon.
- Spacecraft are machines that travel from Earth to the moon or to other space objects.
- Astronauts need special clothing, air, and specially prepared food in order to live on the moon.

Lesson Review

Review the lesson to answer these questions.

1. What is a telescope?
2. What is an astronaut?
3. Why do astronauts need special clothing in order to live on the moon?

People and Science

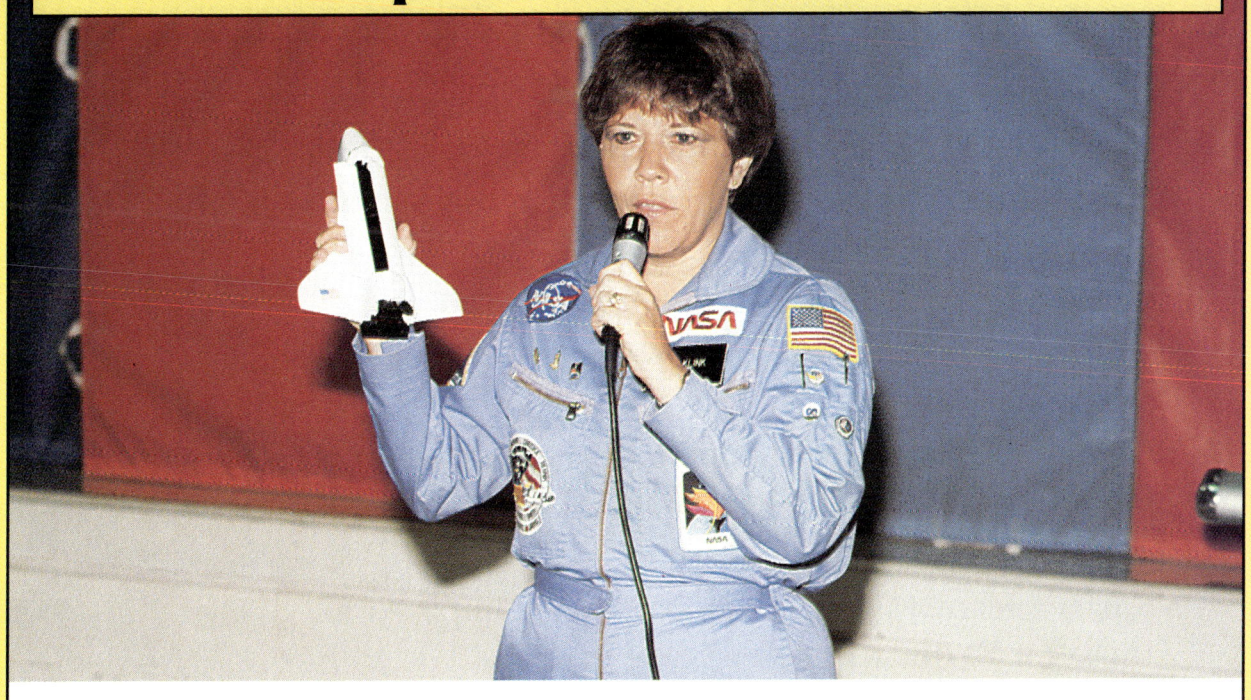

Space Ambassador

How do astronauts bathe? What do astronauts eat? How can I become an astronaut? These are some of the questions that people ask Gail Bossert Klink.

Gail is not an astronaut. She is a space ambassador. Gail tells people about the space program and NASA. Gail talks to students, teachers, community groups, and business people. She wants people to know about the important work NASA is doing. Many people do not know that space research can be used by all of us.

NASA has made many products that we can use. Campers, like astronauts, use special food packets. Cars and planes have safety devices first used in space.

Gail is not a scientist. She teaches Spanish and English. Gail was chosen because she is a good writer and speaker. She tells students that good writing and speaking skills are useful in all jobs.

Many students write to Gail. They thank her for talking to them. One girl wrote that she now wants to be an astronaut.

Chapter 13 Review

Summary

1. Earth is larger than the moon.   13:1
2. Objects look smaller when they are far away.   13:1
3. Earth's gravity is six times greater than that of the moon.   13:2
4. Gravity keeps an atmosphere on Earth.   13:2
5. The moon's pull of gravity is too weak to "hold" an atmosphere.   13:2
6. Temperatures on the moon change quickly.   13:2
7. Wind, ice, and water cause changes on Earth's surface.   13:3
8. Surface features on the moon can be compared to those on Earth.   13:3
9. Regolith is found on the moon.   13:3
10. Scientists use telescopes to study the moon.   13:4
11. Spacecraft are machines that travel from Earth to the moon or other space objects.   13:4
12. Astronauts need special clothing, air, and specially prepared food in order to live on the moon.   13:4

Science Words

rill   crater   regolith   spacecraft
maria   space   telescope   astronaut

Understanding Science Words

Complete each of the following sentences with a word or words from the Science Words that will make the sentence correct.

1. The smooth, dark areas on the moon are called _____.

2. All of the area outside Earth's atmosphere is called _____.

3. Far away objects look larger through a _____.

4. A long, narrow moon valley is called a _____.

5. A person who travels and works in space is called an _____.

6. An object hitting the moon may make a _____.

7. Astronauts traveled to and from the moon in a _____.

8. The outer layer of the moon is called _____.

Questions

A. Recalling Facts

Choose the word or phrase that correctly completes each of the following sentences.

1. Compared to the moon's gravity Earth's gravity is
   (a) 1/6 as much.   (c) 6 times greater.
   (b) 6 times less.   (d) 1/6 more.
2. Moon mountains are sharp because there is no
   (a) weathering.   (b) plant life.   (c) light.   (d) soil.

B. Understanding Concepts

Answer each of the following questions using complete sentences.

1. How does the size of Earth compare to that of the moon? Why does the sun seem to be the same size as the moon?
2. How are the surfaces of Earth and the moon similar? Different?

C. Applying Concepts

Think about what you have learned in this chapter. Answer each of the following questions using complete sentences.

1. Why could plants from Earth not live on the moon?
2. What special needs do astronauts have for living on the moon?

Chapter 14
Earth and Moon Movements

The moon travels around Earth. Sometimes it passes through Earth's shadow. When this happens, the moon appears reddish in color. Scientists found that the moon's surface cools quickly when the moon is in Earth's shadow. How could knowing this fact be helpful to people who travel to the moon?

The moon in Earth's shadow

Movements in Space   14:1

LESSON GOALS

In this lesson you will learn
- Earth revolves and rotates.
- the moon is a satellite of Earth.
- why we always see the same side of the moon.

It is easy to know when you are moving in a car. You can feel when the car turns. You also can see objects outside the car move past you. Earth is also moving. It spins and moves through space around the sun. It is not easy to know Earth moves. We cannot feel Earth turn. For this reason, people used to believe Earth was still. They thought the sun and stars moved around Earth.

The model car in Figure 14-2 is moving around the girl. Each time it moves around her it makes a revolution. **Revolution** is the movement of one object around another object.

Figure 14-1. Movement is easy to sense when in a car.

What is revolution?

Figure 14-2. The model car makes very fast revolutions.

257

Figure 14-3. The top's spinning motion is called rotation.

How long does it take Earth to complete one rotation?

Figure 14-4. Day and night are caused by Earth's rotation.

Earth is a planet. A **planet** is a large space object that revolves around the sun. Earth and eight other planets make revolutions around the sun. In doing this, each planet follows an orbit around the sun. An **orbit** is the path in space that one object follows around another object. The sun and all the space objects that revolve around it are called the **solar system.** It takes Earth one year or 365¼ days to complete one orbit around the sun.

The top in Figure 14-3 is rotating. **Rotation** is the spinning motion of an object. The top rotates one time when it makes one complete spin. Earth also rotates. It rotates or spins once every 24 hours. The rotation of Earth causes day and night.

The moon also moves. It revolves in an orbit around Earth. The moon is a satellite (SAT uh lite) of Earth. A **satellite** is an object that revolves around a larger object. The moon makes one revolution around Earth every 27 days. Earth is also a satellite. Around what larger object does Earth revolve?

Science and Technology

Planetary Explorer

Voyager 2 is a spacecraft that is exploring distant planets. It was launched in 1977 and had traveled almost nine years when it took this photograph of Uranus in 1986. During its close approach to Uranus, *Voyager 2* also sent other information to Earth. Some of the information described what Uranus and its moons and rings are made of. One surprise for scientists was the moons discovered by *Voyager 2*. Scientists knew that Uranus has five moons. *Voyager 2* showed that ten other moons revolve around Uranus.

Voyager 2 carries many testing instruments. These instruments include television cameras, sensors, radio equipment, and computers. The equipment gathers information and sends it to Earth.

Before going to Uranus, *Voyager 2* traveled to Jupiter and Saturn. Next, it will travel to Neptune. Then it will travel into outer space.

Voyager 2 has provided useful information. Scientists have gained new information about Jupiter, Saturn, and Uranus. They are using it to make better models of the planets.

Activity 14-1   Earth and Moon Movements

QUESTION   Why do we see only one side of the moon?

Materials
chair
pencil and paper

What to do
1. Have a partner sit in the chair and pretend to be Earth.
2. Walk in an orbit around "Earth." Keep your left shoulder pointed toward Earth.
3. Record the number of walls that you (the "moon") face as you revolve around "Earth."
4. Stand in one place and rotate slowly.
5. Record the number of walls that the "moon" faces during one rotation.

What did you learn?
1. What motions did the "moon" make?
2. How many walls did the "moon" face while walking around "Earth"?
3. How many walls did the "moon" face during its rotation in Step 4?

Using what you learned
1. How many times does the moon rotate during one orbit?
2. How many sides of the moon would you see if the moon did not rotate?

260

No matter when we look at the moon, the same side always faces Earth. The moon keeps the same side toward Earth as it revolves in its orbit. This happens because the moon rotates once during the same length of time it takes the moon to revolve once around Earth. Think of when you ride a merry-go-round. On the merry-go-round you rotate and revolve in the same length of time.

Figure 14-5. While riding a merry-go-round you rotate and revolve in the same length of time.

Lesson Summary

- Earth revolves around the sun and rotates as it revolves.
- The moon revolves around Earth.
- We see the same side of the moon because it rotates once every time it revolves.

Lesson Review

Review the lesson to answer these questions.

1. What is an orbit?
2. What is the solar system?
3. Why do we always see the same side of the moon?

14:2 Moon Phases

LESSON GOALS

In this lesson you will learn
- half the moon's surface is always facing the sun.
- the names of two of the eight moon phases.

What is moonlight?

The moon does not make its own light. Moonlight is really reflected sunlight. Light from the sun shines on the moon. The light bounces off the moon and shines on Earth. We call the light moonlight.

Figure 14-6. Most of the time we see only part of the lighted side of the moon.

How much of the moon's surface is always facing the sun?

Half of the moon's surface is always facing the sun. Sometimes we can see the whole lighted side of the moon. At other times, we can see only part of the lighted side. The amount of the lighted side that we see changes from night to night because the moon is moving. The lighted part of the moon that we see from Earth is called a moon **phase** (FAYZ).

Moon phases change in a cycle. The cycle lasts for about 29 days. The moon's cycle begins with the new moon phase. During the **new moon** phase, all of the lighted side faces away from Earth. You cannot see the new moon. You see a little bit of the lighted part of the moon on the next night. Each night you see more. People say the moon is waxing. A **waxing moon** has more of its lighted side showing each night.

You see all of the lighted side of the moon during the **full moon** phase. This happens when Earth is between the moon and the sun. The full moon happens halfway through the phase cycle. You see less of the moon each night after the full moon. People say the moon is waning (WAYN ing). A **waning moon** has less of its lighted side showing each night.

How long does the moon's phase cycle last?

What happens to the lighted side of the moon during the new moon phase?

Figure 14-7. All the lighted side of the moon is seen during the full moon phase.

263

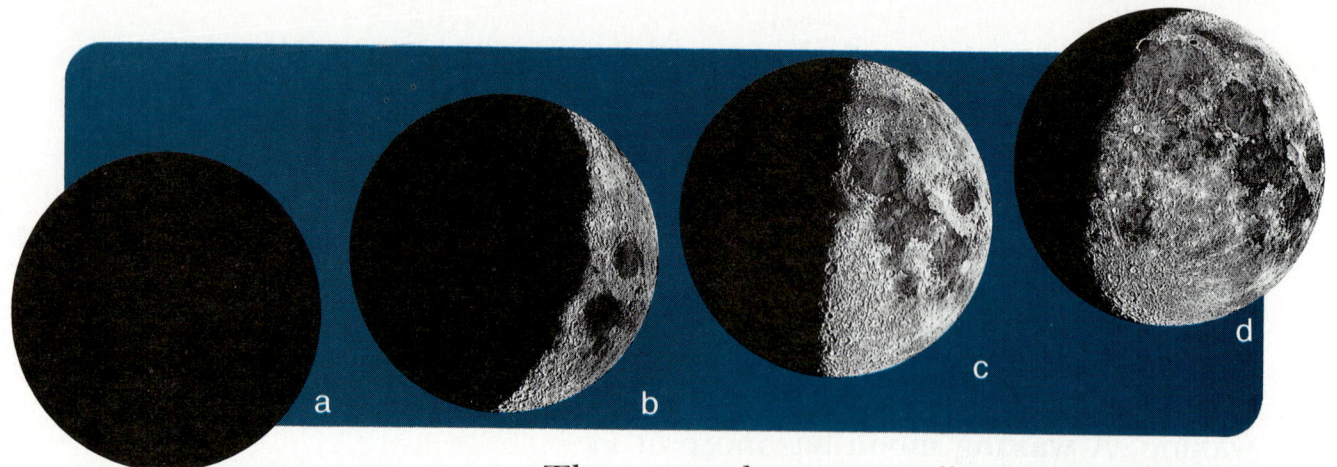

Figure 14–8. There are eight moon phases: new moon (a), waxing crescent (b), first quarter (c), waxing gibbous (d), full moon (e), waning gibbous (f), last quarter (g), and waning crescent (h).

Why do we see phases of the moon?

The moon does not really change shape. We see the phases because both Earth and the moon are moving. Both Earth and the moon rotate and revolve. This movement causes us to see a different amount of the bright part of the moon each day. The total movement or cycle lasts for 29 days. After the cycle is completed it repeats again and again.

There are names for the shapes of the moon during its cycle. Full moon and new moon are two of the eight moon phases. Each of the phases is shown in Figure 14–8.

The cycle begins with the new moon phase shown in (a). All the lighted half of the moon faces away from Earth at the new moon phase. We do not see any of the lighted half of the moon from Earth. Remember, half the moon is always lighted by the sun. We just do not see that light at the new moon phase.

As the moon continues to revolve around Earth we begin to see more and more of the lighted side of the moon. The crescent phase, as in (b) and (h), takes place when we see less than half of a full moon. At the quarter phase in (c) and (g), half of the full moon is visible.

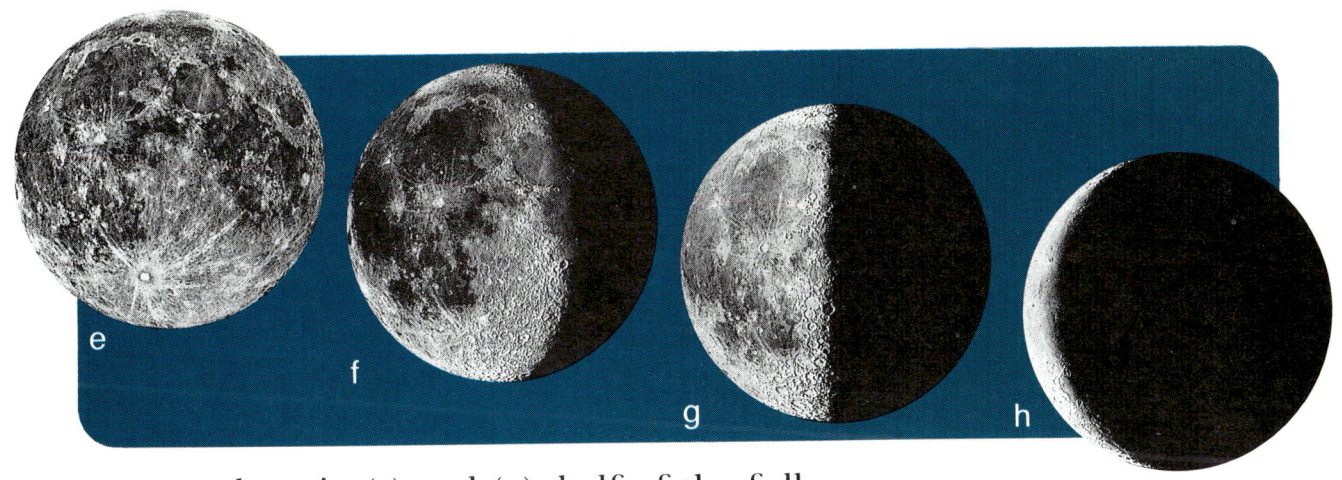

The gibbous phase at (d) and (f) takes place when the moon looks larger than half a full moon but is not yet a full moon. All the lighted side of the moon is seen at the full moon phase in (e). At full moon, half the phase cycle has been completed. Now the cycle continues with less and less of the lighted side visible until once again the new moon phase takes place.

Lesson Summary
- Half the moon's surface is always facing the sun. We see different amounts of the surface in a cycle that repeats every 29 days.
- New moon and full moon are two phases of the moon.

Lesson Review
Review the lesson to answer these questions.
1. How long does the moon phase cycle last?
2. Explain the difference between a waxing moon and a waning moon.

Activity 14-2 Moon Phases

QUESTION What are moon phases?

Materials
flashlight white softball
globe pencil and paper

What to do
1. Hold the flashlight. Have a second student hold the globe so your country faces the flashlight.
2. A third student should hold the ball between the globe and flashlight.
3. Turn on the flashlight. Draw a picture of how much of the lighted side of the ball you would see from the globe. Label your drawing **A**.
4. Move the ball to each place shown below. Draw and label the shapes.

What did you learn?
1. How much light does the ball always get?
2. How did the lighted shapes you saw change as the ball was moved?

Using what you learned
1. What do the flashlight, ball, and globe each stand for?
2. The moon takes about 29 days to complete one cycle of phases. What happens then?

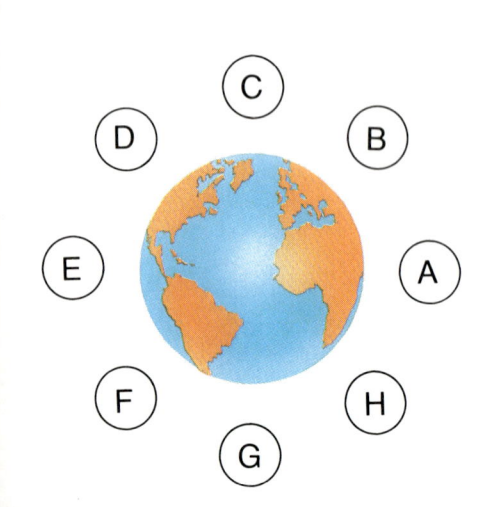

Language Arts Skills

Sequence

All events happen in order. The events that happen can be called steps. The order in which these steps happen is called sequence.

Events in nature follow a sequence or order. Think of the phases of the moon. You know that the moon revolves around Earth. While the moon revolves around Earth, we see different amounts of the moon. These amounts are called phases. Eight different phases of the moon are seen during a cycle that lasts about 29 days.

Look at the pictures at the bottom of the page. Four moon phases are shown. The phases, however, are not in the correct sequence.

- Which picture shows how the moon would look at the beginning of the eight phases?
- Which picture shows the moon halfway through its cycle?
- Which picture shows the second phase?
- Which phase appears just after full moon?

267

Chapter 14 Review

Summary

1. Earth rotates as it revolves around the sun. 14:1
2. The moon is a satellite of Earth. 14:1
3. The same side of the moon always faces Earth. 14:1
4. Half the moon's surface always faces the sun. 14:2
5. Moon phases are seen during a cycle that lasts 29 days. 14:2

Science Words

revolution   rotation   waxing moon
planet   satellite   full moon
orbit   phase   waning moon
solar system   new moon

Understanding Science Words

Complete each of the following sentences with a word or words from the Science Words that will make the sentence correct.

1. The motion of a spinning object is called _____.
2. The lighted part of the moon we see is called a _____.
3. When the lighted side of the moon gets bigger each night we say the moon is a _____.
4. When the whole lighted side of the moon is facing Earth, the phase is called a _____.
5. The path a planet follows around the sun is called an _____.
6. When the lighted side of the moon looks smaller each night, we say the moon is a _____.
7. The movement of one object around another object is called _____.

8. An object orbiting a larger object is called a ⎯⎯⎯⎯⎯.
9. The phase in which the moon is not visible from Earth is the ⎯⎯⎯⎯⎯.
10. The sun and all the objects that revolve around it are called the ⎯⎯⎯⎯⎯.
11. A large space object that revolves around the sun is called a ⎯⎯⎯⎯⎯.

Questions

A. Recalling Facts

Choose the word or phrase that correctly completes each of the following sentences.

1. The object in the center of the solar system is
   (a) Earth.
   (b) the sun.
   (c) the moon.
   (d) a satellite.
2. How long does it take Earth to make one rotation?
   (a) 365¼ days
   (b) 12 hours
   (c) 24 hours
   (d) 180 days

B. Understanding Concepts

Answer each of the following questions using complete sentences.

1. Explain the moon phase cycle.
2. How long does it take the moon to revolve around Earth?

C. Applying Concepts

Think about what you have learned in this chapter. Answer each of the following questions using complete sentences.

1. If the moon does not make light, how can we see it?
2. Why do we see moon phases?

UNIT 7 REVIEW

CHECKING YOURSELF

Answer these questions on a sheet of paper.
1. Why did the astronauts carry oxygen in tanks on their backs when they walked on the moon?
2. Name two ways that lack of gravity causes differences between the moon and Earth.
3. Why are there extreme temperatures on the moon?
4. How were rills and craters formed on the moon?
5. Why does the moon have more craters than Earth?
6. How are igneous rocks formed on Earth and the moon?
7. Compare Earth's soil to regolith on the moon.
8. Explain the difference between rotation and revolution.
9. What object is the center of our solar system?
10. What is moonlight?
11. Name and describe the phases of the moon.
12. Why does the amount of moonlight we see change from night to night?

RECALLING ACTIVITIES

Think about the activities you did in this unit. Answer the questions about the activities.
1. When do different circles seem to be the same size? 13-1
2. How can you make models of moon craters? 13-2
3. Why do we see only one side of the moon? 14-1
4. What are moon phases? 14-2

IDEAS TO EXPLORE

1. Pretend you are a person planning to live on the moon. Write a story that describes one day in your life.
2. Read myths about the moon. Retell one of these myths in your own words. Try writing a new "myth" that explains why the moon's size seems to change.
3. Use resource books to find out about lunar modules. Use cardboard tubes, cardboard, plastic wrap, and aluminum foil to construct a model of a lunar module. Use your model to tell the class about the module.

CHALLENGING PROJECT

Locate a map that shows the moon's surface. Make a model of the moon that shows the moon's features. Write the names of the main features of the moon on slips of paper. Tape these to straight pins and insert them into your moon as labels. Find out how these features got their names. Share your moon and the information you learned with the class.

BOOKS TO READ

The Moon: A Spaceflight Away by David J. Darling, Dillon Press, Inc.: Minneapolis, MN, © 1984.
   Learn how scientists have studied the moon.

On the Moon by Jenny Vaughan, Franklin Watts: Danbury, CT, © 1983.
   Find out more about the moon.

Spacecraft by Michael Jay, Franklin Watts: Danbury, CT, © 1983.
   Artificial objects in the skies are described.

UNIT 8
Health and the Environment

Earnest E. Just was a scientist who studied animal cells. During his lifetime, many scientists believed that all the work of the cell took place in the nucleus. Just proved that all parts of the cell are important. He found that life can exist only when all cell parts work together. Today, cell micrographs show cell parts inside and outside the nucleus that were not known during Just's lifetime. How was Earnest Just's work important to our understanding of cells today?

Earnest Everett Just—1925

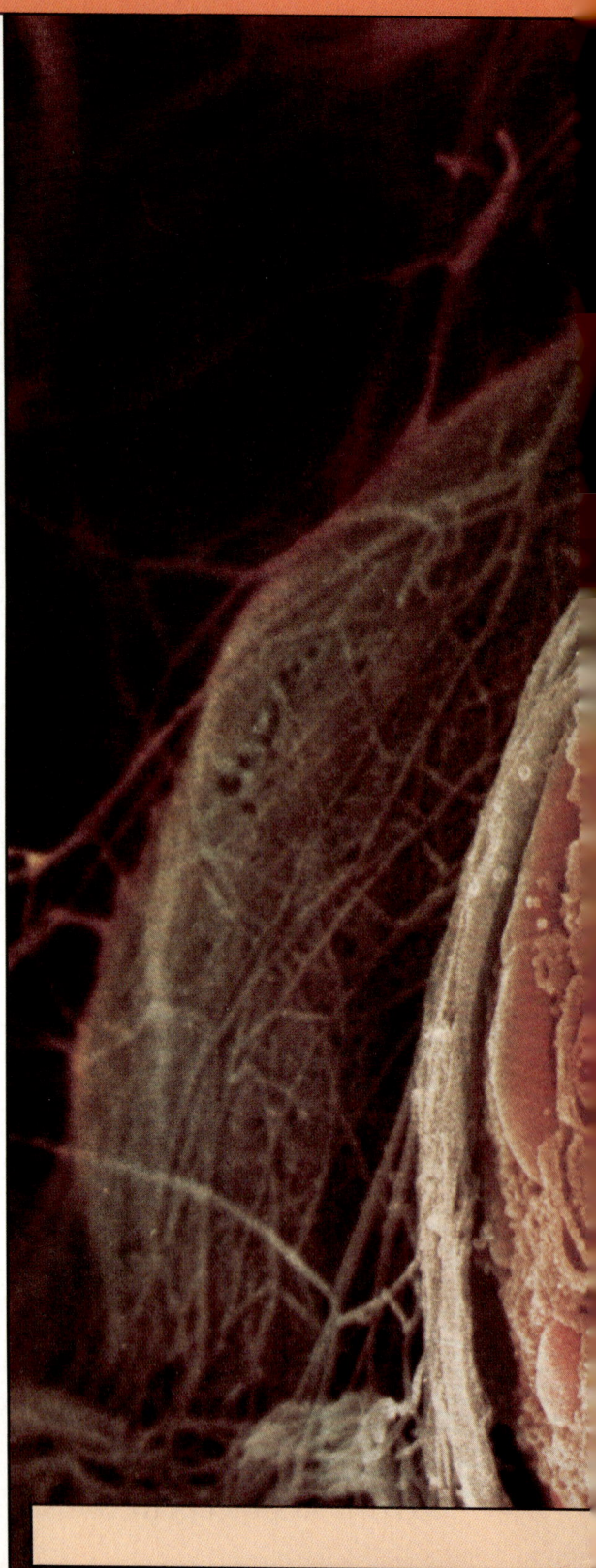

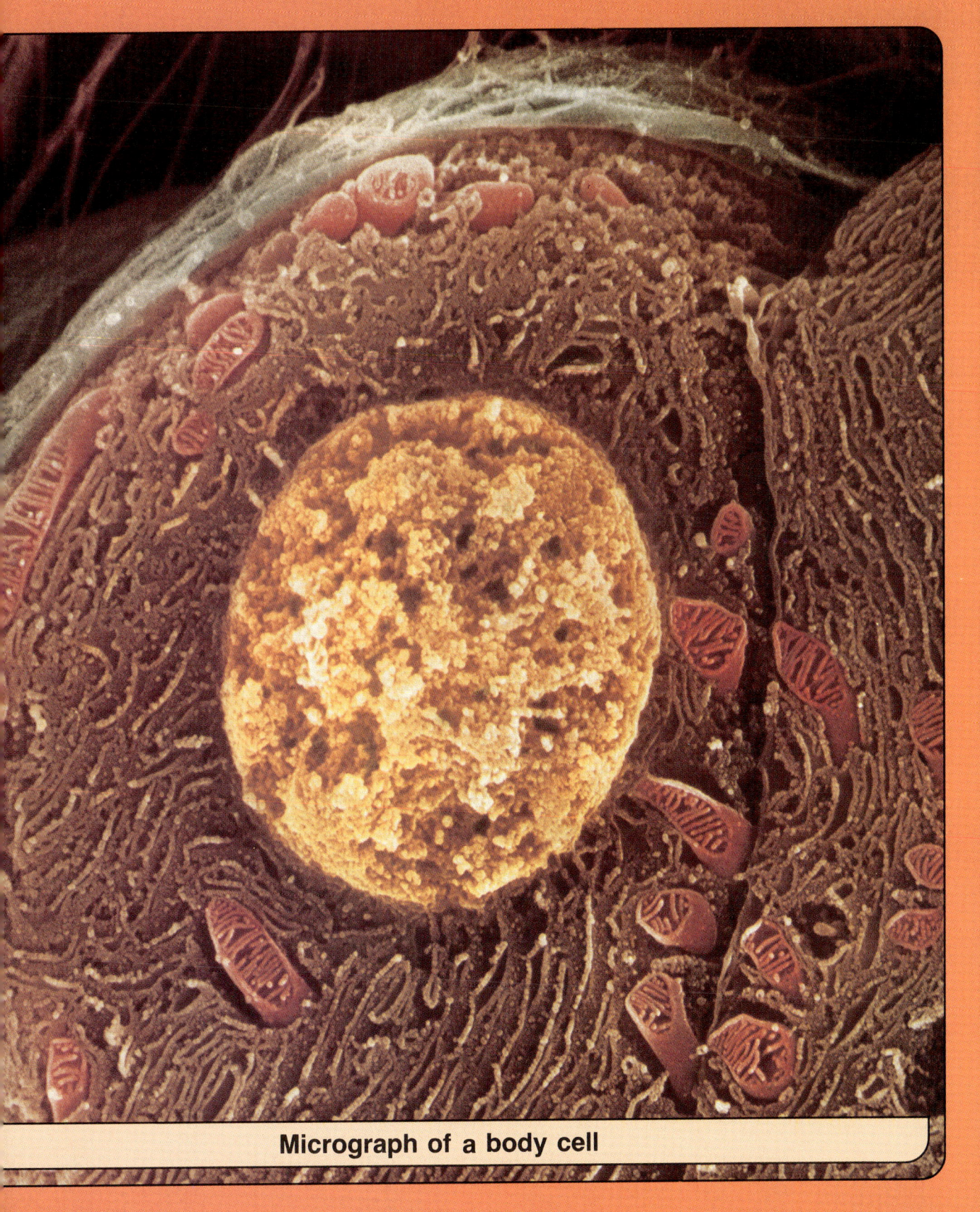

Micrograph of a body cell

Chapter 15
Cells to Systems

Many living things are made of more than one cell. Each cell joins with others of the same type to perform a task. Muscle cells, for example, work together to perform the task of moving an arm. Nerve cells perform the task of sending messages from one part of the body to another. Look at these nerve cells. How is their shape adapted to this task?

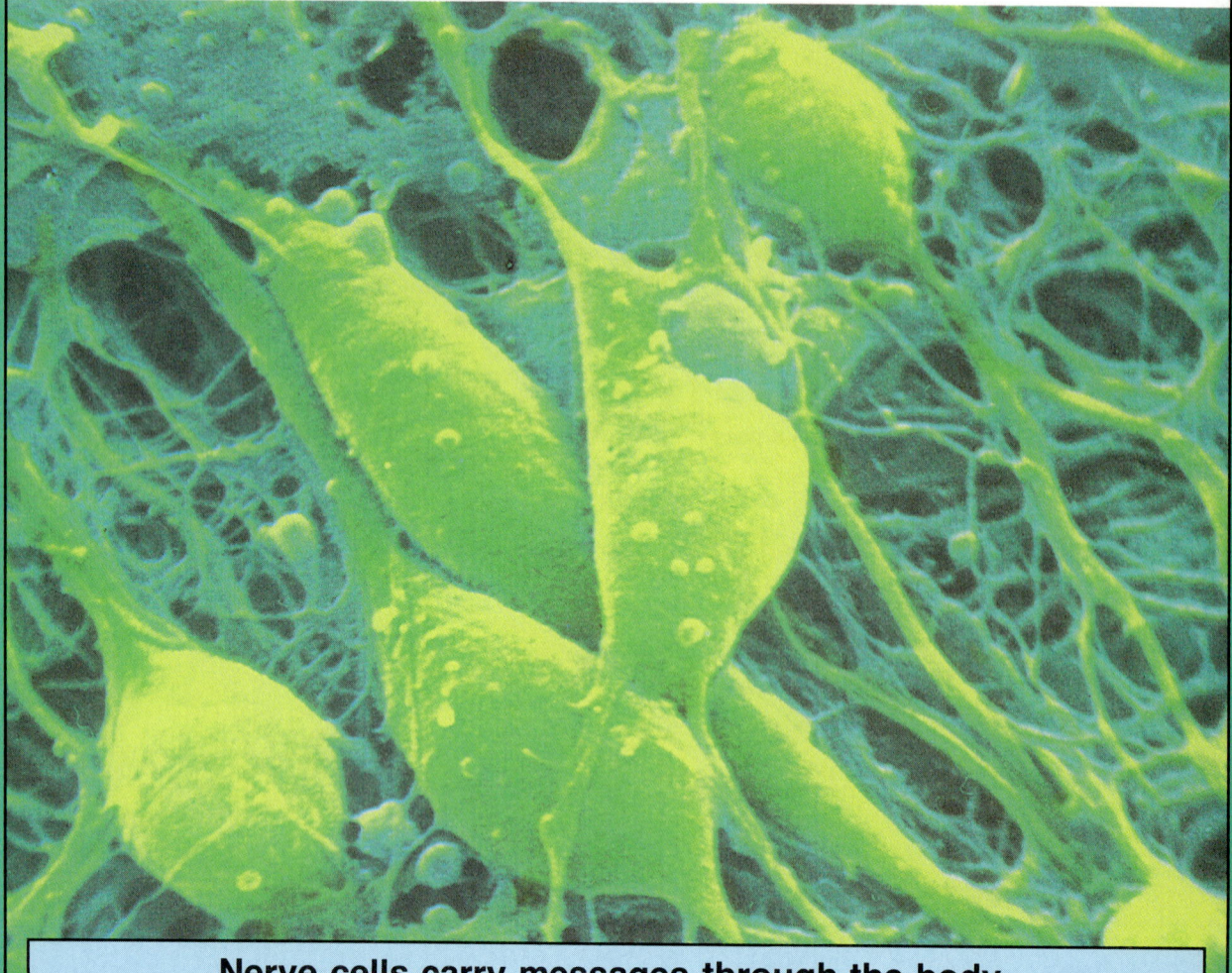

Nerve cells carry messages through the body.

Cells 15:1

LESSON GOALS

In this lesson you will learn
- all living things are made of cells.
- how plant and animal cells compare.
- different kinds of cells are in the body.

A honeycomb is made of many small, boxlike sections. The sections or units are called cells. They are the building blocks of a honeycomb.

Living things are also made of small units called cells. These cells are made of living matter. A **cell** is the smallest unit of living matter. Most cells are so small that scientists use microscopes to look at them.

All living things are made of one or more cells. These cells do not all look the same. Also, they do not all have the same parts. How are the plant cell and the animal cell in Figure 15-1 alike? How are they different?

What is a cell?

What do scientists use to look at cells?

Figure 15-1. All living things are made of cells.

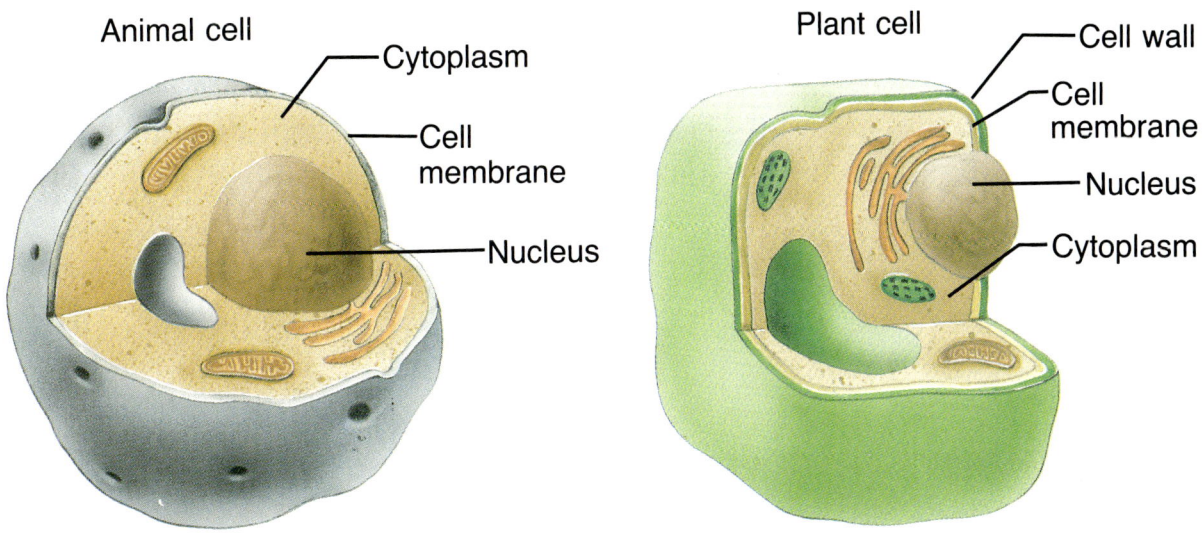

Animal cell — Cytoplasm, Cell membrane, Nucleus

Plant cell — Cell wall, Cell membrane, Nucleus, Cytoplasm

Activity 15-1 Seeing Cells

QUESTION What do different cells look like?

Materials
micro-viewers
micro-view slides (plant and animal cells)
pencil and paper

What to do
1. Place a slide in the micro-viewer.
2. Observe the cells on the slide. Make a drawing of what you see. Record whether the cells are of a plant or an animal.
3. Repeat steps 1 and 2. Continue until all slides are viewed.

What did you learn?
1. How were all the cells alike?
2. How were the plant cells different from the animal cells?

Using what you learned
1. In what ways would the cell wall be important for plant cells?
2. How is a living cell different from the same type of cell once it dies?

a b c

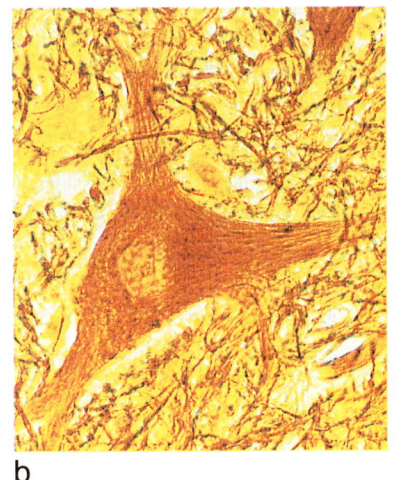

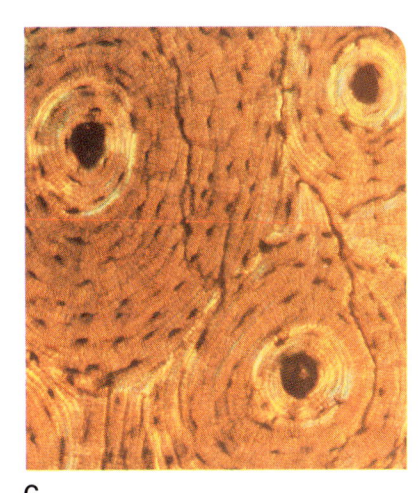

Your body is made of many kinds of cells. Each kind of cell has a special job. Figure 15-2 shows different kinds of body cells.

Each person goes through a life cycle that includes birth, growth, aging, and death. Body cells also go through a life cycle. New cells are formed when other cells divide. The new cells grow, age, and die. Your body grows by adding new cells. New cells also replace dead or damaged cells.

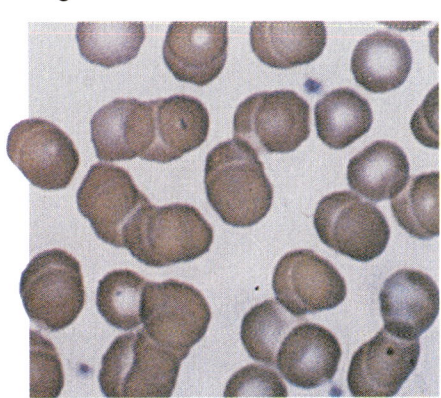

Lesson Summary

- A cell is the smallest unit of living matter.
- Plant cells are different from animal cells because they have cell walls.
- Different kinds of cells have different jobs within the human body.

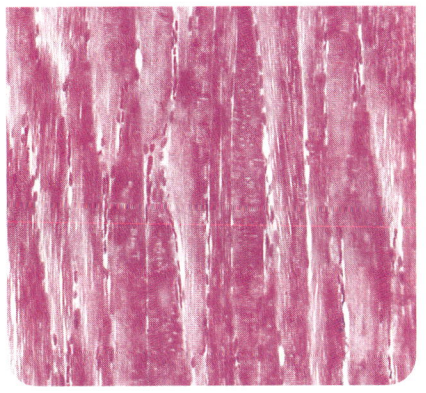

Lesson Review

Review the lesson to answer these questions.
1. How are cells of the body like building blocks?
2. What does a scientist use to look at cells?

d

e

Figure 15-2. There are skin cells (a), nerve cells (b), bone cells (c), blood cells (d), and muscle cells (e) in the body.

277

15:2 Tissues, Organs, and Organ Systems

LESSON GOALS

In this lesson you will learn
- cells form tissues.
- tissues form organs.
- organs form organ systems.

Most organisms have more than one kind of cell. Each kind of cell works with others of the same kind to do a job. In the body, cells work together as groups. Cells working in a group form **tissue** (TIHSH ew). Different kinds of tissue found in the body include muscle, bone, skin, nerve, and blood. A job, such as moving a leg or smiling, is partly performed by muscle tissue when it relaxes or tightens. Other body tissues do different jobs. Nerve tissue carries messages between the brain and parts of the body. You see objects, for example, because messages are carried between parts of your eye and your brain.

Organs

An **organ** is a group of tissues working together. Each kind of tissue has a special job within the organ. Your heart is an example of an organ. It is made of different groups of tissues working together. One of the tissues in the heart is muscle. Another is nerve tissue. What job do you think muscle tissue has in your heart?

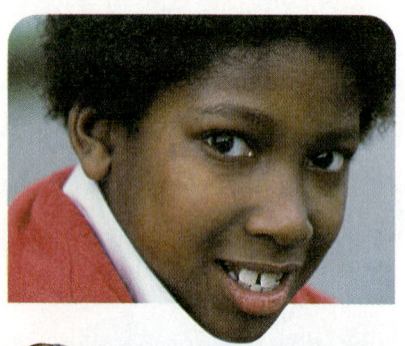

Figure 15-3. Cells work together as tissue to perform a task.

What is an organ?

278

Organ Systems

A group of cells working together form tissue. Tissues are joined to form an organ. A group of organs work together to form an **organ system.** The organs of an organ system carry out a major job in the body. The organs of the respiratory (RES pruh tor ee) system, for example, work to bring oxygen to body cells. They also take carbon dioxide away from the cells.

Why are all the organs of an organ system important?

What job do all the organs of the respiratory system carry out?

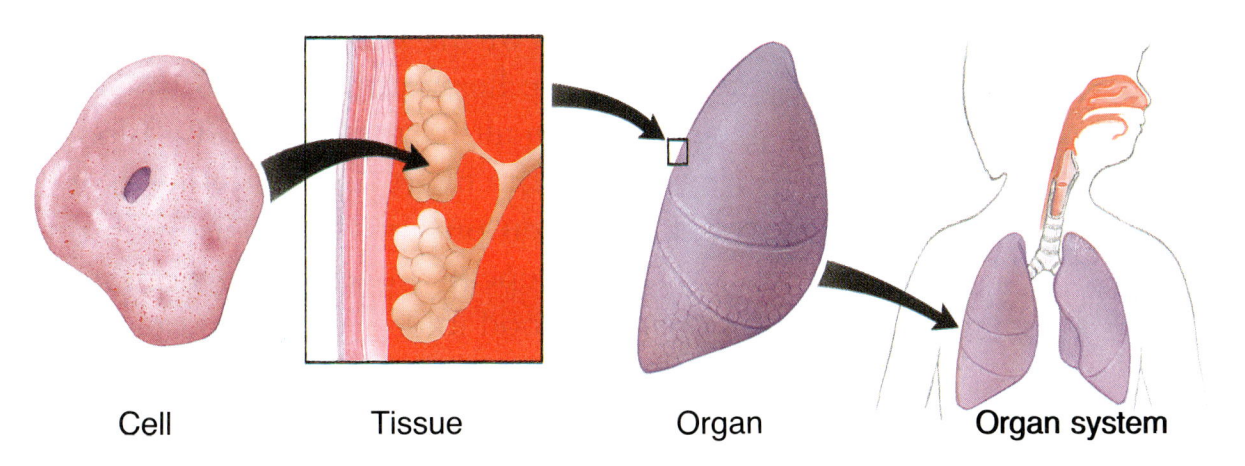

Cell   Tissue   Organ   Organ system

Figure 15-4. Cells form tissue, tissues form organs, and organs form organ systems.

Lesson Summary
- Cells working together in a large group form a tissue.
- A group of tissues working together forms an organ.
- A group of organs working together forms an organ system.

Lesson Review
Review the lesson to answer these questions.
1. Why is nerve tissue important to the body?
2. Why is the heart an organ?

15:3 Circulatory, Skeletal, and Muscular Systems

LESSON GOALS

In this lesson you will learn
- the circulatory system is made of three main parts.
- why the skeletal system is important.
- why the muscular system is important.

The circulatory (SUR kyuh luh tor ee) system is made of the heart, blood vessels, and blood. The heart pumps blood through blood vessels to all parts of the body. Blood is returned to the heart through other blood vessels. It is then pumped again through the body. This is repeated over and over. The blood carries food and oxygen to all parts of the body. It also takes wastes from body cells. Why are these important jobs?

Why is blood important to the body?

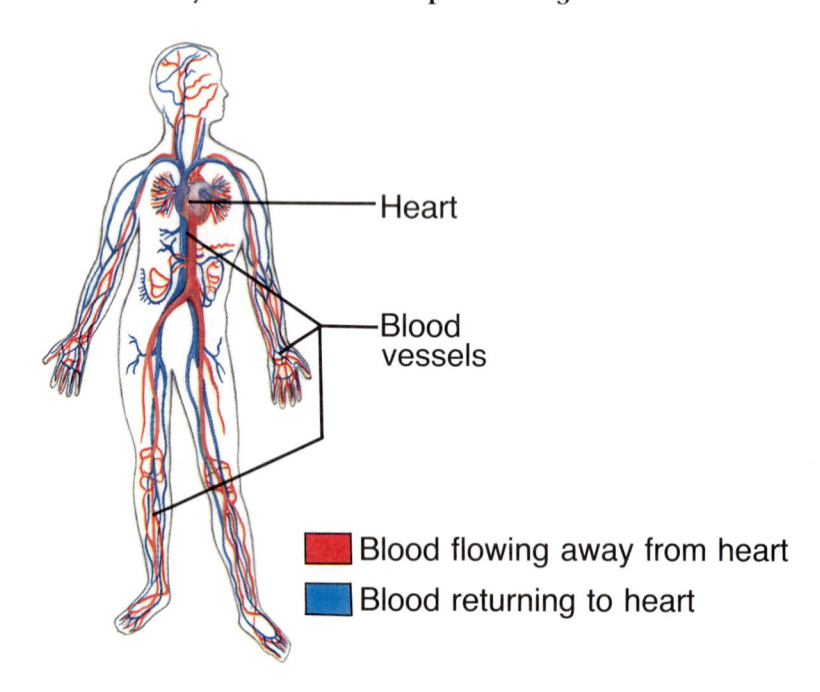

Figure 15-5. The circulatory system carries blood to all parts of the body.

- Heart
- Blood vessels

🟥 Blood flowing away from heart
🟦 Blood returning to heart

Activity 15-2 Circulatory System

QUESTION How does your pulse rate change?

Materials
clock with second hand   pencil and paper

What to do
1. Using one hand, gently place your fingers on the side of your neck just below your jaw.
2. Find your pulse.
3. Count your pulse for 10 seconds. Multiply this number by 6 to get your pulse rate for 1 minute.
4. Count your pulse while at your desk.
5. Record this number.
6. Walk quietly around the room for 45 seconds. Repeat steps 3 and 5.
7. Run in place for 45 seconds. Repeat steps 3 and 5.

What did you learn?
1. When was your pulse most rapid?
2. When was your pulse slowest?
3. Compare your results with those of a classmate. How do they compare?

Using what you learned
1. How long does it take for the pulse rate in step 7 to return to that in step 4?
2. Find the pulse at your wrist. Compare this pulse with the pulse at your neck.

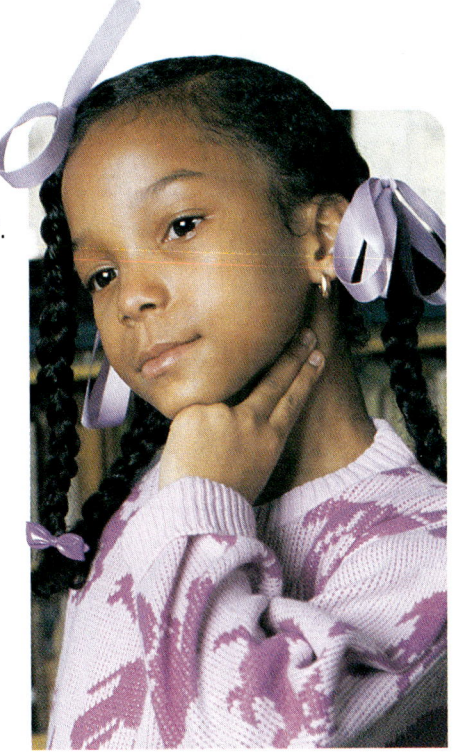

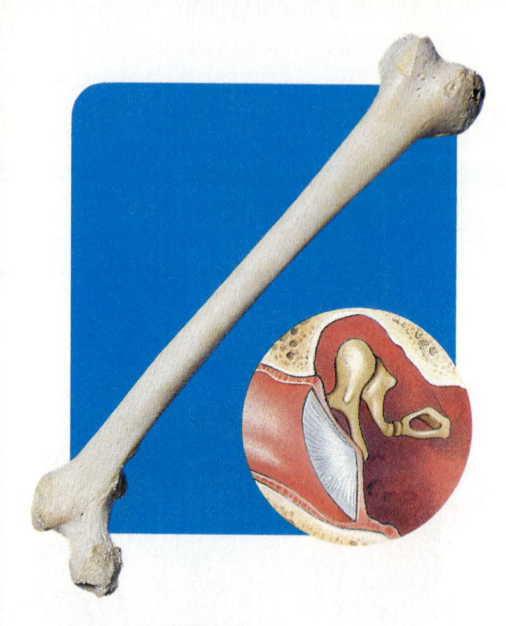

Figure 15-6. There is a great difference in the size of bones.

Why is the skeletal system important?

Skeletal System

The skeletal (SKEL uht ul) system gives the body shape and support. It also protects many organs. The skeletal system is made of bone tissue and other support tissue. Bone tissue forms over 200 bones in your body. These bones range in size from the large bone of the upper leg to the tiny bones of the middle ear. Bones of the skull protect the brain. Compare Figures 15-7 and 15-10. What part of this system protects the lungs? Study Figures 15-5 and 15-9 also. What parts of the skeletal system protect other organs?

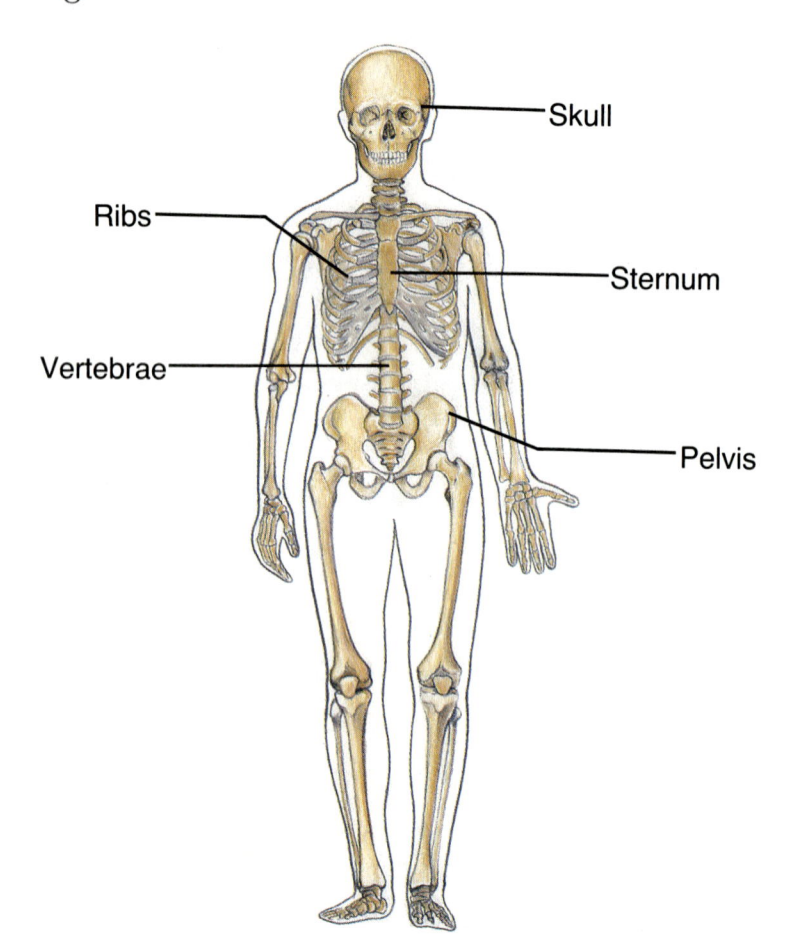

Figure 15-7. The skeletal system gives support and protects body organs.

282

Muscular System

The muscular system is made of muscle tissue. Body parts move because muscles make them move. You use muscles to walk, talk, and eat. What else can you do because you have muscles?

Muscles either contract or relax when they move parts of your body. Suppose you bend your arm. Some of your arm muscles contract, or shorten. Other arm muscles relax, or lengthen. When you drop or lower your arm, the contracting and relaxing of these muscles is reversed. Try bending your leg at the knee. Feel some muscles contract. Feel other muscles relax. Find the muscles that contract or relax when you frown or smile.

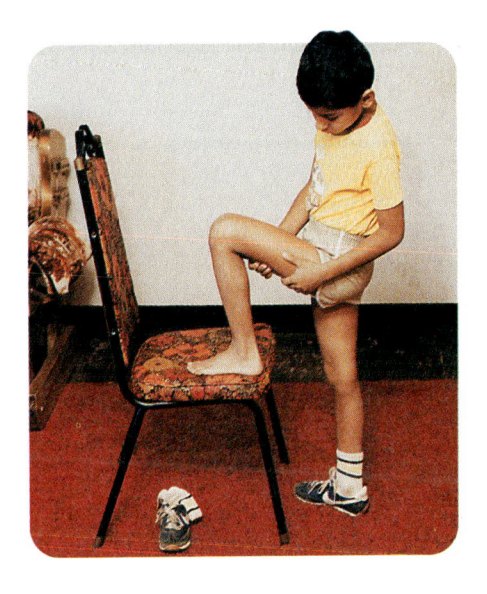

Figure 15–8. You can feel muscles contract when you bend your leg.

What do muscles do as they move parts of your body?

Lesson Summary

- The circulatory system is made of the heart, blood vessels, and blood.
- The skeletal system gives the body shape and support.
- The muscular system moves body parts.

Lesson Review

Review the lesson to answer these questions.

1. What is carried through the circulatory system?
2. In what three ways is the skeletal system important?
3. What happens to leg muscles when you bend your leg?

15:4 Digestive and Respiratory Systems

LESSON GOALS

In this lesson you will learn
- why the digestive system is important.
- why the respiratory system is important.

The digestive (di JES tihv) system changes food so it can be used by your body. When you eat, food moves down a tube and goes into your stomach. As stomach muscles contract, they mix the food with stomach juices. The stomach juices change, or digest, some of the food.

Food passes from the stomach to the small intestine. Vitamins, digested food, and water pass into your blood from the small intestine. The food material then goes to the large intestine. Some of the food cannot be digested. This solid waste material passes through the large intestine and is later removed from the body.

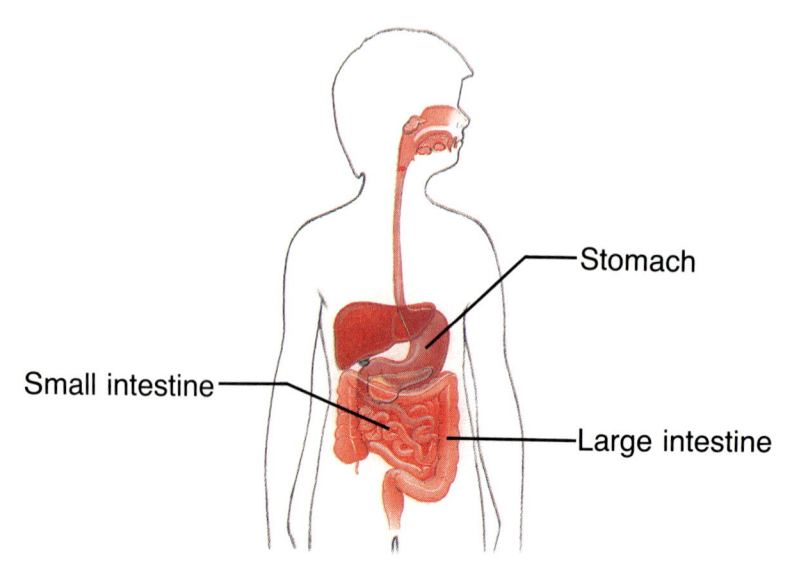

What passes into your blood from the small intestine?

Figure 15-9. Food passes through organs of the digestive system.

Respiratory System

The gases oxygen and carbon dioxide are important. We breathe in oxygen and breathe out carbon dioxide. This is done through the respiratory system. All body cells use oxygen. They use it to change food into energy. When the energy is formed in the cells, carbon dioxide is made. The gas carbon dioxide is a waste product of respiration. This waste gas is removed from your body when you breathe out.

Air enters your body through your nose and mouth. It travels through tubes to your lungs. In the lungs, oxygen from the air passes to your blood. Blood carries the oxygen to your body cells. Blood also carries carbon dioxide from these cells to your lungs. When you breathe out, carbon dioxide leaves your body. What is one difference between the air you breathe in and the air you breathe out?

Why is oxygen important to cells in your body?

Figure 15-10. The respiratory system brings oxygen into contact with blood.

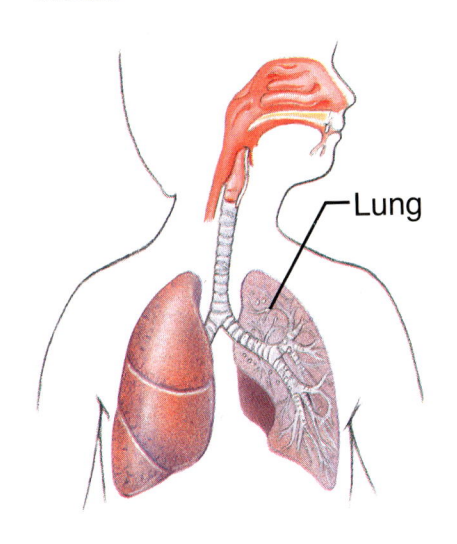

Lesson Summary

- The digestive system changes food so it can be used by the body.
- The respiratory system brings oxygen into the body and rids the body of carbon dioxide.

Lesson Review

Review the lesson to answer these questions.
1. Trace food through the digestive system.
2. Why is oxygen important to all cells in the body?

15:5 Urinary and Control Systems

LESSON GOALS

In this lesson you will learn
- how liquid body wastes are removed.
- the body has two control systems.

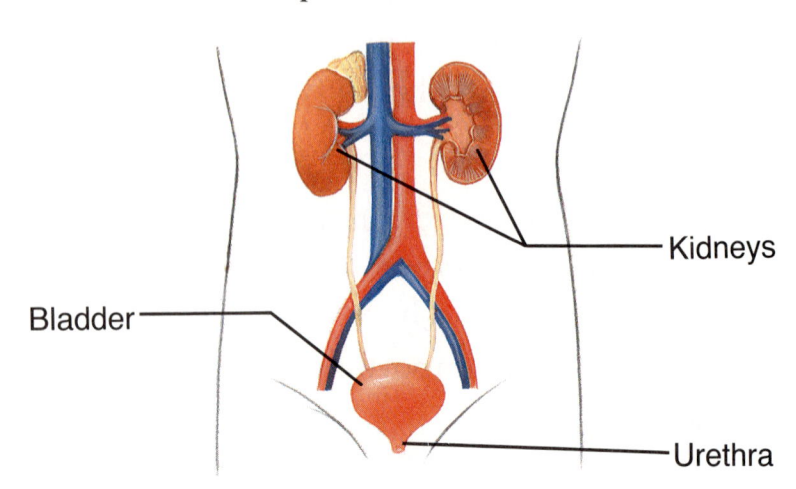

Figure 15-11. Sweat glands release liquid waste to the surface of the skin.

Recall from Lesson 15:4 that not all food can be digested. Solid wastes move through the large intestine and pass out of the body. Removal of this solid waste is the job of the digestive system.

Wastes that are gases are also removed from the body. Carbon dioxide is formed when cells change food into energy. Which organ system removes this waste gas from the body?

Liquid wastes are also produced by body cells. These liquid wastes are picked up by the blood. Some of the liquid wastes are released through sweat glands to the surface of the skin. This liquid waste is called perspiration (pur spir AY shun). Perspiration evaporates from the skin.

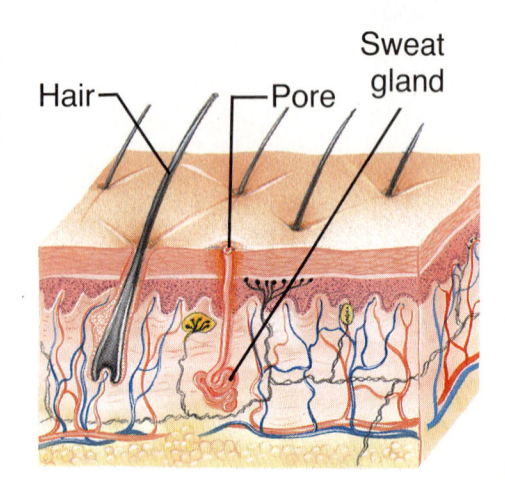

Figure 15-12. The urinary system removes liquid wastes from the body.

Urinary System

Most liquid wastes are removed from the body by the urinary (YOOR uh ner ee) system. As blood moves through organs called kidneys, wastes and water are removed. The waste products and water form urine (YOOR un). The urine passes from the kidneys through tubes to the bladder. It is later released from the body through the urethra (yoo REE thruh).

What organs remove most liquid wastes from your blood?

Control Systems

The control systems of your body keep your body working as one unit. They control your muscles and organs. They control your senses and your thinking. One control system is the nervous system. It is made of the brain, spinal cord, and nerves. The brain and spinal cord are like message centers. Messages from all body parts are sent through nerves to your spinal cord and brain. Nerves in the brain and spinal cord also carry messages to parts of your body.

Figure 15-13. Nerves extend throughout the body and into fingertips.

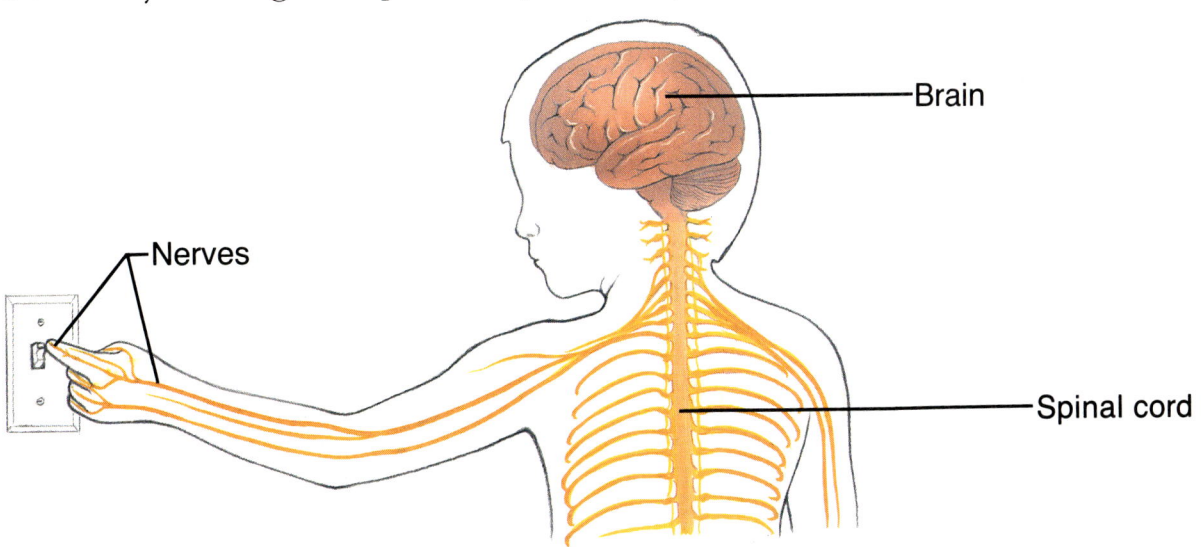

287

What organs make up the endocrine system?

The endocrine (EN duh krin) system is the other control system. It aids the nervous system in the control of your body and is made of organs called glands. The glands make chemicals that pass into your blood. These chemicals cause important changes in your body. Some chemicals are important for proper growth. Others help to digest food.

Figure 15-14. The endocrine system helps to control body growth.

Lesson Summary

- The urinary system removes liquid body wastes.
- The nervous system and endocrine system are the control systems of the body.

Lesson Review

Review the lesson to answer these questions.

1. How are solid, gaseous, and liquid wastes removed from the body?
2. What organs make up the endocrine system?

Language Arts Skills

Cause and Effect

All organ systems work together to keep the body working as a unit. Sometimes a disease or illness affects the body. The disease prevents the body from working in a normal, healthy way.

The girl in the picture has an illness. It may have been caused by germs or in other ways. Something that makes another thing happen is a cause. The thing that is made to happen is the effect.

Cause: germs
Effect: illness

Certain words in a sentence give clues about what the cause or effect may be. These words may include **since, because,** and **as a result.**

Read the following sentence and think about the cause and effect it describes.

Since I stayed overnight with someone who had a cold, I caught a cold also.

- What was the cause?
- What was the effect?
- Which word gives a clue about the cause?

Chapter 15 Review

Summary

1. A cell is the smallest unit of living matter.   15:1
2. Plant cells have cell walls and animal cells do not.   15:1
3. Different kinds of cells have different jobs in the body.   15:1
4. Cells working together in a group form a tissue.   15:2
5. A group of tissues working together forms an organ.   15:2
6. A group of organs working together forms an organ system.   15:2
7. The circulatory system is made of the heart, blood vessels, and blood.   15:3
8. The skeletal system gives the body shape and support.   15:3
9. The muscular system moves body parts.   15:3
10. The digestive system changes food so it can be used by the body.   15:4
11. The respiratory system brings oxygen into the body and gets rid of carbon dioxide.   15:4
12. The urinary system removes liquid body wastes.   15:5
13. The nervous system and the endocrine system are the control systems of the body.   15:5

Science Words

cell   tissue   organ   organ system

Understanding Science Words

Complete each of the following sentences with a word or words from the Science Words that will make the sentence correct.

1. A group of tissues working together form an _____.
2. The smallest unit of living matter is a _____.

3. Cells working together in a group form a _____.
4. The muscular system is an example of an _____.

Questions

A. Recalling Facts

Choose the word or phrase that correctly completes each of the following sentences.

1. Most liquid wastes are removed from the blood by the
   - (a) bladder.
   - (b) kidneys.
   - (c) urethra.
   - (d) sweat glands.
2. Unlike animal cells, plant cells have a
   - (a) nucleus.
   - (b) cytoplasm.
   - (c) cell membrane.
   - (d) cell wall.
3. The endocrine system is made of organs called
   - (a) lungs.
   - (b) glands.
   - (c) muscles.
   - (d) nerves.
4. The skeletal system gives the body shape and support and also
   - (a) sends messages.
   - (b) digests food.
   - (c) protects body organs.
   - (d) pumps blood to the lungs.

B. Understanding Concepts

Answer each of the following questions using complete sentences.

1. What are the control systems of the body? Why is each one important?
2. How are tissues, organs, and organ systems related?

C. Applying Concepts

Think about what you have learned in this chapter. Answer each of the following questions using complete sentences.

1. Trace some food through the digestive system.
2. Tell what happens to the gases oxygen and carbon dioxide when you breathe in and out.

Chapter 16
Staying Healthy

People try to stay healthy by practicing good health habits and controlling the spread of germs. Food that is prepared for eating must be free of harmful germs. Health inspectors check the preparation of different types of food. They make sure the foods are safe to eat. What do you think this inspector wants to learn at this meat packing plant?

A health inspector checks food.

Being Ill 16:1

LESSON GOALS

In this lesson you will learn
- some diseases are caused by germs.
- ways your body defends itself from germs.
- what to do if you are ill.

Think of the last time you were ill. What caused your illness? How can you keep from getting sick again?

A **disease** (dihz EEZ) is an illness. Some diseases, such as a cold or the measles, are caused by germs. Other diseases are not caused by germs. Heart disease is not caused by germs. It may be caused by smoking or the kinds of food you eat.

Diseases caused by germs may be spread from person to person. For example, someone who has a cold may sneeze near you. The germs are spread to you in the air. You may drink from a glass used by someone with a flu. What could you do to keep your cold or flu from spreading to other people?

Figure 16-1. It is important to prevent the spread of germs.

Figure 16-2. Skin protects the body from germs.

What is immunity?

Figure 16-3. A vaccine may be given as a shot.

Your Body's Defense

Your body has ways to defend itself from disease. Your skin is one defense. It keeps germs from getting into your body. Tears are another defense. Germs that get into your eyes are washed away by tears.

Some germs, however, do get into the body. They attack the body and harm cells. The body fights back by making substances that kill the germs. The substances give immunity (ihm YEW nut ee) to the body. **Immunity** is the body's ability to fight certain diseases.

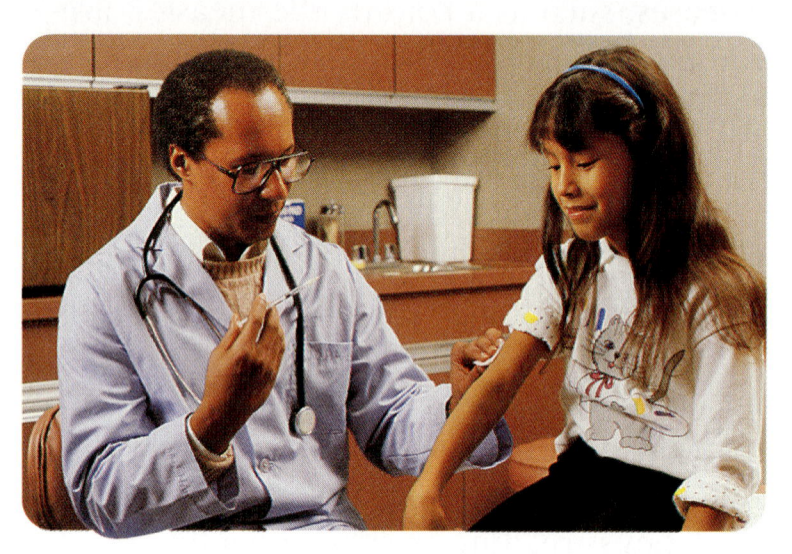

Your body may get immunity in different ways. You can get some diseases only one time. For example, after you have the mumps, your body is immune to those germs. You do not get the mumps again. Sometimes you get a vaccine (vak SEEN) to become immune to a disease. A **vaccine** is dead or weak germs that give immunity to a disease. A vaccine is taken by mouth or given in a shot.

294

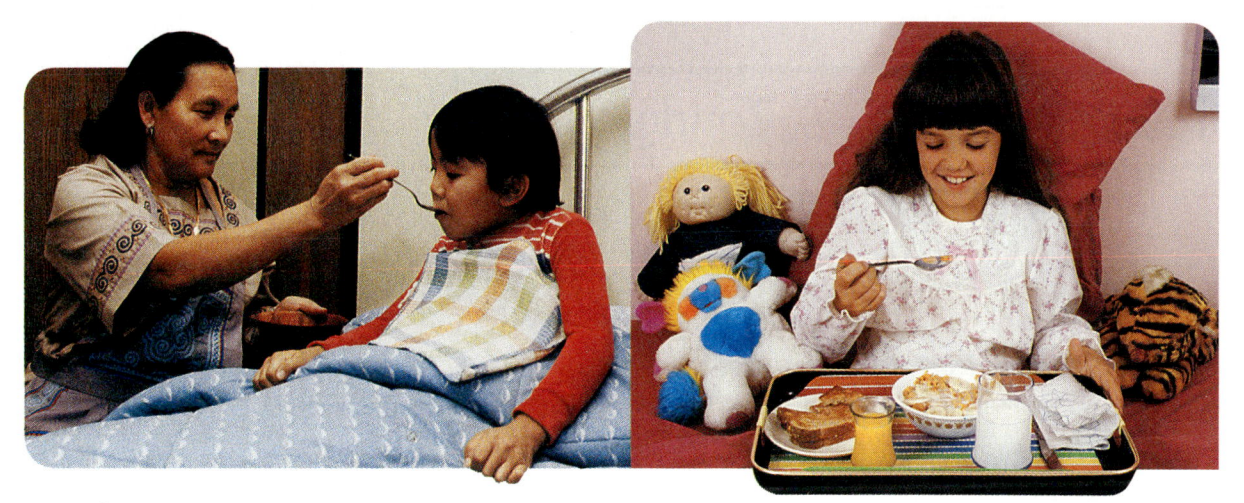

When you are ill, you should drink liquids, eat healthful foods, and get rest. Your body needs six glasses of liquid a day. When you are ill, it needs even more. Healthful food gives your body the energy it needs to repair body cells. Rest and sleep allow your body to heal faster and fight the disease. If an illness continues, you should see a doctor. The doctor may give you medicine to help fight the disease.

Figure 16-4. Liquids, healthful foods, and rest are especially important when you are ill.

Lesson Summary

- Diseases such as flu and measles are caused by germs that enter the body.
- Skin, tears, and substances made by the body help protect it from germs.
- Liquids, healthful foods, and rest are needed when you are ill.

Lesson Review

Review the lesson to answer these questions.

1. What causes colds and flu?
2. How can your body become immune to a disease?
3. What should you do if you are ill?

295

16:2 Eating Well

LESSON GOALS

In this lesson you will learn
- why you should eat healthful foods.
- which foods have nutrients.

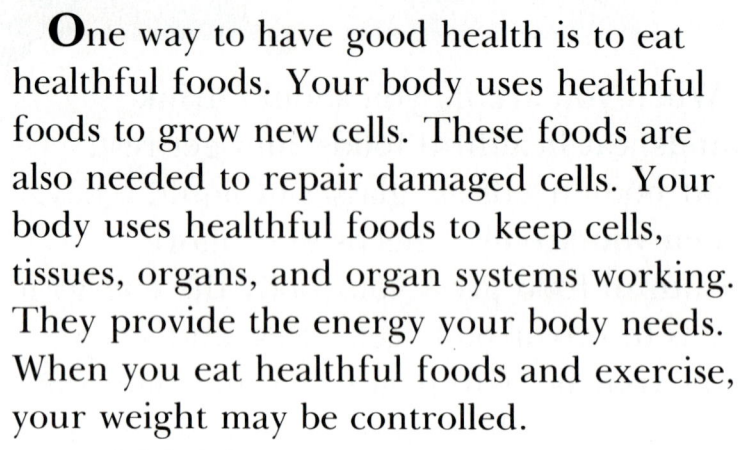

One way to have good health is to eat healthful foods. Your body uses healthful foods to grow new cells. These foods are also needed to repair damaged cells. Your body uses healthful foods to keep cells, tissues, organs, and organ systems working. They provide the energy your body needs. When you eat healthful foods and exercise, your weight may be controlled.

Healthful foods have different nutrients. Recall from Lesson 2:2 that a nutrient is a substance needed by living things for growth. When you eat, the food is changed by the digestive system. Nutrients from the food move into your blood stream. They are carried to cells throughout your body. The nutrients are used by the cells to keep your body healthy. The cells divide as they grow. More cells are produced and your body grows.

Not all foods are healthful. Candy and other foods that contain a lot of sugar or salt are not healthful. These foods contain few nutrients. Your body does not need these foods to grow. These foods can damage your teeth. Too much of these foods can also make you overweight.

Figure 16–5. Nutrients are found in food eaten at breakfast.

How are nutrients used by body cells?

296

Science and Technology

Dissolve Away Decay

Have you ever had a cavity? A cavity is a decayed spot on a tooth. Many people get cavities and go to a dentist to get the tooth repaired. The dentist uses a drill to sand away the decayed part of the tooth. The drill makes a hole in the tooth that the dentist fills with silver or white plastic material.

Some people do not like drills and the noise the drill makes. However, the decayed part of the tooth needs to be removed. The drill is needed for this repair. Teeth that are properly repaired remain healthy.

Some dentists are scientists too. They are learning to fix cavities a new way with a special liquid that dissolves decay. The dentist squirts the liquid on a cavity and the decay becomes soft. Then the dentist washes the decay away. Sometimes the dentist still needs to use the drill before the tooth is filled.

It is important to keep your teeth healthy. You keep your teeth healthy when you brush and floss everyday. Dentists keep your teeth healthy by checking them every six months, and repairing them when needed.

You can choose the foods you eat. To get the nutrients your body needs, you must eat foods from the healthful food groups. Table 16–1 shows the healthful food groups. How many servings from each group should you eat in a day?

Table 16–1 Food Groups and Suggested Servings for Children

Milk	Meat	Fruit-Vegetable	Grain	Combination
1 Serving: 1 cup milk 1 cup yogurt 1 1/2 slice cheese	1 Serving: 2 oz lean meat, fish, poultry 2 eggs 4 tsp peanut butter	1 Serving: 1/2 cup juice 1/2 cup cooked vegetable 1 cup raw fruit or vegetable	1 Serving: 1 slice bread 1 cup dry cereal 1/2 cup cooked cereal	1 Serving: 1 cup soup 1 cup pasta dish 1 cup stew, casserole
Servings: 3	Servings: 2	Servings: 4	Servings: 4	Servings: *

* These count as servings or partial servings of the groups from which they are made.

Lesson Summary

- Your body uses healthful foods to grow and to repair damaged cells.
- Foods from the healthful food groups have the nutrients your body needs.

Lesson Review

Review the lesson to answer these questions.

1. List four reasons why healthful foods are important for the body.
2. What is a nutrient?
3. Why is a food high in sugar not healthful?

Activity 16-1 Healthful Foods in Your Diet

QUESTION What healthful foods have you eaten today?

Materials
food group table
crayons
paper plates
pencil and paper

Meal	Foods Eaten	Food Groups
BREAKFAST		
LUNCH		

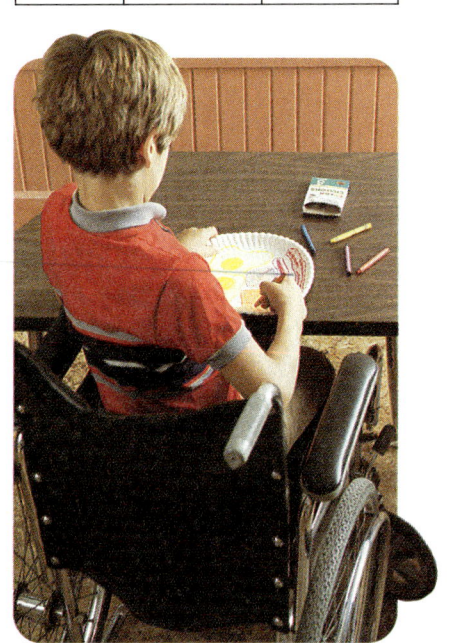

What to do
1. Study Table 16-1 on page 298. Make a chart like the one shown.
2. List the foods you had for breakfast or lunch in the correct column.
3. Using the crayons and paper plates, make a drawing of the foods you ate.
4. Compare your meal with that of a classmate. Decide whether you had a healthful meal.

What did you learn?
1. From which groups did you choose your food?
2. Did you or your classmate have the more healthful meal? How can you tell?

Using what you learned
1. What could you do to make your meal more healthful?
2. Plan a menu of healthful foods for two days.

16:3 Drugs

LESSON GOALS

In this lesson you will learn
- how drugs are used in medicines.
- safety rules to follow for taking medicines.
- what drugs are in drinks and tobacco.

What is a drug?

A drug is a substance that changes the way your body or mind works. Drugs may be used in different ways. Some drugs are used in medicines. The medicines may be used to cure some diseases. For example, if germs cause an earache, some medicines can kill the germs. Your ear will stop hurting. Medicines can be used to control but not cure some diseases. People with heart disease may take medicine to control that disease. Medicine can also be used to make people feel better when they are sick. The medicine can ease coughing, sneezing, or a runny nose.

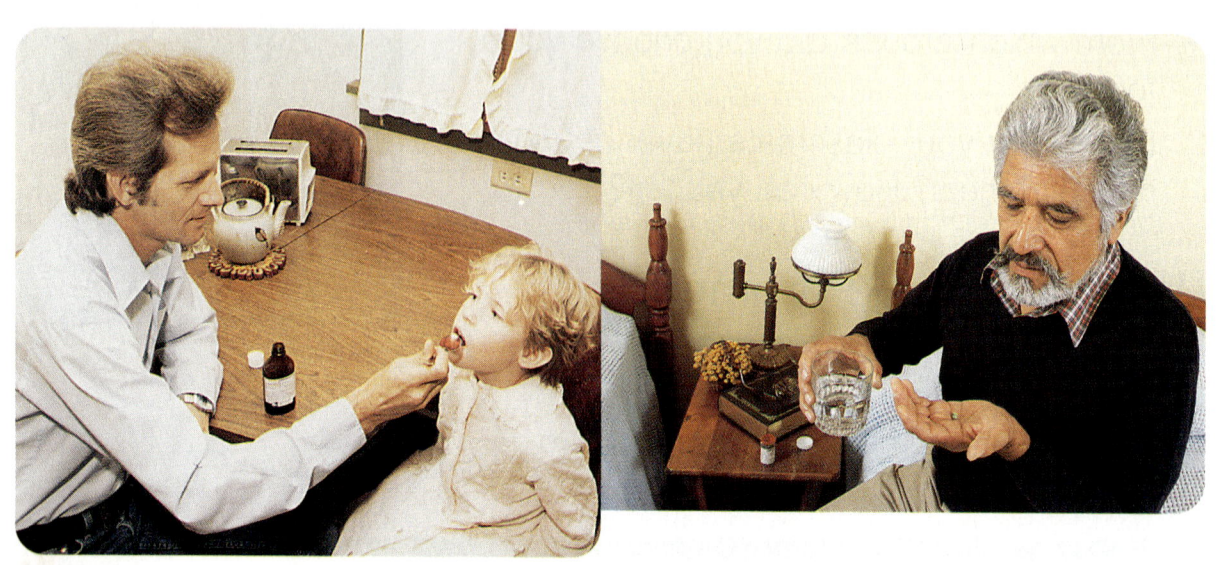

For what three reasons might a medicine be used?

Figure 16-6. Medicines may be used to cure or control a disease.

Figure 16-7. A prescription drug is prepared after a doctor orders it.

Medicines are sold in two ways. Some are sold by prescription (prih SKRIHP shun). A **prescription** is an order by a doctor for a certain medicine. A **prescription drug** is a drug prepared for you after your doctor orders it. Some medicines are sold without a prescription. An **over-the-counter drug** can be bought without a doctor's prescription.

Care must be used when taking any drug. Look at Table 16-2. It lists important safety rules.

What is a prescription?

Table 16-2 Medicine Safety Rules

1. Take medicine only from your parents, a doctor, or other responsible adult.

2. Do not take anyone else's prescription drug.

3. Follow all directions on the medicine.

4. Tell your parents about any strange effects caused by the medicine.

5. **NEVER** take medicine from a stranger.

301

Figure 16-8. Caffeine (a, b) is found in some drinks. Nicotine (c) is found in tobacco.

What effect does alcohol have on the body?

Drugs in Drinks and Tobacco

Some drugs are found in some drinks. **Caffeine** (ka FEEN) is a drug that speeds up the way a body works. Caffeine is found in some soft drinks. It is also found in many coffees and teas. Caffeine can be harmful. It can make people feel nervous. It can also keep them awake at night.

Alcohol (AL kuh hawl) is a drug that slows down the way a body works. Beer, wine, and liquor have alcohol in them. Alcohol can be harmful. It can change the way people act. Alcohol may also make people lose control of their muscles.

Nicotine (NIHK uh teen) is a drug found in tobacco. It is found in cigarettes, cigars, and pipe tobacco. It is also found in chewing tobacco. Nicotine speeds up the way the body works. It makes the heart beat faster. How is nicotine like caffeine?

People can choose to use drugs in healthful ways. For good health, people choose not to drink caffeine and alcohol. For good health, people choose not to smoke or chew tobacco. People who make these choices are working to keep their bodies healthy.

Figure 16-9. People can choose to live healthy lives.

Lesson Summary

- Drugs in medicines may be used to cure diseases, control diseases, or to help people feel better while they are ill.
- Five safety rules must be followed when taking any kind of medicine.
- Caffeine and alcohol are drugs found in drinks. Nicotine is a drug found in tobacco.

Lesson Review

Review the lesson to answer these questions.
1. What is a drug?
2. What is the difference between an over-the-counter drug and a prescription drug?
3. How do caffeine, alcohol, and nicotine affect the body?

16:4 Poisons

LESSON GOALS

In this lesson you will learn
- there are different kinds of poisons.
- important safety rules about poisons.

Many kinds of matter cause injury if they get in your body. These substances are called poisons (POYZ unz). A **poison** is matter that is harmful to the body. Poisons may be solids, liquids, or gases. They may enter the body through contact with the skin or when we breathe them or eat them.

Some plants and animals cause poisoning through contact with the skin. Poison ivy is an example of such a plant. It can cause a rash. Animals, such as some insects, spiders and poisonous snakes, inject poisons into the body when they bite or sting.

Some gases are poisons and enter our bodies when we breathe them. Carbon monoxide, for example, is produced by gasoline engines. This gas is especially dangerous because it does not have an odor.

Many poisons are found in the home because they have important uses. Paint, gasoline, and drain cleaner, for example, are used to protect wood on a house, power a vehicle, or clean a drain. Each product, however, is a dangerous poison. Since poisons are often found in the home, it is important to follow the five safety rules in Table 16-3.

Figure 16-10. Plants, such as poison ivy, may cause a rash if touched.

Why are products that are poisons found in the home?

Figure 16-11. Some products commonly found in the home are poisons.

304

Table 16-3 Poison Safety Rules

1. **NEVER** taste an unknown substance.

2. Label all poisons.

3. Store poisons where young children cannot reach them.

4. Read the label before using any product at home.

5. Place the telephone number of your doctor or the local Poison Control Center near your telephone.

Many communities have Poison Control Centers. These centers give important information about poisons. They will tell a person what to do if poison has been taken by accident. The directions given will depend on the kind of poison taken. It is important to place the telephone number of the nearest Poison Control Center near the telephone. Make sure each family member knows where to find this phone number.

Figure 16-12. Learn the phone number of the nearest Poison Control Center.

Lesson Summary

- Poisons may be solids, liquids, or gases.
- It is important to follow the five poison safety rules.

Lesson Review

Review the lesson to answer these questions.
1. Why is it common to find poisons at home?
2. Where can you call to get help with or information about poisons?

Activity 16-2 Design a Sign

QUESTION   How can you warn people about poisons?

Materials
paper
felt pens or crayons

What to do
1. Work with a partner.
2. Plan a sign to put on poisons. The sign must warn children and adults not to taste the poison.
3. Color your sign.
4. Show it to the class. Tell why you think it would warn people.
5. Ask other members of the class to share their feelings about the sign.

What did you learn?
1. Which signs really tell people about danger and poison?
2. Why do pictures without words sometimes work best?

Using what you learned
1. Make some warning signs and tape them onto poisons at school and at home.
2. How else could people be warned about poisons?

People and Science

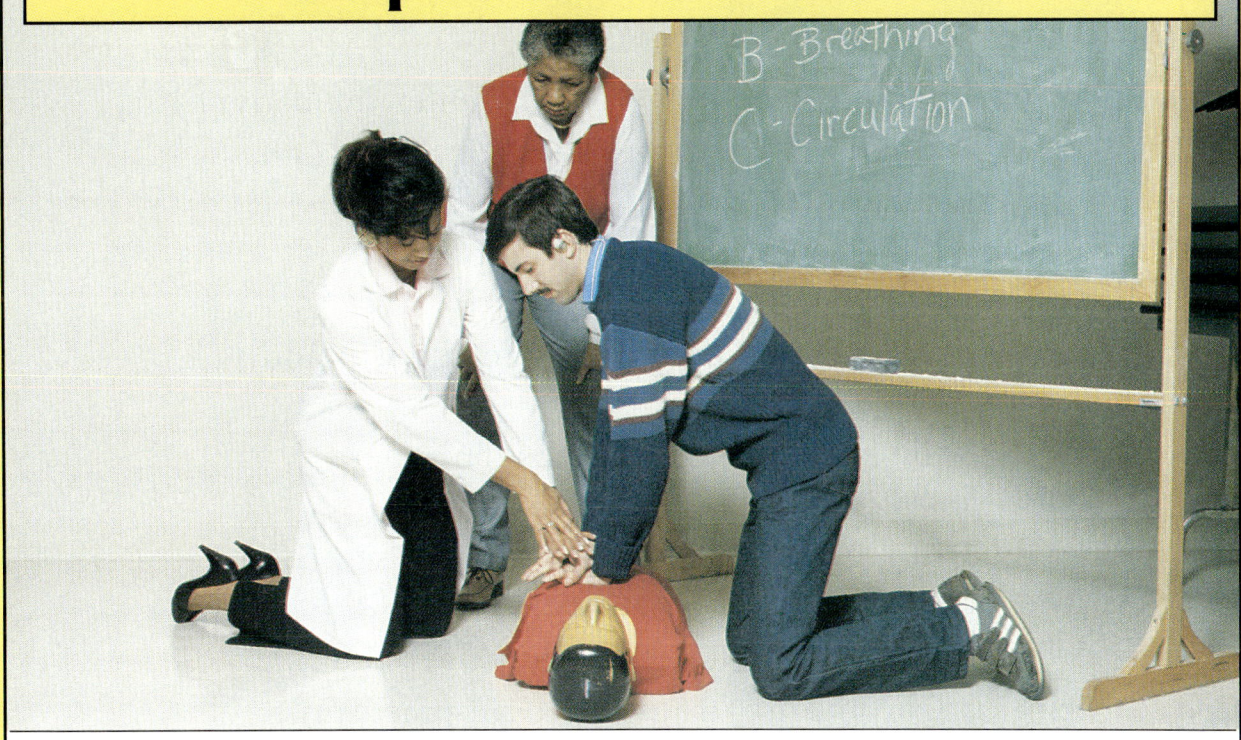

Prepared For Emergencies

Lily Denbo is an Emergency Medical Technician (EMT). She works as part of an ambulance team. When an emergency call is received, Lily and her partner rush to the scene. After giving first aid, they may take the patient to a hospital. There, doctors and nurses take over.

Lily also teaches cardiopulmonary resuscitation (CPR). When a person's heart and lungs stop working, oxygen cannot be carried by the blood to body cells. Without a normal supply of oxygen, cells will die.

The person trained in CPR works to save lives by becoming the patient's heart and lungs for a while. If someone is not breathing, the person trained in CPR has to breathe for them. If the heart has stopped beating, pressing on the chest will keep the person's blood moving. CPR can keep a person alive until trained medical help arrives.

Lily enjoys teaching CPR. She is happy to help people learn to save lives. You never know when someone may need your help.

Chapter 16 Review

Summary

1. Some diseases are caused by germs that enter the body.   16:1
2. The body is protected from germs by skin, tears, and substances made by the body.   16:1
3. Liquids, healthful foods, and rest are especially important when you are ill.   16:1
4. Healthful foods are used by the body for growth and the repair of damaged cells.   16:2
5. Foods from the healthful food groups have the nutrients your body needs.   16:2
6. Drugs in medicines may be used to cure diseases, control diseases, or to relieve distress during illness.   16:3
7. Safety rules should be followed when taking medicine.   16:3
8. Caffeine and alcohol are drugs found in some drinks. Nicotine is a drug in tobacco.   16:3
9. Poisons may be solids, liquids, or gases.   16:4
10. It is important to follow five poison safety rules.   16:4

Science Words

disease	**drug**	**over-the-counter drug**	**nicotine**
immunity	**prescription**	**caffeine**	**poison**
vaccine	**prescription drug**	**alcohol**	

Understanding Science Words

Complete each of the following sentences with a word or words from the Science Words that will make the sentence correct.

1. Matter that is harmful to the body is a _____.
2. An illness is a _____.
3. When you need a medicine, your doctor writes a _____.
4. A drug found in tobacco is _____.
5. The body's ability to fight certain diseases is called _____.

6. A drug that you can get without a doctor's prescription is an _____.
7. Dead or weak germs that give immunity are called a _____.
8. A drug found in some soft drinks, coffee, and tea is _____.
9. A substance that changes the way your body or mind works is known as a _____.
10. A drug prepared after a doctor orders it is a _____.
11. Beer, wine, and liquor contain the drug _____.

Questions

A. Recalling Facts

Choose the word or phrase that correctly completes each of the following sentences.

1. Carbon monoxide is a
    (a) disease.   (b) poison.   (c) nutrient.   (d) harmless gas.
2. An example of food from the meat group is
    (a) an egg.   (b) milk.   (c) soup.   (d) cereal.
3. Two of your body's defenses from germs are tears and
    (a) heart.   (b) skin.   (c) bones.   (d) teeth.
4. An example of food from the milk group is
    (a) orange.   (b) bread.   (c) cheese.   (d) peanut butter.

B. Understanding Concepts

Answer each of the following questions using complete sentences.

1. How do caffeine, alcohol, and nicotine affect the body?
2. Why does the body need healthful foods?

C. Applying Concepts

Think about what you have learned in this chapter. Answer each of the following questions using complete sentences.

1. How should you take care of yourself when you are ill?
2. What are five poison safety rules?

UNIT 8 REVIEW

CHECKING YOURSELF

Answer these questions on a sheet of paper.
1. Why must your body make new cells all the time?
2. What are your body's defenses against disease?
3. What body parts make up the circulatory system?
4. How are medicines helpful to your body?
5. How does your body get immunity?
6. What do muscles do to make body parts move?
7. Give an example of an organ and an organ system.
8. What are five important medicine safety rules?
9. What products contain caffeine, alcohol, and nicotine? How do these drugs affect the body?
10. In what different ways might poisons enter our bodies? Give an example of each type of poison.
11. What are five important poison safety rules?
12. How are plant cells different from animal cells?
13. Which organ systems are the body's control systems?

RECALLING ACTIVITIES

Think about the activities you did in this unit. Answer the questions about these activities.
1. What do different cells look like?   15–1
2. How does your pulse rate change?   15–2
3. What healthful foods have you eaten today?   16–1
4. How can you warn people about poisons?   16–2

IDEAS TO EXPLORE

1. Make a poster that gives information about the drugs caffeine, alcohol, and nicotine. Include artwork and written information about each drug.

2. Work with a partner and plan meals for one day. The meals should have the recommended number of servings from each of the food groups. Share recipes with other student groups.

3. Make a check list that gives information about storing poisons in the home. Share the list with other classes.

CHALLENGING PROJECT

Plan an assembly for your school. Using a play, posters, poems, music, and talks, show other students what you have learned about staying healthy.

BOOKS TO READ

Good Health Fun Book by Gail Aemmer, Carson-Dillon Publishing Co.: Akron, OH, © 1984.
   Do these fun activities and learn about good health.

Health & Hygiene by Rae Bains, Troll Associates: Mahwah, NJ, © 1985.
   Read this book and learn about hygiene and how to stay healthy.

The Healthy Habits Handbook by Slim Goodbody, Putnam Publishing Group: New York, © 1983.
   This interesting book will help you learn good health habits.

Glossary

This book has words that you may not have read before. Many of these words are science words. Some science words may be hard for you to read. You will find the science words in **bold print.** These words may appear two ways. The first way shows how the word is spelled. The second way shows how the word sounds. The list below shows the sounds each letter or group of letters makes.

Look at the word **energy** (EN ur jee). The second spelling shows the letters "ee." Find these letters in the list. The "ee" has the sound of "ea" in the word "leaf." Anytime you see "ee," you know what sound to say.

The capitalized syllable is the accented syllable.

a . . . back (BAK)
er . . . care, fair (KER, FER)
ay . . . day (DAY)
ah . . . father (FAHTH ur)
ar . . . car (KAR)
ow . . . flower, loud (FLOW ur, LOWD)
e . . . less (LES)
ee . . . leaf (LEEF)
ih . . . trip (TRIHP)
i (or i + con + e) . . .
   idea, life (i DEE uh, LIFE)
oh . . . go (GOH)
aw . . . soft (SAWFT)
or . . . orbit (OR but)
oy . . . coin (KOYN)

oo . . . foot (FOOT)
yoo . . . pure (PYOOR)
ew . . . food (FEWD)
yew . . . few (FYEW)
uh (or u + con) . . .
   comma, mother (KAHM uh, MUTH ur)
sh . . . shelf (SHELF)
ch . . . nature (NAY chur)
g . . . gift (GIHFT)
j . . . gem, edge (JEM, EJ)
ing . . . sing (SING)
zh . . . vision (VIHZH un)
k . . . cake (KAYK)
s . . . seed, cent (SEED, SENT)
z . . . zone, raise (ZOHN, RAYZ)

A

alcohol (AL kuh hawl): a drug that slows down the way a body works

astronaut (AS truh nawt): a person who travels and works in space

atmosphere (AT muh sfihr): all the air that surrounds Earth

atom: smallest part of any kind of matter

C

caffeine (ka FEEN): a drug that speeds up the way a body works

cell: the smallest unit of living matter

cirrus (SIHR us) **clouds:** thin clouds formed high in the atmosphere and made of ice

climate (KLI mut): the usual weather in an area year after year

cloud: object that forms in the atmosphere from millions of water droplets, tiny pieces of ice, or both ice and water

community (kuh MYEW nut ee): a group of producers and consumers living together in one area

compound: a kind of matter formed from two or more elements

compound leaf: broad leaf containing leaflets

compound machine: a machine made of two or more simple machines

condensation (kahn den SAY shun): the change from a gas to a liquid

cone: part of some plants in which seeds form

coniferous (kuh NIHF rus) **forest:** forest habitat found in northern regions of the world.

consumer (kun SEW mur): a living thing that cannot make its own food

core: The innermost part of Earth

crater: a hollowed area in the ground

crust: the top layer of Earth

cumulus (KYEW myuh lus) **clouds:** large, puffy clouds

D

decomposer (dee kum POH zur): a living thing that breaks down dead plants and animals into simpler matter

313

desert (DEZ urt): a hot or cold habitat that has very little moisture

dew: water that condenses on objects near the ground

disease (dihz EEZ): an illness

drug: a substance that changes the way a body or mind works

E

element: matter that is made of one kind of atom

embryo (EM bree oh): an undeveloped plant or animal in its early stages of growth

energy (EN ur jee): the ability to do work

erosion (ih ROH zhun): the movement of sediments and rocks to new places

evaporation (ih vap uh RAY shun): the change from a liquid to a gas

F

flower: the part of some plants in which seeds and fruits form

fog: a stratus cloud close to the ground

food chain: the transfer of energy from the sun to producers and then to consumers

food web: all the feeding relationships in a community

force: a push or a pull

freshwater habitat: a water habitat found in ponds, bogs, swamps, lakes, and rivers

friction (FRIHK shun): a force that slows down or stops objects in motion

frost: ice that forms directly from water vapor

fruit: plant part in which seeds grow

fulcrum (FUL krum): point where a lever rocks back and forth

full moon: a phase of the moon in which you see all of the lighted side of the moon

G

gas: matter that has no shape or size of its own

germination (jur muh NAY shun): the beginning of the growth of a plant embryo

glacier (GLAY shur): a large mass of ice that moves

gram: a unit used to measure mass

grassland: a habitat where most of the plants are grasses

gravity (GRAV ut ee): the pulling force between objects

groundwater: water that soaks into the ground

H

habitat (HAB uh tat): an area that supports the life needs of a plant or animal

I

igneous (IHG nee us) **rock:** rock that forms from cooled magma

immunity (ihm YEW nut ee): the body's ability to fight certain diseases

inclined plane: simple machine used to move objects to a higher or lower place

K

kilogram (KIHL uh gram): a unit used to measure large amounts of mass; one kilogram equals 1000 grams

L

lava (LAHV uh): magma at Earth's surface

leaf: the main plant part in which food is made

leaflet (LEE flut): small leaf that is part of a compound leaf

lever: simple machine that can be used to raise or lower an object

liquid (LIH kwud): matter that has a certain size, but does not have a shape of its own

load: the object moved by a lever

M

magma (MAG muh): hot liquid material that forms inside Earth

mantle (MANT ul): layer of Earth located beneath the crust

maria (MAR ee uh): smooth dark areas on the moon

mass: how much there is of an object

matter: everything that takes up space and has mass

metamorphic (met uh MOR fihk) **rock:** rock that has been changed by heat and pressure

315

microscope (MI kruh skohp): an instrument used to make small objects appear larger

mineral (MIHN uh rul): solid matter found in nature but not made by plants or animals

mixture: a combination of two or more different types of matter in which each type of matter keeps its own properties

N

new moon: a phase of the moon in which all of the lighted side faces away from Earth

nicotine (NIHK uh teen): a drug found in tobacco that speeds up the way a body works

nutrient: (NEW tree unt): a substance needed by living things for growth

O

ocean habitat: a water habitat that includes all of Earth's surface covered by saltwater

orbit: the path that one object follows around another object

organ: a group of tissues working together

organ system: a group of organs working together

over-the-counter drug: a drug that can be bought without a doctor's prescription

P

phase (FAYZ): the lighted part of the moon that can be seen from Earth

planet: a large space object that revolves around the sun

plant life cycle (SI kul): the repeated process of the germination, growth of a plant, and formation of new seeds

poison: matter that is harmful to the body

polar region: an area of ice and snow located near the North and South Poles

precipitation (prih sihp uh TAY shun): moisture that falls from the atmosphere

predator (PRED ut ur): an animal that hunts and eats other animals

prescription (prih SKRIHP shun): an order by a doctor for a certain medicine

prescription drug: a drug prepared after it is ordered by a doctor

prey: animals eaten by predators

producer (proh DEW sur): a living thing that makes its own food

property (PRAHP urt ee): a characteristic of an object

pulley: a simple machine that changes the direction or amount of a force

R

rain forest: a hot forest habitat that receives large amounts of rainfall each year

regolith (REG uh lihth): dust and rock pieces that form the outer layer of the moon

reservoir (REZ urv wor): a place where water is stored

revolution (rev uh LEW shun): the movement of one object around another object

rill: a long, narrow moon valley

rock: a solid made of one or more minerals

rock cycle: the changing of rocks into different kinds of rocks

root: the plant part that holds the plant in the ground

rotation (roh TAY shun): the spinning motion of an object

runoff: water that flows across the ground

S

satellite (SAT uh lite): an object that revolves around a larger object

scavenger: (SKAV un jur): an animal that feeds on dead plants and animals

screw: an inclined plane wrapped around a post

sedimentary (sed uh MENT uh ree) **rock:** rock made of sediments that are pressed together

sediments (SED uh munts): small pieces of Earth material

seed: an undeveloped plant that may grow

seed coat: a tough "skin" that protects the other parts of the seed

seedling: a young plant

317

seed plant: a plant that grows from a seed

shelter: a place or object that protects an animal

simple leaf: a broad leaf with one part

simple machine: a machine with few or no moving parts

solar system: the sun and space objects that revolve around it

solid: matter that has a certain size and shape

space: all the area beyond Earth's atmosphere

spacecraft: a machine that travels to the moon or other space objects

stem: part of seed plant that supports the leaves

stored food: food in a seed that is used by the embryo

stratus (STRAT us) **clouds:** clouds that entirely cover the sky

T

telescope: a tool used to make distant objects look bigger

temperate (TEM prut) **forest:** a forest habitat with four seasons—spring, summer, autumn, and winter

tissue (TIHSH ew): a group of cells working together

tundra (TUN druh): a cold, dry habitat with a layer of soil that is frozen

V

vaccine (vak SEEN): dead or weakened germs that give immunity to a disease

W

waning (WAYN ing): said of the moon when it has less of the lighted side showing each night

water cycle: the continuous movement of water through evaporation, condensation, precipitation, and storage

water vapor: water as a gas

waxing: said of the moon when it has more of the lighted side showing each night

weathering: the breaking down or wearing away of rock

wedge (WEJ): a simple machine made of two inclined planes

wheel and axle: a simple machine with a wheel that turns a post

wildlife conservation (kahn sur VAY shun): the protection of habitats and living things

work: what is done when a force moves an object

Index

A

Air: expansion of, 66, 67; and respiratory system, 285
Alcohol, 302
Animals: in communities, 202-205; decomposers, 200-201; facts about, 230-231; food consumption by, 196-199; habitats of, 212-229; predators, 198-199; prey, 198; protection of, 229; and rocks, 105; scavengers, 200, 201; and seed scattering, 18-19
Artificial reefs, 195; *illus.*, 195
Astronaut, 251-252; *illus.*, 251, 252
Atmosphere, 157, 242; *illus.*, 242
Atom, 51; *table*, 52
Axe, 147; *illus.*, 147
Axle, 142; *illus.*, 142

B

Bacteria, 201; *illus.*, 201
Balboa, Vasco de, 236
Bicycles, 149; *illus.*, 149
Blood, 280; *illus.*, 280
Bone, 282; *illus.*, 282
Brain, 287
Breathing, 285
Burning, 76; *illus.*, 76

C

Caffeine, 302
California condor, 209
Can opener, 146; *illus.*, 146
Carbon dioxide, 285
Cardiopulmonary resuscitation, 307
Cause and effect, 289
Cell, 272, 275-277; *act.*, 276; *illus.*, 273, 274, 275, 277
Chapman, John, 2
Cigarettes, 302
Circulatory system, 280-281; *act.*, 281; *illus.*, 280
Cirrus cloud, 162; *illus.*, 162
Climate, 166-170; *act.*, 168
Climate zones, 166
Clouds, 162, 164; cirrus, 162; cumulus, 164; stratus, 164; *illus.*, 162, 164
Community, 202-205
Compound, 75-76; *illus.*, 75, 76
Compound leaf, 33
Compound machines, 146-148; *illus.*, 146, 147, 148
Condensation, 73, 161; *illus.*, 161
Cone, 35; *illus.*, 35
Coniferous forest, 222; *illus.*, 222
Consumer, 196
Control system, 287-288; *illus.*, 287, 288
Core, 88; *illus.*, 88
Cranberries, 53; *illus.*, 53
Crater, 246; *act.*, 248-249; *illus.*, 246
Creating a grahic picture, 185; *illus.*, 185
Crescent moon, 264; *illus.*, 264, 265
Crop rotation, 37
Crust, 87; *illus.*, 87
Cumulus cloud, 164; *illus.*, 164

D

Darwin, Charles, 190
Decomposer, 200-201; *illus.*, 200, 201
Desert, 220-221; *illus.*, 220
Dew, 164
Diet, 296-299; *act.*, 299; *table*, 298
Digestive system, 284; *illus.*, 284
Disease, 293-295, 300
Drugs, 300-303, alcohol, 302; caffeine, 302; nicotine, 302; over-the-counter, 301; prescription, 301; *table*, 301

E

Earth: atmosphere of, 157, 242; core of, 88; crust of, 87; gravity on, 242; layers of, 86-88; mantle of, 88; movements of, 257-261; size of, 239; *act.*, 260; *illus.*, 86, 87, 88, 239, 242, 258
Electricity, 128
Element, 51
Embryo, 8; *illus.*, 8
Emergency medical technician, 307; *illus.*, 307
Endocrine system, 288; *illus.*, 288
Energy, 127-128; food as, 205, 207-208; *illus.*, 127, 128
Erosion, 108; *illus.*, 108
Evaporation, 71, 158-160; *act.*, 72, 159; *illus.*, 158, 160
Extinction of dinosaurs, 89; *illus.*, 89

F

Fact, and opinion, 111
Flower, 34; *illus.*, 34
Fog, 164

Food, 296-299; for astronauts, 252; consumption of, 196-199; in digestive system, 284; and illness, 295; need for, 193-194; and nutrition, 296-299; production of, 37, 193-194; stored, 8, 194; *act.*, 299; *table*, 298
Food chain, 203-205; *act.*, 204; *illus.*, 203, 205
Food web, 206-208; *illus.*, 206, 207, 208
Force, 119-121; and work, 126-128; *act.*, 120; *illus.*, 119, 121, 126
Forest, 222-225; coniferous, 222; rain, 225; temperate, 223; *illus.*, 222, 223, 225
Fossil, 94; *illus.*, 94
Freshwater habitat, 226; *illus.*, 226
Friction, 124; *act.*, 125; *illus.*, 124
Frost, 164
Fruit, 20; *illus.*, 20
Fulcrum, 135-137; *illus.*, 136, 137
Full moon, 263, 265; *illus.*, 263, 265

G

Gas, 58; changes in, 73; *illus.*, 58, 73
Germ, 293, 294
Germination, 10-11; *illus.*, 10
Gibbous moon, 265; *illus.*, 264, 265
Glacier, 104, 108; *illus.*, 104
Gold, 51
Goodall, Jane, 190, 191
Gram, 47
Grassland, 221; *illus.*, 221
Gravity, 122, 242-243; *illus.*, 122
Great Salt Lake, 171
Groundwater, 177; *illus.*, 177

H

Habitat, 212-229; desert, 220-221; forest, 222-225; grassland, 221; importance of, 213-217; and people, 228-229; polar and tundra, 218-219; water, 226-227; *act.,* 214, 224; *illus.,* 212, 213, 215, 216, 217, 218, 219, 220, 221, 222, 223, 225, 226, 227, 228

Hail, 165

Hatchet, 147

Health, 292-306; body's defense, 294-295; and disease, 293-295; and drugs, 300-303; and food, 296-299; and poisons, 304-306; *act.,* 299, 306

Heat: and changes of state, 69, 71; and physical changes, 65-66; *act.,* 70, 72

I

Igneous rock, 91; *illus.,* 91

Immunity, 294

Inclined plane, 138; *act.,* 139; *illus.,* 138

Intestines, 284

Irrigation, 27, 154; *illus.,* 27, 155

J

Just, Earnest E., 272

K

Kidneys, 287

Kilogram, 49

L

Lava, 90-91; *illus.,* 90, 91

Leaf, 32-33; compound, 33; simple, 33; *illus.,* 32, 33

Leaflet, 33

Lever, 135-137; *act.,* 134; *illus.,* 135, 136, 137

Liquid, 55-56, 64; changes in, 71, 72; *act.,* 57, 72; *illus.,* 55, 56, 64

Liquid wastes, 286-287

Load, 135, 136, 137

Lunar rover, 252; *illus.,* 252

M

Machines, 128, 132-148; compound, 146-148; inclined plane, 138, 139; levers, 134, 135-137; pulley, 143-145; screw, 141; simple, 133-145; wedge, 140; wheel and axle, 142; *act.,* 134, 139, 144; *illus.,* 116, 117, 132, 133, 135, 136, 137, 140, 141, 142, 143, 145, 146, 147, 148

Magma, 90-91

Magnet, 122; *illus.,* 122

Mantle, 88; *illus.,* 88

Maria, 245; *illus.,* 245

Mass, 47; and force, 121; measurement of, 47-49; *act.,* 48

Matter, 44-76; changes in, 62-76; combining, 74-76; and heat, 65-66; properties of, 45-49, 63-66; states of, 54-58; 68-73; *act.,* 46, 57, 67, 70, 72; *table,* 52

Measurement, of mass, 47-49; *act.,* 48

Medicine, 300-301; *table,* 301

Metamorphic rock, 94-96; *act.,* 95; *illus.,* 94, 96

Microscope, 201
Minerals, 85-86; *illus.,* 85
Mixture, 74-75; *illus.,* 74, 75
Mold, 200; *illus.,* 200
Moon, 238-266; craters of, 246, 248-249; full, 263, 265; gravity on, 243; movements of, 258-261; new, 263, 264; phases of, 262-266; size of, 239-241; surface of, 244-249; temperatures on, 243; waning, 263; waxing, 263; *act.,* 248-249, 260, 266; *illus.,* 238, 239, 243, 245, 246, 247, 251, 252, 256, 262, 263, 264, 265
Mountains, 170, 244
Muscular system, 282; *illus.,* 278, 283

N

Nervous system, 287; *illus.,* 274, 277, 287
New moon, 263; *illus.,* 264
Nicotine, 302
Noise, 148
North Pole, 218
Nutrient, 29
Nutrition, 296-299; *act.,* 299; *table,* 298

O

Ocean, 226; *illus.,* 226, 227
Ocean floor, 87
Orbit, 258
Organ, 278; *illus.,* 279
Organ system, 279; *illus.,* 279
Over-the-counter drug, 301
Oxygen, 51, 285

P

Paper making, 42; *illus.,* 43
Perspiration, 286
Phases, 262-266; *act.,* 266; *illus.,* 262, 263, 264, 265
Physical change, 64
Plains, 245; *illus.,* 245
Plants, 2-36; food production in, 193-194; growth of, 10-15, 17; leaves of, 32-33; and rocks, 104; roots of, 28-29; seedlings of, 11-15; seeds of, 4-20; stem of, 30; water transport in, 31; *act.,* 6, 14, 17, 31, 197; *illus.,* 24, 25, 26
Planting, 18
Plant life cycle, 35-36; *illus.,* 36
Poison, 304-306; *act.,* 306; *illus.,* 304; *table,* 305
Poison Control Center, 305
Polar habitat, 218; *illus.,* 218
Polar zones, 166
Pollution, of water, 183-184
Precipitation, 165; and climate, 167, 168, 170; *act.,* 168; *illus.,* 165
Predator, 198-199; *illus.,* 198, 199
Prescription, 301
Prescription drug, 301
Producer, 193-194
Production of diamonds, 77; *illus.,* 77
Properties, 45-49; changes in, 63-66; of minerals, 85; of rocks, 86; *act.,* 46
Pulley, 143-145; *act.,* 144; *illus.,* 143, 144, 145
Pulse rate, *act.,* 281

R

Rain, 165

Rain forest, 225; *illus.*, 225
Regolith, 247
Reservoir, 179, 183
Respiratory system, 279, 285; *illus.*, 285
Revolution, 257; *illus.*, 257
Rill, 245
Rock, 82-110; and Earth layers, 85-88; and erosion, 108; formation of, 90-96; igneous, 90-91; location of, 86-88; metamorphic, 94-96; on moon, 247; sedimentary, 92-94; weathering of, 101-105, 110; *act.*, 93, 95, 102; *illus.*, 84, 85, 86, 91, 92, 94, 96, 100, 101, 103, 104, 105, 109, 110
Rock cycle, 109; *illus.*, 109, 110
Roots, 28-29; *illus.*, 28, 29
Rotation, 258; *illus.*, 258
Runoff, 176; *illus.*, 176
Rust, 75; *illus.*, 75

S

Safety glasses, 148
Satellite, 258; weather, 163; *illus.*, 163
Saturn V **Rocket,** 236; *illus.*, 237
Scavenger, 200, 201; *illus.*, 200
Screw, 141; *illus.*, 141
Sediment, 92; *illus.*, 92
Sedimentary rock, 92-94; *act.*, 93; *illus.*, 92, 94
Sedimentologist, 97; *illus.*, 97
Seed, 4-20; germination of, 10-11; parts of, 6-9; scattering, 16-20; *act.*, 6, 17; *illus.*, 5, 8, 9, 10, 11, 16, 18, 19, 20
Seed coat, 9, 11

Seedlings, 11-15; *act.*, 14; *illus.*, 12, 13
Seed plants, 24-36; cone of, 35; flower of, 34; leaves of, 32-33; life cycle of, 35-36; roots of, 28-29; stems of, 30; *act.*, 31; *illus.*, 24, 25, 26
Sequence, 267
Shelter, 216; *illus.*, 216
Similarities and differences, 59; *illus.*, 59
Simple leaf, 33
Simple machines, 133-145; inclined plane, 138, 139; levers, 134, 135-137; pulley, 143-145; screw, 141; wedge, 140; wheel and axle, 142; *act.*, 134, 139, 144; *illus.*, 132, 133, 135, 136, 137, 140, 141, 142, 143, 145
Skeletal system, 282; *illus.*, 282
Skyscrapers, 123; *illus.*, 123
Sleet, 165
Snow, 165; *illus.*, 165
Soil formation, 106, 247; *act.*, 107
Solar system, 258
Solid, 54-55, 56, 64; changes in, 64, 69; *act.*, 57, 70; *illus.*, 55, 68, 69
Solid waste, 284, 286
South Pole, 218
Space ambassador, 253; *illus.*, 253
Spacecraft, 250-251
Spatial relationships, 239-241; *act.*, 240
Spinal cord, 287
States of matter, 54-58; changes in, 68-73; *act.*, 57, 70, 72; *illus.*, 54, 55, 56, 58, 68, 69, 71, 73
Stems, 30; *act.*, 31; *illus.*, 30
Stomach, 284
Stored food, 8, 194
Stratus cloud, 164; *illus.*, 164

T

Taking notes, 129
Teeth, 199; decay of, 297; *illus.,* 199, 297
Telescope, 250
Temperate forest, 223; *illus.,* 223
Temperature, 167
Tissue, 278; *illus.,* 278
Tobacco, 302
Tropics, 166; *illus.,* 166
Tundra, 219-220; *illus.,* 219

U

Uranus, 259; *illus.,* 259
Urethra, 287
Urinary system, 287
Urine, 287
Using a graph, 21; *illus.,* 21

V

Vaccine, 294; *illus.,* 294
Valley, 245
Voyager 2, 259

W

Waning moon, 263; *illus.,* 265
Wastes, 284, 286-287
Water, 174-179; condensation of, 73; and erosion, 108; evaporation of, 71, 72; groundwater, 177; pollution of, 183-184; and runoff, 176; transport in plants, 31; and weathering of rocks, 100, 101-104
Water cycle, 180-184; *act.,* 182; *illus.,* 181
Water habitats, 226-227; *illus.,* 226, 227
Water storage, 179; *act.,* 178; *illus.,* 179
Water tower, 179; *illus.,* 179
Water vapor, 158; condensation of, 161, 164; evaporation of, 158-160; freezing of, 164; *act.,* 159
Waxing moon, 263; *illus.,* 264
Weather, 156-165; clouds, 162-164; precipitation, 165; *illus.,* 156, 157, 162, 164, 165
Weathering, 101-105, 110; *act.,* 102; *illus.,* 101, 103, 104, 108, 110
Wedge, 140; *illus.,* 140
Wheel and axle, 142; *illus.,* 142
Wildlife conservation, 229
Wind, 104, 108
Work, 126-128; and machines, 128, 132-148

PHOTO CREDITS

COVER: Commercial Image/21st Century Robotics

VIII, Commercial Image; **2,3,** Ralph Perry/Aperture; **4,** Charles C. Johnson; **5,** Gerard Photography; **6,** (l) Gerard Photography, (r) Commercial Image; **8,** (l) Leonard Lee Rue III/Bruce Coleman, Inc., (r) Tom Bean; **10,** Runk/Schoenberger from Grant Heilman; **11,** Commercial Image; **12,** Tom Pantages; **13,** Grant Heilman Photography; **14,** Cobalt Productions; **16,** (l) William D. Popejoy, (r) Johnny Johnson/DRK Photo; **18,** Patti Murray/Earth Scenes; **19,** (tl) J.N. Skeen/Bruce Coleman, Inc., (tr) Commercial Image, (b) Ruth Dixon; **20,** Runk/Schoenberger from Grant Heilman; **24,** Frank S. Balthis; **25,** (l) M.P.L. Fogden/Bruce Coleman, Inc., (r) David Overcash/Bruce Coleman, Inc.; **26,** (l) Dwight R. Kuhn, (r) Grant Heilman Photography; **27,** James N. Westwater; **28,** Frank S. Balthis; **29,** (l) Dwight R. Kuhn, (r) Bob Firth; **30,** (l) Lynn M. Stone/Earth Scenes, (r) Dwight R. Kuhn; **32,** Doug Martin; **33,** Gerard Photography & Hickson-Bender Photography; **34,** (l) David M. Stone, (r) Barry L. Runk from Grant Heilman; **35,** Grant Heilman Photography; **37,** Charlton Photos; **42,43,** Tom Tracy Photography; **44,45** (t) Commercial Image; **45,** (b) Cobalt Productions; **47,** (l) Bob Firth, (tr) John Shaw/Tom Stack & Associates, (br) Steve Lissau; **48,** Cobalt Productions; **49,** (r) FPG, (l) Keith Gunnar/Bruce Coleman, Inc.; **50,** George Anderson; **51,** Jack Sekowski; **53,** Courtesy of Ocean Spray Corporation; **54,55,** Jack Sekowski; **56,57,** Cobalt Productions; **62,** Gary Milburn/Tom Stack & Associates; **63,** Commercial Image; **64,** Jack Sekowski; **65,66,** Cobalt Productions; **68,** Elaine Shay; **69,** (t) Larry Hamill, (b) Milt & Joan Mann; **70,** Bogart Photography; **71,** Jack Sekowski; **72,** Cobalt Productions; **73,** Terry Domico/Earth Images; **74,** Doug Martin; **75,** (l) Jack Sekowski, (r) Ray Ellis/Photo Researchers, Inc.; **76,** Don Rutledge/Tom Stack & Associates; **77,** Royce Bair/ The Stock Solution/ High Pressure Press at facility of Sii Megadiamond in Provo, UT; **82,83,** Lucian Niemeyer/LNS Arts, inset David L. Perry; **84,** file photo; **85,** Doug Martin; **86,** (l) Craig Kramer, (c) Linda Young, (r) University of Houston; **87,** Roger K. Burnard; **89,** Breck P. Kent; **90,** (l) file photo, (r) Steve Lissau; **91,** (tl) Linda Young, (tr) Doug Martin, (bl) Elaine Shay, (br) Linda Young; **92,** (tl) FlexPhoto, (tr) Elaine Shay, (b) James N. Westwater; **93,** Cobalt Productions; **94,** (tl) Michael Collier, (tr) Transparency #K10234 Courtesy Department Library Services, American Museum of Natural History, (bl) University of Houston, (br) Doug Martin; **95,** Cobalt Productions; **96,** (l) University of Houston, (r) Craig Kramer; **97,** Doug Martin; **100,** Steve Lissau; **101,** Roger K. Burnard; **102,** Cobalt Productions; **103,** (t) FlexPhoto, (b) David L. Perry; **105,** (l,r) Commercial Image, (c) Courtesy Rock Of Ages Corporation; **106,** FlexPhoto; **107,** Cobalt Productions; **108,** (l) Roger K. Burnard, (r) David L. Perry; **110,** James N. Westwater; **116,117,** H.M. DeCruyenaere, inset North Wind Picture Archives; **118,** David R. Frazier; **119,** (l) Commercial Image, (r) Tom McGuire; **120,** Cobalt Productions; **121,** (t) Commercial Image, (b) Jack Sekowski; **122,** (l) Jack Sekowski, (r) Doug Martin; **123,** Marc PoKemper/CLICK/Chicago; **124,** (t) Commercial Image, (b) Doug Martin; **126,** (r) David Hiser/Aspen, (l) Commercial Image; **127,** Jack Sekowski; **128,** (t) Robert J. Ashworth/Photo Researchers, Inc., (b) Tom Campbell/FPG; **132,** Gerard Photography; **134,** Jack Sekowski; **135,** Gerard Photography; **137,** Jack Sekowski; **139,** Cobalt Productions; **140,** Doug Martin; **141,** Commercial Image; **142,** (tl,tr) Cobalt Productions, (b) file photo; **143,144,** Cobalt Productions; **145,** Pamela J. Willits; **146,** Courtesy Libby, McNeill & Libby, Inc.; **147,** (t) Kent & Donna Dannen/Photo Researchers, Inc., (b) file photo; **148,** (t) Frank Cezus, (b) Cobalt Productions; **149,** Doug Martin; **154,155,** Frank S. Balthis; **156,** Jack Sekowski; **157,** Commercial Image; **158,** Gerard Photography; **159,** Cobalt Productions; **160,** (tl,tr) Gerard Photography, (b) Jack Sekowski; **161,** (l) Ted Levin/Earth Scenes, (r) Harry Cutting/Animals Animals; **162,** (t) Johnny Johnson, (b) Richard Kolar/Earth Scenes; **163,** (l) NOAA, (r) NASA; **164,** (l) John Lemker/Earth Scenes, (r) E.R. Degginger/Earth Scenes; **165,** (t) John Shaw/Tom Stack & Associates, (b) Breck P.

Kent/Earth Scenes; **166,** Breck P. Kent; **170,** David R. Frazier; **171,** Courtesy of Salt Lake County Flood Control/Hwy. Division; **174,** L.L.T. Rhodes/Earth Scenes; **175,** (tl,tr) Gerard Photography, (b) Jack Sckowski; **176,** (t) Michael P. Gadomski/Earth Scenes, (b) Jack Wilburn/Earth Scenes; **178,** Cobalt Productions; **179,** Zig Leszczynski/Earth Scenes; **180,** Bob Firth; **182,** Cobalt Productions; **183,** (l) E.R. Degginger/Earth Scenes, (r) James N. Westwater; **184,** Pat Lanza Field/Bruce Coleman, Inc.; **190,191,** Dr. Chris Boehm/Northern Kentucky University, inset Cambridge University Library; **192,** A.B. Shapiro, M.D./Animals Animals; **193,** (tl) Elaine Shay, (tr) Dwight R. Kuhn, (b) Patti Murray/Earth Scenes; **194,** Gerard Photography; **195,** Jeff Rotman; **196,** (t) Michael P. Gadomski/Bruce Coleman, Inc., (br) Mitch Reardon/Photo Researchers, Inc., (bl) Patti Murray/Animals Animals; **197,** Jack Sekowski; **198,** (l) Len Rue, Jr./DRK Photo, (r) Breck P. Kent; **199,** (l) Chip Clark, (tr) Leonard Lee Rue III/Animals Animals, (br) Stephen J. Krasemann/DRK Photo; **200,** (tl) Gregory K. Scott/Photo Researchers, Inc., (bl) Mitch Reardon/Photo Researchers, Inc., (r) Dwight R. Kuhn; **201,** Courtesy Rex Educational Resources Co.; **205,** Jack Sekowski; **207,** David C. Fritts/Animals Animals; **209,** Zoological Society of San Diego/Ken Kelley; **212,** John Gerlack/DRK Photo; **213,** (t) David M. Stone, (b) Roger K. Burnard; **214,** Cobalt Productions; **215,** Lee Lockwood/Black Star; **216,** (l) Karli Wallin/FPG, (r) Alvin E. Staffan; **217,** (l) Frank S. Balthis, (c) Bruce Coleman/Bruce Coleman, Inc.; **220,** (t) Sandra Grant/Photo Researchers, (b) Stephen J. Krasemann/DRK Photo; **221,222,** (t) Leonard Lee Rue III/FPG; **222** (b), **223** (t), Breck P. Kent; **223,** (b) Paul W. Nesbitt; **224,** Commercial Image; **228,** (tl) Jack Riesland/Berg & Associates, (tr) Lawrence Migdale/Photo Researchers, Inc., (b) David Hiser/Aspen; **229,** ODNR; **236,237,** NASA, inset The Granger Collection; **238,239,** NASA; **240,241,** Jack Sekowski; **242,** NASA; **243,** From "The World Book Encyclopedia" © 1986 World Book, Inc.; **244,** (l) NASA, (r) James N. Westwater; **245,** (l) Courtesy Hansen Planetarium, (r) David M. Dennis; **246,** (tl,tr) NASA, (b) Kenneth W. Fink/Berg & Associates; **247,** NASA; **248,** Cobalt Productions; **250,** (t) Kitt Peak Nat'l. Observatory, (b) NASA; **251,252,** NASA; **253,** Doug Martin; **256,** Dennis diCicco; **257,** (t) Commercial Image, (b) Jack Sekowski; **258,** (t) Commercial Image, (b) NASA; **259,** JPL; **260,261,** Cobalt Productions; **262,** H.M. DeCruyenaere; **263,** NASA; **264,265,** From "The World Book Encyclopedia", © 1986 World Book, Inc.; **266,** Commercial Image; **272,273,** © Lennart Nilsson, from "Our Victorious Body," 1987 by Merloyd Lawrence Publishing Co./Dell Publishing Co.; **274,** CNRI/Science Photo Library; **276,** Cobalt Productions; **277,** (tl,tc,cr) Biophoto Associates/Science Source, (tr) Eric Grave/Science Source, (br) Dr. Brian Eyden/Science Photo Library; **278,** (t) David Falconer/Frazier Photolibrary, (b) Jack Sekowski; **281,** Cobalt Productions; **282,** Jack Sekowski; **283,** Allen Zak; **288,** file photo; **292,293** (l), Jack Sekowski **293** (r) Cobalt Productions; **294,** (t) First Image, (b) Commercial Image; **295,** (tl) Allen Zak, (tr) Jack Sekowski, (b) Commercial Image; **296,** First Image; **297,** Latent Image; **298,** Jack Sekowski; **299,** Cobalt Productions; **300,** (l) Allen Zak, (r) Jack Sekowski; **301,** Allen Zak; **302,** FlexPhoto; **303,** (l) Jack Sekowski, (r) Latent Image; **304,** (t) Dagmar/Earth Scenes, (b) FlexPhoto; **305,** Commercial Image; **306,** Cobalt Productions; **307,** Doug Martin.